BASIC GREEK
IN 30 MINUTES A DAY

NEW TESTAMENT GREEK WORKBOOK FOR LAYMEN

BASIC GREEK IN 30 MINUTES A DAY

NEW TESTAMENT GREEK WORKBOOK FOR LAYMEN

JAMES FOUND

with BRUCE OLSON, MDiv, Editor

BETHANYHOUSE
Minneapolis, Minnesota

Note: The pronunciation system used in this book is not the same as modern Greek pronunciation; it is only one of several different systems that are in use for pronouncing ancient Greek.

Basic Greek in 30 Minutes a Day
Copyright © 1983
James Found
2007 edition

Cover design by Eric Walljasper

Published by Bethany House Publishers
11400 Hampshire Avenue South
Bloomington, Minnesota 55438

Bethany House Publishers is a division of
Baker Publishing Group, Grand Rapids, Michigan.

Printed in the United States of America

ISBN 978-0-7642-0336-7 (2007 edition)

ISBN 978-0-87123-285-4 (original edition)

JAMES FOUND has served as a director of Christian education in the Lutheran Church—Missouri Synod—in the United States and abroad. In 2006 James retired from teaching Outreach and Missions at Concordia University in St. Paul, Minnesota. Today he is often on the road presenting the workshop Sharing Faith Naturally in Conversation as a team member of the Oswald Hoffman School of Christian Outreach. James and his wife make their home in Roseville, Minnesota.

CONTENTS

CONTENTS

NEW TESTAMENT GREEK WORKBOOK FOR LAYMEN

Why the sub-title?

NEW TESTAMENT GREEK --- Every Greek word used in this book is found in the Greek New Testament. You will not have to learn any words that you will not need for studying scripture.

WORKBOOK --- The author is convinced that "learning by doing" will lead to the greatest understanding and retention for the student. On almost every page of this book you will find yourself filling in blanks, matching words, and even using guesswork as tools for successful learning.

FOR LAYMEN --- The author is also convinced that there are a great many practical concepts about the Christian faith that can be learned even with the easy introduction to Greek found in this workbook. This book will not make you into a Greek "scholar", but you will reap the benefits of understanding the Bible better from learning the basic Greek presented here.

What are these benefits?

After completing this workbook, you will:

1. be able to pronounce Greek words fluently and feel "at home" with the alphabet.

2. know the meanings of hundreds of New Testament words.

3. understand the background of dozens of religious terms through seeing the Greek components that form them.

4. see relationships between Bible words that are not easily apparent in English translation.

5. be able to use Greek dictionaries and other valuable reference books.

6. understand the general outlines of Greek grammar.

Could you give me some examples?

1. Did you know that the word "bishop" developed over centuries by gradually changing the pronunciation of the word from which we get "episcopal"? And that this word "episcopal" is made up of two parts: epi, which means "over" in Greek, and scope, which means "look"? And that the original Greek form of this word was used to designate the person appointed to "over-look" or "watch-over" the Christians in a given place?

2. Did you know that the English words "holy", "sanctify", and "saints" are all translations of various forms of a single Greek word-family?

What is unique about the approach of this workbook?

1. The student reads entire words right from the start, using Greek letters that resemble the English letters. This builds confidence and fluency, and removes the fear of mastering the Greek alphabet.

2. Scripture quotations are used very early in the book.

3. The student's vocabulary is built up quickly and easily through much use of Greek words that resemble English words of similar meaning ("cognates").

4. Technical terms are avoided as much as possible.

Who should use this workbook?

This workbook is meant especially for the person who does not have the time to take two years of college-level Greek. It is also valuable for the person who would like to take college-level Greek, but is unsure about whether he would be able to understand it---this book should give him the confidence to proceed into a standard academic course. Finally, the author believes this book could be used as the first few weeks of a full-fledged college Greek course. After completing this book, the student will be at a high level of confidence and motivation which will carry him through the drudgery of learning rules and memorizing grammatical endings.

What are the author's qualifications?

The author taught in the public schools, in the field of music, for eighteen years; he is now a Director of Christian Education. "Languages" and "language-learning theories" were major hobby interests which led him to study the basics of many modern languages. When a fresh commitment to Christ led to many opportunities to lead Bible studies, he began to study Greek on his own (using the textbook, NEW TESTAMENT GREEK FOR BEGINNERS, by J. Gresham Machen). Even before finishing that book, he was already sharing many of the materials and approaches found in this workbook with youth Bible studies, with small groups of adults, and with the eighth graders in a Christian school. The excitement and appreciation of those who used these materials are what have caused him to believe they could be of value to a wider audience.

An explanation of the approach used in this book is included on page 305, for the benefit of the Greek specialist.

PART I

READING AND THE ALPHABET

After completing Part I, you will be able to:

1. pronounce all the Greek letters.

2. read Greek words quickly and fluently.

3. know over 200 Greek words.

4. use the words you have learned in context in Bible passages.

Exercise One

READING ENGLISH WORDS IN GREEK

The words on this page are English words, but they are written in Greek letters. As you begin to read, simply imagine that you are reading "fancy" English lettering. Answers for exercises are given in the answer pages at the end of the book (p. 307).

INSTRUCTIONS: Read all three words in each box, then circle the word that corresponds to the picture. Check your answers with the answer page in the back of the book.

βεδ
δοττεδ
βετ

Note that there is a small tail at the bottom of the letter "β" (b), and note the curved form of the letter "δ" (d).

δαδ
βατ
ταβ

The letter "a" is written like a circle crossing itself: (α)

κατ
κιτ
κοτ

Note that the letter "i" is not dotted, and is curved: (ι)

κιδ
βιτ
καβ

Some of the words on these pages are spelled "wrong", and must be sounded out to get the meaning. There is no "c" in the Greek alphabet, so we must spell "cab" as "kab".

Note uneven shape of s (ς)
Notice the way you say the letter "o" in the first two of these words. That's the way you'll always say it later on when pronouncing Greek words.

βοςς
κοςτ
δοτ

Exercise Two

MORE ENGLISH WORDS IN GREEK LETTERS.

This page introduces four Greek letters that do not look like English letters. There is a pronunciation guide at the bottom of the page.

Circle the word that corresponds to the picture.

πετ		ρωπ	
ποτ		ρωδ	
τοπ		ρωβ	

πιτ		κριβ	
τιπ		δριπ	
διπ		δαρτ	

ποπ		καρτ	
πωπ		κορκ	
βωτ		παρροτ	

τωδ		πιν	
κωδ		καν	
κωτ		παν	

ρατ		βων	
ραββιτ		κωτ	
βρεδ		κων	

PRONUNCIATION GUIDE

π = p ρ = r

ω = long "o" ν = n

Note the two kinds of "o":   o as in "log", ω as in "pope".

Exercise Three

ADDITIONAL GREEK LETTERS

Refer to the pronunciation guide at the bottom of the page.

Circle the word that corresponds to the picture.

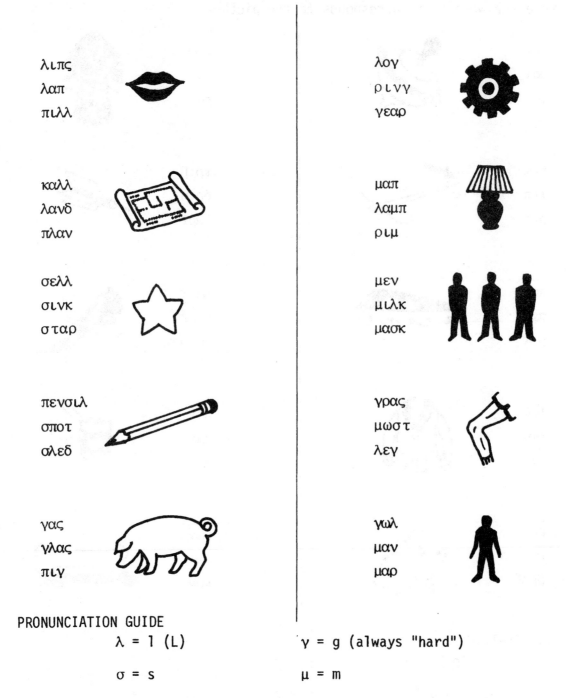

λιπς
λαπ
πιλλ

λογ
ρινγ
γεαρ

καλλ
λανδ
πλαν

μαπ
λαμπ
ριμ

σελλ
σινκ
σταρ

μεν
μιλκ
μασκ

πενσιλ
σποτ
σλεδ

γρας
μωστ
λεγ

γας
γλας
πιγ

γωλ
μαν
μαρ

PRONUNCIATION GUIDE

λ = 1 (L)   γ = g (always "hard")

σ = s   μ = m

Note: The sound for "s" is written ς at the end of a word, but is
       written σ anywhere else.

16

Exercise Four

NAMES FROM THE BIBLE

These are spelled as they appear in the Greek New Testament.
Match the Greek to the English equivalent.

I. ___ βαραββας   a. Anna   NOTES:
    ___ Αραβια   b. Cana   I've omitted some capital
    ___ ρεβεκα   c. Barabbas   letters and accents at this
    ___ Αννα   d. Nain   stage for simplicity. All
    ___ Κανα   e. Arabia   we're after is recognition.
    ___ Ναιν   f. Rebecca

II. ___ Αβελ   g. Barnabas   Ααρων would be
    ___ Αδαμ   h. Abel
    ___ Ααρων   i. Samaria   pronounced: Ah-roan.
    ___ βαρναβας   j. Adam
    ___ δαν   k. Dan
    ___ σαμαρια   l. Aaron

These have different "endings" in Greek and English:

III. ___ Ιταλια   a. Mark   All the a's in Greek words
     ___ Μαρκος   b. Messiah   should sound like the a in
     ___ Μαρια   c. Mary   father; so pronounce σατανας
     ___ σατανας   d. Italy
     ___ Μεσσιας   e. Satan   sah-tah-nahss

These are pronounced differently in Greek and English:

IV. ___ σιμων   f. Isaac   Greek doesn't have a letter
    ___ σολομων   g. Abraham   for the "h" sound. Pronounce
    ___ Αβρααμ   h. Peter   each "a" in Αβρααμ separate-
    ___ πετρος   i. Simon   ly: Ah-bra-ahm.
    ___ Ισαακ   j. Solomon
    ___ Ανδρεας   k. Andrew   Ισαακ would be: Izz-ah-ahk.

For your quick reference, all the Greek letters are listed on Page 76.

Exercise One

SOME POINTERS ON PRONUNCIATION

Circle correct answer.

Since all "a's" are pronounced like the "a" in "father":

1. Αβελ would be: a) Ah-bell   b) Abe-ell.

All e's are like the "e" in "pet":

2. πετρος would be: a) pe-tross   b) Pee-truss

All i's are often pronounced like the "i" in "machine":
    (Sometimes i's are pronounced as in pin)

3. Ιταλια would be: a) Ea-ta-lee-ah   b) Eye-tal-ee-ah

All o's are pronounced like the "o" in "log":

4. σολομων would be: a) sah-lah-mun   b) saw-law-moan

All ω's are pronounced like the "o" in bone:

5. σιμων would be: a) sigh-mun   b) see-moan

Exercise Two

DIPHTHONGS: Two vowels together, pronounced as one sound.

αυ sounds like "ow", as in cow
αι sounds like "eye"
οι sounds like "oi", as in foil
ου sounds like "oo", as in boot

English words used as examples:

   1. Three strikes and you're αυτ.
   2. In Holland, water is held in by a δαικ.
   3. Let's flip a κοιν.
   4. You eat soup with a σπουν.

I. Matching sounds, using English words. Match the letter of the picture or English word to the corresponding word spelled with Greek letters.

_ 1. αιλ

_ 2. οιλ

_ 3. αυλ

_ 4. μουν

a)   b) aisle   c) petroleum   d)

II. SOME GREEK NAMES WITH DIPHTHONGS.
Match the English name and the Greek pronunciation with the equivalent Greek name in the left column.

_ _ 5. λουκας

_ _ 6. κλαυδια

_ _ 7. σαδδουκαιος

_ _ 8. παυλος

_ _ 9. γαλιλαια

_ _10. καισαρος

e. Claudia
f. Galilee
g. Paul
h. Luke
i. Sadducee
j. Caesar

k. Lew-kahss
l. klow-dee-ah
m. pow-loss
n. gah-lee-lie-ah
o. sah-dew-kye-yoss
p. kye-sar-oss

Exercise Three

I. COGNATES (Words with similar spellings that mean about the same in Greek and English). Match the Greek words and their definitions.

_ 1. αρωμα

_ 2. μαννα

_ 3. μετροπολις

_ 4. εγω

a. my "self"; this is the Greek word for "I"; related to our word egotist.
b. bread from heaven
c. something sweet-smelling
d. very large urban area. (πολις is Greek for "city")

II. COGNATES with slight spelling changes. Match the English words with their Greek equivalents.

_ 5. βαπτισμα

_ 6. αγωνια

_ 7. λαμπας

_ 8. λεων

_ 9. σκορπιος

_10. λεπρος

_11. γενεαλογια

e. leper
f. agony
g. baptism
h. lamp
i. lion
j. scorpion
k. genealogy

Exercise Four

PRONUNCIATION CHECK

Select the correct pronunciation for each Greek word

___ 1. Μεσσιας   a) Mess-sigh-us   b) Mess-see-us

___ 2. σατανας   a) Sah-tah-nus   b) Say-tah-nus

___ 3. σιμων   a) See-moan   b) Sigh-moan

___ 4. πετρος   a) Pee-tross   b) Pe-tross

___ 5. Ισαακ   a) Iz-ah-ock   b) Eye-zack

___ 6. παυλος   a) Paw-luss   b) Pow-loss

___ 7. γαλιλαια   a) Gah-li-lay-uh   b) Gah-lee-lye-ah

___ 8. λουκας   a) Lew-cuss   b) Low-cuss

SIX GREEK WORDS

These are all real Greek words. Copy the Greek word on the long blank
after the English word.

 οικος    βιβλος    λαμπας

 σκορπιος    πετρα    λεων

house _____   rock _____

scorpion _____   lamp _____

book _____   lion _____

PRONUNCIATION CHECK OF THE NEW WORDS.

___ 9. πετρα   a) te-trah   b) pe-trah

___ 10. βιβλος   a) Bye-bloss   b) Bi-bloss

___ 11. σκορπιος   a) Score-pee-oss   b) Oh-core-pie-oss

___ 12. λαμπας   a) lahm-pahss   b) lamb-pace

___ 13. οικος   a) oy-cuss   b) oo-cuss

___ 14. λεων   a) Le-on   b) leh-own

Exercise Five

PHRASES

The English word "in" is a preposition. The Greek word for "in" is εν.

Guess at the meaning of the following phrases, and write a or b in the blank.

a	b

__ 1. σκορπιος εν οικῳ

The word after a preposition, such as οικῳ, will end differently than it does at other times. You must be able to recognize the meaning of a word no matter how it ends. (The actual endings will be the subject of Part II of this book.) The little mark under the last letter of the word οικῳ, above, is a small letter "ι". Do not pronounce it. Pronounce the ω as if there were no small ι there. (oy-coe)

__ 2. λαμπας εν σκορπιῳ

__ 3. βιβλος εν οικῳ

__ 4. οικος εν βιβλῳ

__ 5. πετρα εν βιβλῳ

The Greek word for "on" is επι.

	a	b
__ 6. λεων επι βιβλῳ		
__ 7. σκορπιος επι πετρᾳ		
__ 8. οικος εν πετρᾳ		
__ 9. λαμπας εν οικῳ		
__ 10. λαμπας επι οικῳ		

START YOUR DICTIONARY. Set aside one page in a notebook for each letter in the Greek alphabet. There are 24 letters all together; you'll find the entire alphabet listed on page 76. You do <u>not</u> need to put names or obvious cognates in your dictionary, but start <u>by</u> putting in the words you learned on the previous page. Then add every new word in this book as you come to it. YOU WILL NEED TO REFER TO YOUR DICTIONARY CONSTANTLY IN ORDER TO PROCEED THROUGH THIS BOOK!

ACCENT

Greek New Testaments published today are written in small letters with accent marks included in the proper places. This workbook will usually omit the accent marks. When you take an academic course in Greek, you will find that the accent is very important. In order to give you a little exposure to accents, they will be used in this workbook on pages such as this one that present quotations from the scripture.

The Greek accent is written in three ways, but all sound the same---a stress, just like English. The three ways are: ╱ ╲ and ⌒ .

SCRIPTURE QUOTES

Be sure to pronounce the Greek word, even if you know what the answer should be. Fill your English answer in the blank, and check your answers with your Bible. Your challenge is to recognise the Greek word even though its ending may be different than the way it was presented on a previous page.

1. Therefore everyone who hears My words and does them is like a wise

    οἰκίαν   ἐπὶ   πέτραν

    man who built his _____ _____ the _____. Matt.7:24

          Πέτρος   ἐπὶ   πέτρᾳ
2. Thou art _____, and _____ this _____ I will build
    my church.   Matt.16:18

                              ἐν   βίβλῳ
3. For David himself says _____ the _____of Psalms...Luke 20:42

                                                    λαμπὰς
4. A great star fell from heaven, burning as if it were a _____.

                                                    Rev.8:10

                                        σκορπίον
5. If he asks for an egg, will he give him a _____? Luke 11:12

Exercise One
MORE COGNATES FROM THE NEW TESTAMENT

Select the correct definition for each Greek word.

__1. διαβολος   __4. μεμβρανα

__2. δογμα   __5. βαρβαρος

__3. στιγμα   __6. σκανδαλον

Add these words to your dictionary

a. foreigner, barbarian
b. brand-mark, stigma
c. looks like "diabolic"; it's the Greek word for "devil".
d. looks like "scandal"; used in scripture to mean "offense" or stumbling block.
e. a rule; dogma.
f. animal skin: membrane.

One more scripture quote:

6. Your adversary, the _διάβολος_ _____ walks around like a roaring

    λέων
    _____, seeking to devour.   1 Pet. 5:8

MORE EXAMPLES FROM SCRIPTURE

Pronounce each Greek word and write its English equivalent on the line underneath it. Check your answers from your Bible.

1. (There is) one Lord, one faith, one _βάπτισμα_ _____. Eph.4:5

The word for "and" in Greek is και, pronounced "kye".

2. (Jesus said): _Ἐγὼ_____ _καὶ_____ the father are one. John 10:30

3. (In garden of Gethsamane): _καὶ___ being in great _ἀγωνία_____, he prayed.
                                                                    Luke 22:44

4. Jesus went into Bethany, to the _οἰκίᾳ_____ of _Σίμωνος_____ the

    λεπροῦ
    _____. Matt.26:6

5. _Ἀνδρέας_____, the brother of _Σίμωνος_____ _Πέτρου_____ was one of

    the two who heard this from John and followed him; so he first found

    his own brother _Σίμωνα_____ _καὶ_____ said to him, "We have

    found the _Μεσσίαν_____. John 1:40 & 41

Exercise Two

SOME MORE COGNATES

Match the definitions from the right column with the corresponding Greek
word in the left column. Add these words to your dictionary.

___ 1. λινον

___ 2. διαλεκτος

___ 3. δωμα

___ 4. σιων

___ 5. κιναμωνον

___ 6. τιτλος

a. insignia, inscription, title

b. house-top; we use it to refer to a
   housetop that is round.

c. linen

d. dialect: a variety of speech.

e. Zion; one name for Jerusalem.

f. cinnamon (a certain spice).

Exercise Three

CONTINUING WITH THE ALPHABET

These are English words spelled with Greek letters. Write these words
in English.

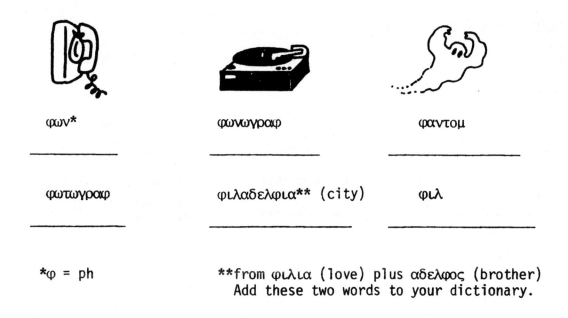

φων*

_____

φωτωγραφ

_____

φωνωγραφ

_____

φιλαδελφια** (city)

_____

φαντομ

_____

φιλ

_____

*φ = ph

**from φιλια (love) plus αδελφος (brother)
  Add these two words to your dictionary.

Exercise Four

Follow the same directions as for Exercise Three.

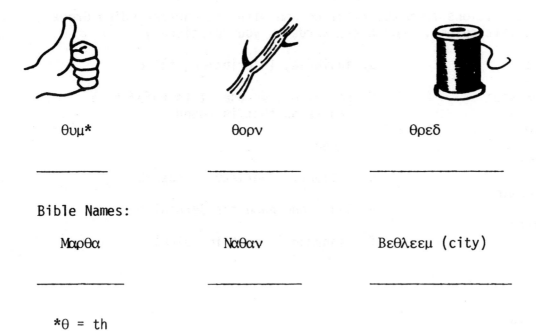

θυμ*   θορν   θρεδ

_____   _____   _____

Bible Names:

Μαρθα   Ναθαν   Βεθλεεμ (city)

_____   _____   _____

*θ = th

Exercise Five

MATCHING. Real Greek names:

Match the English words with their Greek equivalents. (Add these words to your dictionary)

___ 1. γολγοθα   ___ 5. φιλιππος

___ 2. ρουθ   ___ 6. στεφανος

___ 3. φαραω   ___ 7. Μαθουσαλα

___ 4. Ματθαιος   ___ 8. φαρισαιος

a. Ruth
b. Pharisee
c. Golgotha
d. Methuselah
e. Matthew
f. Philip
g. Pharaoh
h. Stephen

NEW WORDS

Match these Greek words with their definitions. (Add these words to your dictionary)

___ 9. θεος

___10. φωσφορος

___11. παρθενος

___12. καθολικος

___13. οφθαλμος

a. Means universal, world-wide; a church body uses this word in its name, but it is also used in the Nicene Creed to indicate the all-encompassing nature of the body of Christ.

b. Virgin. A temple in Athens was named using the word. (The Parthenon)

c. God. We get our word "theology" by combining this word with λογος. (word, study of)

d. Phosphorus. (φως = light, φορος = bearing)

e. Eye. Basis for English word for eye-doctor.

Exercise Six

NEW GREEK WORDS TO GUESS

Match the English words and definitions with their Greek equivalents. (Add these words to your dictionary)

___ 1. λιθος

___ 2. λογος

___ 3. ανθρωπος

___ 4. ορφανος

___ 5. καρδια

___ 6. θρονος

a. Man. We get the word anthropology from this word.

b. Word. The word "logic" is related, and so is the "-logy" which we put on the end of scientific terms.

c. Stone. Lithography was a printing process that involved etching onto a piece of limestone.

d. Chair for a king: throne.

e. Person without parents: orphan.

f. Heart. Compare our medical word "cardiac".

Exercise Seven

USING THE NEW GREEK WORDS

Match the picture with the Greek phrase which describes it.

	a	b

___ 1. ανθρωπος εν οικῳ

___ 2. καρδια εν ανθρωπῳ

___ 3. λιθος εν καρδιᾳ

___ 4. λογος επι βιβλῳ

___ 5. λογος επι λιθῳ

	a	b

__ 6. θρονος εν οικῳ

__ 7. λιθος επι θρονῳ

__ 8. καρδια εν ορφανῳ

__ 9. ορφανος επι θρονῳ

Answer yes or no:

__10. ανθρωπος και ορφανος εν οικῳ

__11. πετρα και λιθος επι οικῳ

Exercise Eight

PRONUNCIATION CHECK

Match these Greek words with their respective pronunciations.

__ 1. βιβλῳ   a) Bib-low   b) Bib-loo

__ 2. φιλιππος   a) thill-lip-oss   b) fill-lip-oss

__ 3. ρουθ   a) Rooth   b) Pooth

__ 4. Ματθαιος   a) Mott-thigh-oss   b) Matt-they-oss

__ 5. φαρισαιος   a) far-iss-eye-oss   b) Fair-iss-ay-oss

__ 6. ανθρωπος   a) on-thrah-poss   b) on-throw-poss

__ 7. πετρα   a) Pee-traw   b) Pe-trah

__ 8. οικων   a) oy-cone   b) oy-coon

__ 9. ανθρωπῳ   a) on-throw-poo   b) on-throw-poe

__10. λιθου   a) li-thoo   b) li-thowe

__11. βιβλος   a) Bye-bloss   b) Bi-bloss

MEANING CHECK

Match these Greek words with their corresponding pictures.

__12. βιβλος

__13. οικος

__14. λαμπας

__15. πετρα

__16. ανθρωπος

__17. καρδια

__18. λιθος

__19. λογος

__20. θρονος

__21. ορφανος

__22. σκορπιος

 a
 b
 c
 d
 e
 f
 g
 h
 i
 j
 k

Pronounce each Greek word, and then write its English equivalent on the line below.

What ____^{ἄνθρωπος}____ among you, when his son asks him for a loaf, will

he give him a ____^{λίθον}____?   Matt. 7:9

^{ἐν}____ the beginning was the ____^{λόγος}____, ____^{καὶ}____ the ____^{λόγος}____ was with ____^{θεόν}____.

^{καὶ}____ the ____^{λόγος}____ was ____^{θεός}____.   John 1:1

SCRIPTURE VERSES

Try to identify the Greek word no matter what ending is put on it.
Write in the English equivalent under each Greek word. Check your
answers from your Bible.

1. Resist the __διαβόλῳ__ __καὶ__ he will flee from you.   James 4:7

2. But that which comes out of the mouth proceeds from the __καρδίας__ ,

   and that "defiles" the __ἄνθρωπον__ . Matt. 15:18

Some of the names in the following passages may "throw" you:

3. Leaving the next day, (Paul) came to __Καισάρειαν__ , __καὶ__

   entered into the __οἶκον__ of __Φιλίππου__ . Acts 21:8

The blanks underlined with two lines mean the word is "plural" --
add an "s".

4. __Παῦλος__ , knowing that some of them were __Σαδδουκαίων__ __καὶ__

   the others __Φαρισαίων__ , cried in the council: men, brothers,

   __ἐγὼ__ am a __Φαρισαῖος__ , a son of __Φαρισαίων__ . Acts 23:6

Though many of the following words are "cognates", the words customarily
used to translate them may surprise you. Check your Bible after writing
in your guess.

5. (Christ, the cornerstone, is also a) __λίθος__ of stumbling

   __καὶ__ a __πέτρα__ of __σκανδάλου__ . 1 Pet. 2:8

6. It happened __ἐν__ those days that there went out a __δόγμα__ from

   __Καίσαρος__ __Αὐγούστου__ that the entire domain be enrolled.
                                                      Luke 2:1

32

7. (Paul writing): When you come, bring the cloak I left in Troas

         κάρπῳ   καὶ   βιβλία   μεμβράνας

  with Carpus , _____ the _____ , especially the _____ .

                                                2 Tim. 4:13

        ἐγὼ   στίγματα   ἐν

8. For _____ bear the _____ of Jesus ____ my body. Gal. 6:17

                                            ἀρώματα

9. When the sabbath had ended (the women) brought _____ that

  they might come and anoint him.   Mark 16:1

Exercise One

SOME COMPOUND WORDS

Some of these were put together by the Greeks themselves; others by English-speakers using Greek words as roots.

Instructions: From the word-list at right, select the two words that you think were used to form the English words, and then write these Greek words in the two long blanks.

Select the meaning from below the word-list that best fits each word, and write the corresponding letter in the blank. Be sure to add all Greek words on this page to your dictionary.

__ 1. microscope   _____ + σκοπος   μετρον (measure)

__ 2. micrometer   _____ + _____   θεος   (God)

                                        κοσμος (world, universe)

__ 3. sophomore   _____ + _____   μικρος (small)

__ 4. Timothy   _____ + _____   μακρος (large)

__ 5. microcosm   _____ + _____   σοφος (wise)

                                        μωρος (foolish "moron")

__ 6. theosophy   _____ + _____   τιμιος (honored, precious)

__ 7. macroscopic   _____ + _____   λογος (word,"study of")

__ 8. cosmology   _____ + _____   σκοπος (watcher).

__ 9. macrocosm   _____ + _____

a. This name means "honored of God". b. Large enough to see with the naked eye. c. A religious system that claims to have direct knowledge of God, without Bible or Jesus. d. The entire universe. e. Something to look at tiny things with. f. A student who knows little, but regards himself as very smart. g. Used to measure small things. h. Study of the universe. i. "The universe in a drop of water".

___ 10. energy   _____ + _____   μονος (only)

___ 11. monolith   _____ + _____   φιλος (friend)

    εν   (in)

___ 12. monologue   _____ + _____   βιος (life)

___ 13. philosophy   _____ + _____   λογος (word,"study of")

___ 14. philanthropy   _____ + _____   εργον (work)

    ανθρωπος (man)

___ 15. photograph   _____ + _____   σοφια (wisdom)

___ 16. anthropology   _____ + _____   γραφω (write)

___ 17. biology   _____ + _____   λιθος (stone)

    μεγα   (large)

___ 18. megalith   _____ + _____   φωτος (light)

___ 19. lithograph   _____ + _____

a. Showing your love of mankind through your generosity. b. A huge rock. c. Marks made on paper through exposure to the light. d. A stone structure standing alone. e. Study of man. f. A printing process which involves etching upon stone. g. The ability to put work in a task. h. Love of wisdom. i. Study of life. j. A conversation by one person.

The following compounds are found in the New Testament. Match to the number of the English word above and from the previous page:

___ A. τιμοθεος   ___ B. φιλοσοφια   ___ C. ενεργεια   ___ D. φιλανθρωπια

SCRIPTURE EXAMPLES

Disregard any unfamiliar endings and simply write in the meaning of the main part of the Greek word. Check your answers with your Bible.

θεὸς   μωρὰ   κόσμου

But _____ has chosen the _____(things) of the _____ in order

σοφούς

to confound the _____. 1 Cor. 1:27

ἐν   κόσμῳ

All that is ___ the _____ --- the lust of the flesh and the lust of

ὀφθαλμῶν   βίου

the _____ and the pride of _____ --- is not of the father

κόσμου

but of the _____. 1 John 2:16

While you have _____ (φῶς), believe in the _____ (φῶς), that ye may be sons of _____ (φωτὸς). John 12:36

Greater love than this has no one: that anyone should lay down his life for his _____ (φίλων); you are my _____ (φίλοι), if you do the things I command you. John 15:13, 14

The following have word order different from English:

If anyone build on the foundation with gold, silver, _____ _____ (λίθους τιμίους) wood, hay, stubble...   1 Cor. 3:12

Who can forgive sins but _____ _____ (μόνος θεός)? Luke 5:21

Exercise One

MORE ALPHABET

Say the number "8". Spell in English:_____.
The Dipthong "ei" sounds like "ay". It also does in Greek. The
words in the left column are English words spelled with Greek letters.
Match with the corresponding word in the right column.

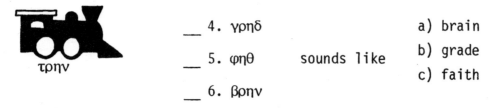

τρειν

___ 1. βρειν   a) faith

___ 2. γρειδ   sounds like   b) brain

                                            c) grade

___ 3. φειθ

The Greek letter η also sounds like "ay"; so "8" = ειτ = ητ.
Same directions as previous section.

τρην

___ 4. γρηδ   a) brain

___ 5. φηθ   sounds like   b) grade

                                            c) faith

___ 6. βρην

IDENTIFY THESE BIBLE NAMES. The Words in the middle column are simply
to help you read the Greek words in the left column. Match the Greek
words with their English equivalents from the right column.

___ 7. δανιηλ   dah-nee-ale   a) Israel

___ 8. Ισραηλ   Iss-rah-ale   b) Gabriel

                                                  c) Daniel

___ 9. γαβριηλ   Gah-bree-ale

Note: When names with "η" are written in English letters, the letter
"e" is used.

COGNATES

Match these Greek cognates with their meaning from the right column.
(Add these words to your dictionary)

___10. ειϰων   a. allegory

___11. αμην   b. alleluia

___12. αλληλουια   c. father (compare our word "paternity")

___13. ανατολη   d. icon. These images are valued in the
        Eastern Orthodox Church.

___14. αλληγορεω   e. This word means East; a region of the
        ancient world was named Anatolia.

___15. σεισμος   f. Means earthquake. Compare our word seismo-
        graph.

___16. πατηρ   g. This word means: "It is true!". Used to end
        a prayer.

___17. προφητης   h. Looks like "Bible", but means book in general
        in Greek.

___18. αηρ   i. camel

___19. βιβλος   j. prophet

___20. σωτηρ   k. parable

___21. παραβολη   l. orphan

___22. θεραπεια   m. air

___23. ορφανος   n. therapy

___24. καμηλος   o. Saviour. Theologians use the word
        "soteriology"--the study of salvation.

Exercise Two

PRONUNCIATION CHECK

Match each Greek word with its correct pronunciation.

___ 1. γαβριηλ   a) Gah-bree-ail   b) Gay-bree-ell

___ 2. αμην   a) aim-men   b) ah-mane

___ 3. δανιηλ   a) Dah-nee-ell   b) Dah-nee-ale

___ 4. πατηρ   a) Pah-tare   b) potter

___ 5. προφητης   a) praw-fay-tace   b) prophetess

___ 6. ισραηλ   a) Is-rye-all   b) Iz-rah-ale

___ 7. ενεργεια   a) en-er-jee-ah   b) en-air-gay-uh

___ 8. σεισμος   a) size-mos   b) saze-moss

SCRIPTURES WITH η-WORDS.

Pronounce the Greek word, write its English equivalent beneath it and check your answers with your Bible.

καὶ
___ the twenty-four elders and four creatures fell and worshipped ____ θεῷ

who was seated ____ ἐπὶ the _____ θρόνῳ, saying, _____ Ἀμὴν, _____ Ἀλληλουϊά. Rev. 19:4

> (The two dots above the ι in Alleluia tell you to pronounce both the ι and the α, rather than running them together into a diphthong.)

When Jesus was born, wise men from the _____ ἀνατολῶν came to Jerusalem,

saying... we have seen his star in the _____ ἀνατολῇ and have come to worship him. Matt. 2:1-2

> An older name for the country we now call Turkey: Anatolia

How much more will your _____ πατὴρ ____ ἐν heaven give good gifts to those asking him? Matt. 7:11b

Blind guides! Straining at a gnat, and swallowing a _____ κάμηλον. Matt. 23:24

_____ Ἀμὴν _____ ἀμὴν I say to you: If anyone keeps my _____ λόγον he shall not see

death. John 8:51

SCRIPTURES SHOWING VARIOUS ENDINGS

Pronounce the Greek word, write its English equivalent beneath it and
check your answers with your Bible.

1. For _____ θεὸς so loved the _____ κόσμον that he gave his only son...

John 3:16

When some words end with -ου, this may indicate "possession" ---
so use the word "of" when translating. βιβλου = of book.

2. _____ καὶ the peace _____ _____ θεοῦ, which passes all understanding, will

keep your _____ καρδίας and minds ___ ἐν Christ Jesus.   Phil. 4:7

If there already is a preposition, don't add the word "of":

3. Grace to you and peace from ἀπὸ _____ θεοῦ our _____ πατρὸς. Eph. 1:2

   (The word πατρος is the word πατηρ (father), contracted to
   πατρ, with an ending added.)

Some words must end with ῳ when written after the word εν:

4. ____ καὶ to show...the mystery hidden _____ ἐν θεῷ _____ who created everything,

   to make known...the wonderfully-varied _____ σοφία _____ θεοῦ.

Eph. 3:9-10

5. He was ___ ἐν the _____ κόσμῳ, _____ καὶ the _____ κόσμος was made by him,

   _____ καὶ the _____ κόσμος did not οὐκ know him.   John 1:10

Or the word may end that way without any word εν being there:

6. _____ Ἀβραὰμ believed ____ θεῷ and it was reckoned to him as righteousness.

Rom. 4:3

In the next example, there is an -ου indicating possession; I had to
write in the word "the", since you don't know that word yet.

7. Beware lest anyone capture you through _____ φιλοσοφίας and empty deceit,

   according to the traditions of _____ ἀνθρώπων, according to the elements

   ___ (the) _____ κόσμου and not according to Christ. Col. 2:8

39

LESSON SIX

Exercise One

ENGLISH WORDS THAT WERE CREATED FROM GREEK WORDS

Instructions: Find the Greek word in the second column that reminds you
of an English word in the first column. Print that Greek word on the
long blank provided. Then select the definition below which corresponds
to the English word, and print the letter of the definition in the short
blank. Copy these Greek words in your dictionary.

___ 1. phonetics _____   τοπος (place)

___ 2. galactic _____   σκολιος (crooked)

___ 3. phosphorescent _____   φωνη (sound)

___ 4. arterio-sclerosis _____   γαλακτος (of milk)

___ 5. topical _____   φοβος (fear)

___ 6. neon _____   φως (light)

___ 7. phobia _____   σκληρος (hard)

___ 8. scoliosis _____   νεος (new)

a. Hardening of arteries. b. The fear of something. c. Pertaining to
our galaxy, the "Milky Way". d. Placed into categories. e. Curvature
of the spine. f. Study of the sounds of languages. g. A rare gas named
after its "new-ness". h. Glows in the dark.

___ 9. plastic _____   κλεπτω (steal)

__10. anthracite _____   ορθος (straight)

__11. necromancy _____   δενδρον (tree)

__12. kleptomaniac _____   πλαστος (formed)

__13. dendrite _____   γραμμα (letter)

__14. acoustics _____   ανθρακος (coal)

__15. grammar _____   νεκρος (dead)

__16. orthodontist _____   ακουω (hear)

i. The forbidden occult practice of attempting to contact the dead.
j. One who straightens teeth. k. Study of language rules. l. A type
of coal. m. Branch-like end of a nerve cell. n. Substance that can
be formed into any desired shape. o. Science of sound. p. Habitual
thief.

__17. Thanatopsis _____   κρανιον (skull)

__18. leukocyte _____   μεγας (large)

__19. gerontology _____   μελας (black)

__20. idiosyncracies _____   εσωτερος (inner)

__21. esoteric _____   γερων (old)

__22. melanoma _____   ιδιος (self)

__23. megaphone _____   θανατος (death)

__24. cranium _____   λευκος (white)

__25. trauma _____   τραυμα (wound)

q. White blood cell. r. Device that makes sounds louder. s. Secrets known only to an inner group. t. Head-bone. u. Medical practice for the aged. v. Tumor containing dark pigment. w. My personal quirks. x. A poem giving the author's thoughts about death. y. We use this word for the condition brought on by shock.

τραύματα
(The Good Samaritan) approached and bandaged his _____ with oil.
———————— Luke 10:34
(See Exercise 1, #25)

SCRIPTURES

γάλακτος
1. You have need (of) _____, not solid food. Heb. 5:12

ἐγώ   φῶς   κόσμου
2. Jesus said, ____ am the _____ ___ the _____. John 8:12

φωνὴν   θρόνου
3. I looked and heard the _____ of many angels around the _____.
Rev. 5:11

(throne has an -ου ending because it comes after a preposition---"around". Do not add "of".)

Introducing a new capital letter: Γ is the capital of γ.

τόπον   Γολγοθᾶ   Τόπος
4. They came to a _____ called _____, which means _____

Κρανίου
____ __ _____. Matt. 27:33

(Use the word "of" with the word that ends in -ου. There is no word for "a" in Greek, but we need to use this word so our trans- lation sounds like smooth English: of a skull.)

ἐν   φόβῳ   θεοῦ
5. ...perfecting holiness ____ the _____ ___ _____. 2 Cor. 7:1

6. ...you have put off the old ἄνθρωπον _____ with it's practices, καὶ ____

    have put on the νέον _____ ... Col. 3:9-10

7. But when the kindness and φιλανθρωπία θεοῦ _____ _____ _____ our saviour
    appeared, he saved us. Titus 3:4

8. Master, I knew that you were a σκληρὸς _____ ἄνθρωπος _____.
                                           Matt. 25:24

9. And I saw a μέγαν λευκὸν θρόνον _____ _____ _____ and one seated on it...and I saw

    the νεκρούς _____ both great and μικρούς _____ standing before the θρόνου _____,

    καὶ βιβλία ____ _____ were opened. Rev. 20:11-12

10. (Jesus partook of flesh and blood) so that through θανάτου _____ he

    might destroy him who had the power θανάτου ___ _____, that is, the

    διάβολον _____, and free those who through φόβῳ θανάτου _____ __ _____ were en-
    slaved all their lives. Heb. 2:14-15

Exercise One

MORE COGNATES

Matching: Select the best definition for each Greek word. Keep your
dictionary current!

__ 1. φαρμακεια

__ 2. οινος

__ 3. δεσποτης

__ 4. εθνικος

__ 5. θησαυρος

__ 6. αποστασια

__ 7. ναρδος

__ 8. μουσικος

__ 9. τραυμα

__10. καταστροφη

__11. πορνη

__12. ειδωλον

__13. σκολιος

__14. μαθητης

__15. σωμα

__16. μαγος

a. A perfume-like ointment: NARD

b. Means "wound"; we use it to refer to going
   into shock after an accident.

c. Crooked. We call a crooked spine SCOLIOSIS.
   Also used figuratively.

d. Prostitute; we made the word Pornography from
   this.

e. Idol, false god. Combined with the Greek word
   for worship, λατρεια, we get the word meaning
   idolatry: ειδωλολατρεια

f. μαθ in Greek referred to learning in general,
   not just to the highly-disciplined subject
   we call by that name today (math). The word
   you're matching to means one under discipline;
   a learner; usually translated "disciple" in
   the New Testament.

g. This word means body. Our English word psycho-
   somatic means that our bodies are affected
   by the state of our minds.

h. One who makes sounds by singing or playing
   an instrument.

i. Refers to the race of the person; comes from
   Greek word εθνος, which means "nation". ETHNIC.
   (often translated "Gentile")

j. Means "treasure"; we use it to refer to a book
   which is a treasury of words: a THESAURUS.

k. This word originally referred to drugs mixed
   for magic; now we use it for a drugstore or
   PHARMACY. The word φαρμακος is translated
   "sorcerer".

l. One who practices magic. Our term for the "wise
   men" who visited the child Jesus is a respell-
   ing of this word into English: Magi.

m. Wine

n. Tyrannical ruler: DESPOT

o. Apostasy (falling away from the faith)

p. Means "turned-down", and refers to disasters
   like earthquakes where everything topples.

Exercise Two

A SPECIAL USE FOR THE LETTER "I"

Some languages pronounce the name "Jesus" differently than we do. For example, in German it's spelled "Jesus", but pronounced "yay-zoose". Greek also has the "y" sound in names where we're accustomed to the "J" sound. But Greek doesn't spell those names either with a "Y" or with a "J". Greek uses the letter "I" for this purpose.

For example: Ιωβ. Pronounce it yōb. It's the Old Testament figure noted for his suffering. We call him "Job".

IDENTIFY:

		Greek pronunciation	Match to meaning
__	1. Ιακωβ	yah-kobe	a) Jesus
__	2. Ιωνας	yoe-nass	b) Jacob
__	3. Ιησους	yay-zoose	c) Jonah

MATCHING NAMES:

Select the best definition for each Greek word.

__ 4. Ιερεμιας

__ 5. Ιησους

__ 6. Ιορδανης (pronounce: your-dah-nace)

__ 7. Γενεσις

__ 8. κορινθος

__ 9. Ναθαναηλ

a. Our Lord and Saviour

b. A city to which Paul wrote two letters (after Romans in New Testament).

c. First book in the Bible; it means "beginnings". (lineage, generations)

d. The river that John the Baptist used for baptizing. (Jordan)

e. A disciple whom Jesus saw beneath a tree (John 1:45-49).

f. Prophet located after Isaiah in the Old Testament.

__ 10. Ιουδαια

__ 11. Ιουδας

__ 12. Νικοδημος

__ 13. κορνηλιος

__ 14. ποντιος πιλατος

__ 15. θομας

g. The doubting disciple

h. The Roman governor who OK'd Christ's crucifixion.

i. A name for the Holy Land: Judea

j. He came to Jesus by night (John 3).

k. He betrayed Christ for 30 silver pieces.

l. He was swallowed by a great fish.

m. Peter preached the gospel to him (Acts 10).

MATCH PRONUNCIATIONS TO GREEK NAMES:

___16. Ιησους

___17. Ιακωβ

___18. Ιερεμιας

___19. Ιακωβος

___20. Ιωαννης

___21. Ιουδαια

a. ye-re-mee-as

b. yay-zoose

c. you-dye-ah

d. ya-kobe

e. ya-co-boss. (This is the Greek word
   for "James")

f. yo-on-ace. (Greek for "John")

Exercise Three

PRONUNCIATION CHECK

Select the correct pronunciation for each Greek word.

___ 1. Ιερουσαλημ*   a) eye-row-salem   b) Yeh-rue-sah-lame

___ 2. Ιερεμιας   a) ear-em-my-us   b) Yeh-rem-ee-us

___ 3. Ιησους   a) Yay-zoose   b) Ee-ayze-oose

___ 4. Ιορδανης   a) Yor-dan-us   b) Yor-dah-nace

___ 5. Ιωαννης   a) Eye-oh-annas   b) Yoe-on-ace

___ 6. Ιουδαια   a) You-die-uh   b) Yoe-day-uh

___ 7. Ιουδας   a) Yah-dass   b) Yew-dass

___ 8. Ιακωβ   a) Yah-cob   b) Yah-cobe

___ 9. Ιωνας   a) Yoe-nass   b) Yon-us

___10. Ιωβ   a) ee-ob   b) Yobe

___11. φαρμακεια   a) farma-kaya   b) farma-key-uh

___12. θησαυρος   a) theos-ourus   b) Thay-sour-us

___13. γενεσεως   a) Jen-ess-iss   b) Gen-ess-eh-oce

___14. μουσικος   a) moo-zee-koss   b) myu-zik-us

   *means Jerusalem.

MEANING CHECK

Select the best definition for each Greek word.

___15. φαρμακεια

___16. γενεσεως

___17. καταστροφη

___18. θεος

___19. φιλοσοφια

___20. προς

___21. φιλος

___22. λογος

___23. σοφια

___24. κοσμος

___25. θησαυρος

___26. φιλαδελφια

___27. αδελφος

___28. σωτηρ

___29. εθνων

a. love of wisdom

b. god

c. everything fallen down

d. of lineage, generation; related to Greek name for first book of the Bible.

e. has something to do with drugs; in Bible times, that would mean drugs in the occult.

f. friend, related to (love, friendship)

g. wisdom

h. world

i. word

j. treasure

k. forth

l. nations or Gentiles

m. brother

n. saviour

o. brotherly love

SCRIPTURES

As you check your answers to the following in your Bible, you may be surprised at how these familiar cognates are sometimes used. Also, note a new capital letter: Δ = δ.

Matthew 1:1 βίβλος _____ of the γενέσεως _____ of Ἰησοῦ _____ Christ, son of

Δαυὶδ _____ ...

There was a ἄνθρωπος _____ sent from θεοῦ _____ ; his name was Ἰωάννης _____

John 1:6

46

Outside are the dogs _____ the φαρμακοὶ _____ the πόρνοι
_____ _____

_____ the murderers _____ the εἰδωλολάτραι _____ those φιλῶν
καὶ   καὶ   καὶ
_____ _____
                                                  (add -ing)

καὶ
_____ doing falsehood. Rev. 22:15

Servants, submit to your δεσπόταις with all φόβῳ, not only to the
_____   _____

good... but also to the σκολιοῖς. 1 Pet. 2:18
_____

Land of Ζαβουλὼν _____ land of Νεφθαλίμ, by the way of the sea,
_____ καὶ   _____

beyond the Ἰορδάνου, Γαλιλαία of the ἐθνῶν... Matt. 4:15
_____ _____   _____

When you pray don't use vain repetitions as the ἐθνικοί do. Matt. 6:7
                                                _____

Ἰησοῦς
_____ took bread, blessed it and gave it to his μαθηταῖς,
                                                    _____

saying, take, eat, this is my σῶμα. Matt. 26:26
                              _____

47

Exercise One

SOME COMMON PREPOSITIONS

Select the word from the word-list that would best translate the preposition (underlined word) in each sentence. Write the letter of the
English word you've chosen in the short blank at the front of each
sentence.

WORD LIST

__ 1. θρονος is <u>εν</u> οικῳ.

__ 2. βιβλος is <u>επι</u> θρονῳ.

a. on _____

__ 3. σκορπιος is entering <u>εις</u> οικον.

b. beside _____

__ 4. Ανθρωπος is leaning <u>αντι</u> οικου.

c. in _____

__ 5. Ανθπωπος is walking <u>προς</u> οικον.

d. from _____

__ 6. λεων is running <u>δια</u> οικου.

e. through _____

__ 7. Δενδρον is growing <u>παρα</u> οικῳ.

f. out of _____

__ 8. σκορπιος is climbing <u>εκ</u> δενδρου.

g. toward _____

__ 9. Καμηλος is walking away <u>απο</u> οικου.

h. against _____

i. into _____

Write the correct Greek preposition after each word in the word-list,
and add the new words to your dictionary.

In Part II of this book you will learn the endings that are put on
nouns, and there will be a list of which endings to use after particular
prepositions. For Part I, it is sufficient for you to grasp only the
meaning of the words.

Exercise Two

SENTENCES WITH PREPOSITIONS

Write the letter of each picture in front of the corresponding sentence.

__ 1. Δανιηλ is sitting επι θρονῳ.

__ 2. Δεσποτης is whipping someone εν οικῳ.

__ 3. Ειδωλ is placed παρα θησαυρῳ.

__ 4. Καμηλος is going απο οικου.

__ 5. λεων is lying παρα πετρᾳ.

__ 6. Διαβολος is going εκ καρδιας.

__ 7. Καμηλος is going δια οικου.

__ 8. Γαβριηλ is going εις οικον.

__ 9. κρανιον is leaning αντι βιβλον.

__10. Μαθητης is coming προς δενδρον.

__11. λεων is coming εκ οικου.

__12. βιβλος is placed επι λιθῳ.

__13. προφητης is leaning αντι δενδρου.

__14. Διαβολος is coming εις οικον.

__15. Μαθητης is coming προς θησαυρον.

SCRIPTURES USING PREPOSITIONS

Pronounce the Greek word and then write its English equivalent beneath it.

1.   καὶ   ἐν   Ἰησοῦς (a)   ἀπὸ
   _____ ___ those days, _____ came _____ Nazareth (in)

   Γαλιλαίας   καὶ   εἰς
   _____ _____ was baptized (by going) _____ the

   Ἰορδάνην (b)   Ἰωάννου (c)   καὶ   ἐκ
   _____ by _____. _____ immediately, coming up _____

   of the water he saw the heavens opened... Mark 1:9 & 10

   FOOTNOTES: Pronounciations of words starting with I: a) Ἰησους =
   yay-zoose; b) Ιορδανην = your-dah-nane; c) Ιωαννου = Yo-ah-new

                    καρδία   πρὸς θεόν
2. Beloved, if our _____ condemn us not, we have boldness ____ _____.
                                                      1 John 3:21

                                  παρὰ
3. ...Innumerable as the sand which is _____ the seashore.
                                                      Heb. 11:12

            διὰ
4. ...so that _____ death he might destroy him who had the power of

                    διάβολον
   death, that is, the _____, and free those who were held in

        φόβω   διὰ
   slavery by _____ of death _____ all their lives. Heb. 2:14-15

                                        εἰς   Ἰησουν
5. Don't you know that whoever was baptized _____ Christ _____

            εἰς
   was baptized _____ his death? We are buried with him therefore

   διὰ   βαπτίσματος   εἰς
   _____ _____ _____ death, so that as Christ was raised

   ἐκ   νεκρῶν   διὰ   πατρός
   _____ the _____ _____ the glory of the _____, we

                        ἐν
   also might walk _____ newness of life. Rom. 6:3-4

50

LESSON NINE

Exercise One

WORDS FORMED BY COMBINING WITH PREPOSITIONS

Some of these combinations were actually formed by the Greeks; others are English words formed from Greek roots. Put the word that appears after the plus sign in your dictionary.

WORDS FORMED WITH παρα (alongside): RESULTANT ENGLISH WORDS:

__ 1. παρα + αλληλων (each other)

__ 2. παρα + γραφω (write)

__ 3. παρα + βαλλω (throw)

__ 4. παρα + νοια (mind)

__ 5. παρα + σιτος (food)

__ 6. παρα + εν + θεις (put)

a. Throwing an everyday example alongside a spiritual truth gives us a PARABLE. *παραβολη

b. A creature that gets its food by living near another creature is called a PARASITE.

c. When a person's mind is beside itself with fear: PARANOIA.

d. Two lines which are alongside one another are parallel.

e. Writing this sign ⁋ alongside a sentence = a new PARAGRAPH.

f. Putting words within brackets next to what they're explaining.

WORDS FORMED WITH επι (on):

__ 7. επι + στελλω (send)

__ 8. επι + γραφω (write)

__ 9. επι + φανος (lantern)

__10. επι + δερμα (skin)

__11. επι + γλοττις (tongue)

__12. επι + δημος (people)

__13. επι + γραμμα (written)

__14. επι + ταφος (tomb)

__15. επι + κεντρον (center)

__16. επι + σκοπος (watcher)

g. Church festival about Jesus shining forth with the truth of who He is: EPIPHANY. *επιφανεια

h. It hangs above your tongue: epiglottis

i. Outer layer of skin: EPIDERMIS

j. Message sent on to someone: an EPISTLE. *επιστολη

k. Inscription on statue: EPIGRAPH

l. Words on a gravestone: EPITAPH

m. Bishops watch over the church in the EPISCOPAL system. επισκοπος

n. A disease coming upon many at the same time: EPIDEMIC.

o. Writing upon a subject with a short witty poem: EPIGRAM

p. Place above center of an earthquake: EPICENTER.

Note: Underlined words above appear in Greek forms in the New Testament. Asterisk* words above are used beginning on page 53. Put them in your dictionary.

REFER TO PICTURE OF PREPOSITIONS ON PAGE 48 TO WORK OUT THESE:

__17. εκ + κεντρον (center)

__18. απο + στελλω (send)

__19. απο + γη (earth)

__20. απο + λογος (word)

__21. δια + μετρον (measure)

__22. δια + σπορα (seed)

__23. παρα + ουσια (being)

__24. αντι + νομος (law)

__25. αντι + θεις (placed)

q. Measurement thru circle: DIAMETER

r. Point of orbit far from earth: apogee.

s. One who's sent out on a mission: emissary or APOSTLE. αποστολος

t. Theological term for Christ's coming to be with us: PAROUSIA. *παρουσια

u. ANTINOMIANS feel we shouldn't pay attention to the law.

v. An ECCENTRIC is off-center.

w. People scattered through the world like sown seed: DIASPORA.

x. One idea placed in contrast against another: ANTITHESIS.

y. Words to defend your view against criticism. APOLOGY. *απολογια

Note: Underlined words above appear in Greek forms in the New Testament. Asterisk* words above are used on following pages. Put them in your dictionary.

Exercise Two

GUESS THE MEANINGS

Write the appropriate Greek word on the long blanks:

man _____	law _____	see _____
write _____	treasure _____	shining _____
skin _____	seed _____	throne _____
grave _____	earth _____, _____	

Exercise Three

PRONUNCIATION CHECK

Select the correct pronunciation for each of these Greek words.

___ 1. αλληλους   ___ 6. Ιησους   a. pah-rah-bo-lay   f. gace

___ 2. θησαυρους   ___ 7. λεγει   b. yay-zoose   g. ah-lay-loose

___ 3. επιφανεια   ___ 8. μετρειτε   c. met-ray-teh   h. leggay

___ 4. θεῳ   ___ 9. γης   d. theh-oh   i. pa-roo-see-a

___ 5. παρουσια   ___10. παραβολη   e. e-pee-fah-nay-a   j. Thay-sow-rooce

MEANING CHECK

Select the best definition for each of these Greek words.

__11. επι	__18. λογος	k. against	w. through
__12. φανος	__19. εκ	l. on	x. from
__13. επιφανεια	__20. παρα	m. of God	y. next-to
__14. θησαυρος	__21. απο	n. torch	z. Christ's coming
__15. παραβολη	__22. δια	o. of law	
__16. θεου	__23. αντι	r. parable; a story of comparison.	
__17. νομου	__24. παρουσια	s. treasure, storehouse	
		t. shine upon	
		u. out	
		v. word	

SCRIPTURES

Pronounce the Greek words and write their English equivalents beneath.
Check answers in your Bible.

Don't lay up for yourselves   θησαυρους   επι   γης   _____ _____ _____ Matt. 6:19

For where your θησαυρος _____ is, there will your καρδια _____ be also.
Matt. 6:21

We know that whatever the νομος _____ says, it says to those under the

 νομω _____, that every mouth may be stopped and the whole κοσμος _____ be

accountable to θεω _____; because by εργων νομου _____ ___ _____ no flesh

shall be justified before Him. Rom. 3:19-20

The Lord Jesus will destroy the lawless one by the επιφανεια _____

of his παρουσιας _____. 2 Thess. 2:8

Therefore comfort αλληλους _____ with these λογοις _____. 1 Thess. 4:18

The greeting is in my hand: _Παύλου_ . This is my mark in every

ἐπιστολῇ ; this is how I _γράφω_ . 2 Thess. 3:17

Παῦλος , _ἀπόστολος_ of Christ _Ἰησοῦ*_ , _διὰ_ the will _θεοῦ_ ,

to the saints in _Ἐφέσῳ_ , faithful _ἐν_ Christ _Ἰησοῦ_ ; grace to you

καὶ peace _εἰρήνη*_ _ἀπὸ_ _θεοῦ_ our _πατρὸς_ _καὶ_ the Lord _Ἰησοῦ_

Christ. Blessed be the _θεὸς_ _καὶ_ _πατὴρ_ of our Lord _Ἰησοῦ_

Christ. Eph. 1:1-3

*ει and η in the same word: ειρηνη (ay-ray-nay)
*Ιησου pronounced Yay-zoo

Exercise One

MORE OF THE ALPHABET

English Words:

 αξ   ταξι    sounds like English "x"

Our word "doxology": comes from the Greek word δοξα(glory) + λογος = words of glory. Now combine παρα plus δοξα and you get παραδοξα.

English: _____

In English, we sometimes say "an" instead of "a", when the next word starts with a vowel. Greek makes a similar change with the preposition εκ (out of). When εκ comes before a vowel, it is written εξ instead.* The meaning stays the same:

εκ κοσμου = out of world; εξ οικου = out of house;

εξ(out of) + οδος(way or path) = _____(book of Bible)

*in other words, an ς has been added to εκ, making εκς; then that word is respelled as εξ.

Exercise Two

THE THROAT-CLEARING SOUND

This is the sound used in the German word "ach". It is written χ.

That looks like an "x"---but you know it can't be the "x" sound, because we just had the x-sound above, and it looked like this: ξ.

Now pronounce the famous German composer's name: Johann Sebastian βαχ.

Did you do OK? Then let's see how good you are at <u>starting</u> words with that sound:

Match to meanings at right---and no fair not attempting to pronounce the words:

___ 1. Χασμα

___ 2. Χριστιανος

___ 3. Χορος

___ 4. Χρονος

a. Greeks used this to refer to groups of dancers; we refer it to singers, but we do base a word on it that means planning the steps for a dance: choreography.

b. a follower of the Lord Ιησους Χριστος

c. a deep crack in the earth

d. time; the basis for our word chronology.

___ 5. Χερουβιμ   e. Chaldean (a person from south of Babylon)

___ 6. Χαρτης   f. Canaan (spelling influenced by the Hebrew
                           original).
___ 7. Χαλδαιος
                        g. Means "exact likeness" in Greek; we use it to
___ 8. Χαρακτηρ   refer to distinguishing marks of personality.

___ 9. Χανααν   h. Means "paper" in Greek; for us, a map on paper.

                        i. Cherubim; certain types of angels.

Exercise Three

ABOUT THE WORD CHRIST:

There's a Greek word, Χρισει, which means anoint (pour oil on):

                                                       Χρισει
1. In the Old Testament the prophet Samuel takes oil and _____
   David as King.

2. In Luke 4:18, Jesus quotes Isaiah and applies it to Himself: "The

                                               εχρισεν
   Spirit of the Lord is upon me, because he has _____ me to
   preach good news to the poor..."   (past tense)

3. After the resurrection, the disciples knew Jesus was the anointed
   one; as shown by their prayer in Acts 4:27: ...the people of Israel
   were gathered together against your holy servant Jesus, whom you

           εχρισας
   didst _____.

4. Χρισειν, then, means "to _____". Someone who's been anointed

   is called a χριστος, spelled in English _____. This means
   the same as the Old Testament word "Messiah" - an annointed King who
   was to come, to save and rule God's people.

Exercise Four

THE WORD FOR GRACE

χαρις means "grace": "For by χαριτι are you saved..." Eph. 2:8.
χαρισματα means "things you get by grace". See what your Bible does
with 1 Cor. 12:4 - "Now there are varieties of χαρισματων, but the same
Spirit".

From the word χαρισματα comes the English word _____, one who
believes in the spiritual "gifts".

Exercise Five

THE "PS" SOUND

ψ is pronounced like ps.   ENGLISH EXAMPLE: λιψ
If we turn to the Bible book after Job, we can read a ψαλμος.
ψυχικος (soulish), without the ος, is spelled in English as _____.
ψευδος (lie) is used in English words such as _____.

SCRIPTURES

           ἄνθρωπος Ἀδὰμ   εἰς   ψυχὴν
The first _____ _____ was made ____ a living _____.
                                          1 Cor. 15:45

        ἐκ   πατρὸς   διαβόλου   καὶ
You are ____ your _____ the _____, _____ you do the

                πατρὸς   ψεῦδος
desires of your _____...when he speaks a _____, he speaks

                                     ψεύστης
according to his own nature, because he is a _____ and the

πατὴρ
_____ of it.   John 8:44

COMBINATIONS OF ψευδος WITH WORDS YOU KNOW:

                            ψευδαδέλφοις
2 Cor. 11:26   In perils among _____
                               _____

                        ψευδαπόστολοι
2 Cor. 11:13   For such are _____
                           _____

                  ψευδοπροφητῶν
Matt. 7:15   Beware of _____
                       _____

                  ψευδόχριστοι
Matt. 24:24   For there shall arise _____
                             _____

WORDS FROM THE PREVIOUS PAGES

Stir up the _____ _____ which is in you... 2 Tim. 1:6
           χάρισμα   θεοῦ

The _____ were first called _____ _____ _____.
    μαθητὰς   Χριστιανούς ἐν Ἀντιοχείᾳ
                                 _____   Acts 11:26

Δόξα   θεῷ   ἐν   καὶ ἐπὶ γῆς εἰρήνη
_____ to _____ ____ the highest, _____ _____ _____ _____,
(capital δ)

goodwill towards _____. Luke 2:14
                 ἀνθρώποις

Exercise Six

ANOTHER NEW LETTER - ζ

ζ is pronounced like dz---like adz.

MATCH: Select the correct definition for each of these Greek words.

__ 1. ζωον   (dzoe-on)   a. zeal

__ 2. ζηλος   (dzay-loss)   b. an animal. The word from
                                    which we get "zoo"
__ 3. ζηλωτης   (dzay-low-tace)
                                 c. zealot

The capital of ζ is Z. The capital of λ is Λ.

MATCH: Select the correct definition for each of these Greek words.

__ 4. Ζεβεδαιος (dze-bed-eye-oss)   d. Zachaeus

__ 5. Ζακαριας   (dzah-kah-ree-ahss) e. Lazarus

__ 6. Ζακχαιος   f. Zebedee

__ 7. Λαζαρος   (lodz-a-ross)   g. Zacharias

__ 8. Ζωη   h. life

SCRIPTURES

’Ιησοῦς   εἰς   βηθανίαν   Λάζαρος
_____ came ____ _____ where _____ lived, whom

’Ιησοῦς   ἐκ   νεκρῶν
_____ had raised   ____ _____ . John 12:1

(no word "the" in the original before the last word, but you can supply
 it for the sake of smooth English)

Καὶ   ἐγὼ   Βεελζεβοὺλ   δαιμόνια
____ if ____ through _____ cast out _____ , then through

whom do your sons cast them out?   Matt. 12:27

*Φίλιππος   Ναθαναὴλ   καὶ
_____ found _____ _____ said to him, "We have found the

          **Μωϋσῆς   ἐν   νόμῳ   καὶ   προφῆται
one that _____ (____ the _____) ____ the _____
wrote about: _____ , son of _____ , ____ _____ .

’Ιησοῦν   ’Ιωσὴφ   ἀπὸ   Ναζαρέτ

                                                    John 1:45

    * Φ is the capital of φ

    ** The two dots mean - pronounce the υ separately.

Exercise One

WORDS ABOUT THE BODY.

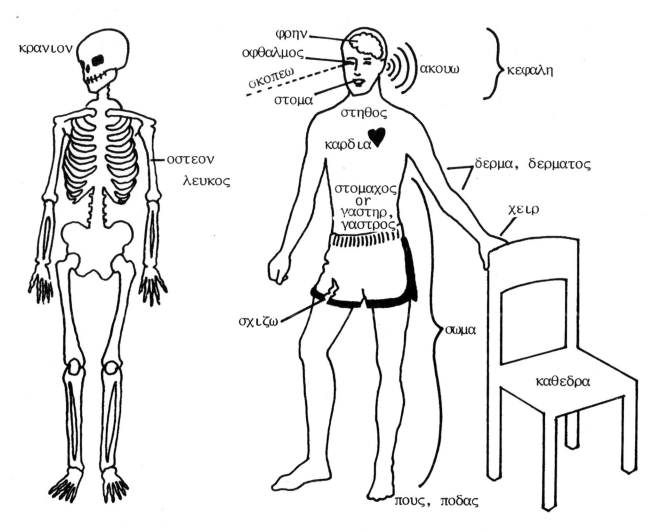

(The words that are in pairs above are two forms of the same word.)
Fill in the blanks with Greek words from the picture above:

see _____   stomach _____   skull _____

body _____   hear _____   stomach area _____ _____

white _____   head _____   rip or tear _____

bone _____   brain _____   eye _____

mouth _____   chest _____   heart _____

skin _____   hand _____   chair _____

foot _____

Fill in the long blanks with Greek words from the picture on page 61. Select the best definition from the words in the right column for the English words in the left column.

__ 1. podiatrist_____   a. adjusting joints by hand

__ 2. phrenology _____   b. under the skin

__ 3. ophthalmologist _____   c. guessing mental ability
                                       from head-shape
__ 4. dermatologist _____
                                    d. instrument for making obser-
__ 5. hypodermic _____   vations within the chest

__ 6. osteopath _____   e. foot-doctor

__ 7. cathedral _____   f. stomach cramps, inflammation

__ 8. gastritis _____   g. bone-doctor

__ 9. chiropractor _____   h. the mind seems to be torn in-
                                       to two personalities
__10. schizophrenia _____ + _____
                                    i. eye-doctor
__11. stethoscope _____ + _____
                                    j. this is the church where the
                                       bishop had his "seat", or
                                       headquarters

                                    k. skin-doctor

Exercise Two

THE "H" SOUND

The "h" sound: shown by a backwards comma over the first letter of a word that starts with a vowel:

ὡσαννα (hosanna) ἁλληλουια (hallelujah)

When an h sound is not wanted, the comma will go the other way:

ἀγαπη (means love), ἀνωθεν (means "again", "from above")

Match these Greek words with their English equivalents.

__ 1. ὁλος   a. hour

__ 2. ὡρα   b. Hebrew

__ 3. ὁδος   c. whole

__ 4. Ἑβραιος   d. path

Exercise Three

Write the Greek word in the long blank. Match the English words to the meanings below.

__ 1. holocaust _____   ἡγεμον (governor)

__ 2. homogenized _____   ὁμος (similar)

__ 3. eschatology _____   ἑτερος (unlike)

__ 4. hegemony _____   ὁλος (entire)

__ 5. Michael _____   σχολη

__ 6. School _____   Μιχαηλ

__ 7. heterodox _____   εσχατος (final)

__ 8. homophonic _____

a. Combined with γενος, kind, it indicates mixing together until each sample of the material is of the same kind. b. Study of the end-times as described in the Bible. c. Combined with καυσις, burning, it refers to the near-extermination of a race during World War II. d. Combined with φωνη, it is a musical term, meaning that all the sounds are happening at the same time, as chords. e. The name of a head angel in the Bible. f. Overlordship, taking the rule over. g. Place for instruction. h. Different from the accepted standards of church doctrine.

φωνὴ   ὁδὸν κυρίου
A _____ crying in the wilderness, prepare the _____ _____.
                                                                        Matt. 3:3

   (There is no "the" in the original before the last word but
    smooth English requires that you add one.)

Exercise Four

THE LETTER "U"

The U sound. Put lips like oo and try to say ee. Scholars give various pronunciations ranging from "oo" in book to "u" in unity.

The Greek word τυπος became English _____ (model or symbol).

Κυριος means "Lord" as in the liturgical song called the Kyrie. Opening a church song book, we'd sing a ὑμνος _____.

Paul warns Timothy to keep away from false μυθαις _____.

In all these examples, Greek υ became English ___. But in the case of the Old Testament King δαυιδ, Greek υ became English _____.

Diphthongs with υ. ευ (pronounce "ewe") is a prefix meaning good. υι (wee) is found in the Greek word υἱος, which means "Son". (pronounced hwee-oss)

SCRIPTURES

Pronounce the Greek words and write its English equivalent beneath.

υἱὸς   θεοῦ   λίθοι
If you are the _____ ___ _____, command these _____ to become

bread. Matt. 4:3

λόγος   Χριστοῦ   σοφίᾳ
Let the _____ ___ _____ indwell you richly, in all _____

καὶ   ψαλμοῖς
teaching ____ admonishing one another with _____,

ὕμνοις   χάριτι   ἐν
_____, and spiritual songs, singing with _____ ___

καρδίαις   θεῷ
your _____ to _____. Col. 3:16

Exercise Five

WORDS WITH υ WHICH BECAME A "Y" IN ENGLISH:

Select the best definition for each of these Greek words.

___ 1. αποκαλυψις
___ 2. αβυσσος
___ 3. τυραννος
___ 4. κηρυγμα
___ 5. κρυπτος
___ 6. μαρτυρ
___ 7. πρεσβυτερος
___ 8. δυναμις
___ 9. ψυχη
___10. φυσικος
___11. ψυχικος
___12. αποκρυφος
___13. ὑπνος
___14. γυμνασια
___15. δυναστης

a. This is a theological term, meaning proclamation, from the word κηρυξ (announcer). Theologians use it to refer to the basic content of gospel message, with the English word "kerygma".
b. This word originally meant a "witness"; now we use it in particular to refer to those who lost their lives because of standing up for the truth. Martyr.
c. An oppressive ruler: tyrant.
d. A crypt is an underground room; means "hidden".
e. A form of κρυπτος hidden, plus απο, gives us certain books that were found "hidden" and scattered in the Greek Old Testament, but were not part of the Hebrew original. Now published in a separate section. Apocrypha.
f. καλυψ "covering" plus απο away from = take the cover off; revelation: Apocalypse.
g. Power. Compare our word dynamite.
h. An older person; source of the word Presbyterian, church rule by elders.
i. Soul: PSHCHE.
j. Soulish: PSYCHIC.
k. Physical.
l. Means "sleep"; source of our word hypnosis.
m. Training, discipline; became our word GYMNASIUM.
n. A great depth: abyss.
o. Means "ruler". Our word DYNASTY.

SOME PREPOSITIONS THAT CONTAIN A υ

συν = with   ὑπο = under or by   ὑπερ = over or for

SCRIPTURES:

For you have died, and your life is hid ___ ___ σὺν Χριστῷ ___ ___ ἐν θεῷ.
                                                                                Col. 3:3

Sin shall not rule over you, since you are not ___ ___ ὑπὸ νόμον but

___ ___ ὑπὸ χάριν. Rom. 6:14

The ___ μαθητὴς is not ___ ὑπὲρ his teacher, nor the servant ___ ὑπὲρ

his ___ κύριον. Matt. 10:24

Exercise Six

COGNATES WITH THESE PREPOSITIONS USED AS PREFIXES: Select the best
definition for each of these Greek words.

__ 1. συναγωγη
__ 2. συνοδια
__ 3. hypnotism
__ 4. ὑπερβολη
__ 5. συνδρομη
__ 6. hypodermic
__ 7. hyperactive
__ 8. συμφωνια
__ 9. ὑποκριτης
__ 10. ὑποκρισις

a. A walking together, cooperation: synod.
   (includes the word ὁδος, path)

b. A rushing together; we use the English
   derivative to mean a collection of symptoms:
   Syndrome.

c. Over-active.

d. Harmonious sounds; a form of συν plus φωνη
   became English Symphony.

e. Under the skin.

f. συν plus αγω (lead) gives us the word for a
   Jewish gathering place.

g. Outstanding; exaggeration; A term used in
   English literature: hyperbole. Add the
   Greek word ὑπερ plus a form of βαλλω,
   throw

h. Comes from ὑπνος, which means "sleep".

i. hypocrisy

j. hypocrite

Exercise One

PICTURE OF A FIELD

Write the Greek words from the picture in the blanks.

1. Botany is the study of plants. Plants = _____

2. Greek word for rainbow became the name of a flower: _____

3. Chrysallis, the hard, gold-colored shell around a caterpillar which is turning into a butterfly comes from this word meaning gold: _____

4. This flower-name comes from the Greek word for star: _____

5. Helium; this element got its name because it was first discovered on the sun: Sun = _____.

6. Seed: _____ _____

7. Crystal: _____

8. River: _____

9. Valuable substance we drill for in rocks (petroleum) comes from this word for rock: _____.

10. Air-filled (pneumatic) comes from this word which means wind or spirit: _____.

11. A hippopotamus is a horse_____ of the river_____.

12. Science of farming, agriculture, comes from the word for field:_____

COMPOUND WORDS: Write the Greek words from the picture on page 66 that were combined to form these English words

13. thermometer _____ + _____

14. anemometer _____ + _____

15. hippopotamus _____ + _____

16. astrology _____ + _____

17. astronomy _____ + _____

18. petrology _____ + _____

19. lithography _____ + _____

20. ichthyologist _____ + _____

21. chlorophyll _____ + _____

22. agronomy _____ + _____

23. dendrology _____ + _____

24. xylophone _____ + _____

Exercise Two

THE FAMOUS SECRET CODE OF EARLY CHRISTIANS.

= ιχθυς

Write the English equivalent of each of these Greek words in the blanks.

ι is for Ιησους _____

χ is for Χριστος _____

θ is for Θεου ____ _____

υ is for υἱος _____

ς is for σωτηρ _____

SOME SCRIPTURES: It is important that you carefully pronounce each Greek word in this section because the scripture exercises are the only exercises from which you learn how to use accents. Of course, write in the English equivalents.

     παραβολή   σπόρας   λόγος θεοῦ
This then is the _____. The _____ is the _____ _____.
                       Luke 8:11

  φύλλα   ξύλου   θεραπείαν   ἐθνῶν
The _____ of the _____ were for the _____ of the _____.
                       Rev. 22:2

ὑπακούω. The Greek word, ακουω, hear, plus ὑπο, under, is usually translated "obey" in the New Testament. (This is not a cognate) I enjoy this
picturesque notion of "hearing and submitting" and this helps me remember
the word.

            ἄνεμοι   ὑπακούουσιν

Even the _____ and the sea _____ him! Matt. 8:27

Here's the same concept in a noun form and a participle form (that is,
an -ing word):

            υἱός   ὑπακοήν

Though he were a _____, yet he learned _____ from the things he

suffered, and by completing everything he became the source of salvation

       ὑπακούουσιν

to all those _____ -ing him. Heb. 5:8, 9

Νικη was the name of the ancient Greek goddess of victory; there is a
statue from ancient Greece with this name, and an American anti-aircraft
missile of the 1950's was named after her.

       νίκη

This is the _____ that overcomes the world: our faith. 1 John 5:4

Can you put the word "victory" into verb form? You would get a word that
means "to have victory", to "conquer", to "overcome". The following full
quote includes both noun and verb forms based on νικη:

         νικᾷ   νίκη

That which is born of God _____ the world; and this is the _____

   νικήσασα

which _____ the world, our faith. 1 John 5:4

Combine a verb form of νικη with ὑπερ (over), and the result is Rom. 8:37:

          ὑπερνικῶμεν

But in all these things we _____ through him who loves us.

        (literally, we "over-conquer")

Exercise Three

WORDS CREATED FROM GREEK NUMBERS

Write the Greek word in the long blank. Match the English words to the meanings below.

__ 1. dekameter _____

__ 2. prototype _____

__ 3. hexagon _____

__ 4. proton _____

__ 5. myriads _____

__ 6. chiliasm _____

__ 7. decathlon _____

__ 8. πεντεκοστη _____

__ 9. δευτερονομος _____

πρωτος (1st)   δωδεκα (12)

δευτερος (2nd)   χιλιοι (1000)

τριτος (3rd)   μυριαι (10,000)

τεσσαρες (4)

πεντε (5)

ἑξ (6)

ἑπτα (7)

οκτα (8)

δεκα (10)

a. A basic atomic particle.
b. A holiday 50 days after Easter: Pentecost.
c. Combined with μετρον, measure; it means 10 meters
d. The approach to end-time studies that sees Christ returning during the thousand-year time-span of Revelation 20. The equivalent term with a latin root is Millenialism.

SCRIPTURE EXAMPLES

e. Moses reads the law (νομος) to the people a second time at the end of their 40 years of wandering in this book of the Bible: Deuteronomy.
f. Combined with τυπος; it means "the first of its kind".
g. Combined with αθλεω (compete), it is an Olympic contest made up of ten events.
h. Lots and lots!
i. Six-sided figure.

Pronounce the Greek. Write in the English equivalent. Remember, if a word is double-underlined, it is plural.

ἐπὶ   δώδεκα   θρόνους
(Jesus speaking to his disciples): You shall sit ____ _____ _____

δώδεκα   Ἰσραήλ
judging the _____ tribes of _____ . Matt. 19:28

τρίτον   δένδρων
And the _____ part of the _____ was burnt. Rev. 8:7

ἑπτὰ   λαμπάδες   θρόνου
(And I saw) _____ _____ burning with fire before the _____

ἑπτὰ   πνεύματα   θεοῦ
which are the _____ _____ ____ _____ . Rev. 4:5

Exercise Four

SCIENTIFIC WORDS

I. Geology

Match these Greek words with their English equivalents.

___ 1. αμεθυστος   a. Crystal

___ 2. χαλκηδων   b. Chrysolite

___ 3. χρυσολιθος   c. Topaz

___ 4. ορος   d. Amethyst

___ 5. σαπφειρος   e. Sapphire

___ 6. τοπαζιον   f. Chalcedony

___ 7. κρυσταλλος   g. This word means <u>mountain</u>; the geological word for mountain building is orogeny.

II. Life Science

Select the best definition for each of these Greek words.

___ 8. ασπις

___ 9. νωτος

___10. χιτων

___11. φυτεια

___12. φυλη

___13. κητος

___14. συκομορεα

___15. γαμεω

___16. γενος

___17. θωραξ

___18. πλασσω, and related words πλασμα and πλαστος

___19. ορνις

___20. αυξω

h. A whale is a Cetacean
i. A type of tree: sycamore
j. This word is used in classifying to label the major divisions of living things: Phyla. In Greek it means tribe.
k. Asp (a snake)
l. This word means "back". The elastic rod of cells in the embryo where the backbone is going to be is called a notochord.
m. A classification-word for the next category above "species"; it means "kind". Genus.
n. This word means "marry", and is found in many scientific terms dealing with reproduction, such as "gamete".
o. This word means "plant", and is the last part of many terms used in botany, such as bryophyte, saprophyte.
p. A tunic(type of garment) became the name for a certain type of clam: the chiton.
q. Means "grow" in Greek; used to refer to the chemical substance at the growing edge of plant roots and stems: auxin.
r. Bird. Source of the word Ornithology.
s. Means "formed"; varieties of this word refer to the fluid part of substances, to an organized particle, as in chloro<u>plast</u>, also "plastic" surgery.
t. The middle part of an insect's body; means "breastplate" in Greek.

Exercise One

COMBINING THROAT-LETTERS

When there are two "throat-letters" (such as "g"), the first is pronounced like the "ng" in singer.

αγγελος
means "messenger"

English version:

_____

Pronounce the first γ like "ng".

Pronounce the second γ like a <u>hard</u> g.

Exercise Two

COMBINING PREFIXES WITH αγγελος

__ 1. αρχη (chief) + αγγελος = αρχαγγελος

__ 2. ευ (good) + αγγελιον (message) = ευαγγελιον

Match to correct explanation above:

a. good news
b. a chief angel---archangel.

Examples of ευ + αγγελος

As a Noun   ___ 3. ευαγγελιον   (good message)

As a Verb   ___ 4. ευαγγελιζω   (give a good message)

Another Noun   ___ 5. ευαγγελιστης (one who gives a good message)

Match to these English translations (commonly used in Bible):

a. proclaimer   b. gospel   c. preach

Exercise Three

CHANGING TO ENGLISH LETTERS. In the blank write the appropriate English word.

ευαγγελιστης (good-message-giver) Take off the ending (ης), change υ to v, and write γγ as ng, and you get: _____

ευαγγελιζω (tell good news)
change the last letter to a silent e: _____

Now try Luke 2:10-11: Pronounce the Greek and translate into English.

ἄγγελος

And the _____ said (to the shepherds), "Do not fear; for behold

εὐαγγελίζομαι

I _____ to you about a great joy which will be to all

the people."

εὐαγγέλιον   δύναμις

I am not ashamed of the _____ for it is the _____

θεοῦ

___ _____ unto salvation for all who believe. Rom. 1:16

Exercise Four

OTHER WORDS FORMED WITH αρχη (chief or old or beginning)

Select the best definition for each of these Greek words.

___ 1. πατριαρχης

___ 2. αρχαιος

___ 3. αντιχριστος

___ 4. αρχιτεκτων

a. We use this term to mean someone who plans a building; in Greek it means the master builder.

b. Patriarch: an honored male ancestor.

c. Archaic

d. A powerful figure of the end-time who sets himself against Jesus.

Pronounce the Greek and translate into English.

χάριν   θεοῦ

According to the _____ __ _____ given to me, I laid a foundation as

σοφὸς   ἀρχιτέκτων

a _____ _____; others built upon it...No other foundation

'Ιησοῦς Χριστός

can be laid besides the one that is laid, who is _____ _____.

1 Cor. 3:10-11

Exercise Five

WORDS WITH αι WHICH BECAME e WHEN THEY WERE TAKEN INTO ENGLISH.
Match these Greek words with their English equivalents.

__ 1. αιων   a. demon   g. <u>hemoglobin</u>
                                                     (means "blood")
__ 2. Αιγυπτος   b. gangrene

__ 3. δαιμων   c. Egypt

__ 4. αινιγμα   d. eon

__ 5. γαγγραινα   e. enigma
                              (puzzle)
__ 6. ἁιρετικος
                           f. heretical
__ 7. αἱμα

FIRST JOHN, CHAPTER ONE

The blanks in the following quotation are for words you have learned so
far; sometimes the meanings might be variations of the meanings you have
so far associated with these words.

That which was ⎯⎯⎯ (ἀπ'*) the ⎯⎯⎯ (ἀρχῆς), which we heard, which we saw with our

⎯⎯⎯⎯⎯ (ὀφθαλμοῖς), what we beheld and our ⎯⎯⎯⎯ (χεῖρες) touched, concerning the

⎯⎯⎯ (λόγου) of ⎯⎯⎯ (ζωῆς) --- ⎯⎯ the (ζωὴ) ⎯⎯ appeared, ⎯⎯ (καὶ) we saw ⎯⎯ (καὶ)

⎯⎯⎯⎯⎯ (μαρτυροῦμεν) ⎯⎯⎯ (καὶ) announce to you the eternal ⎯⎯⎯ (ζωὴν) which was with

the ⎯⎯⎯⎯ (πατέρα) ⎯⎯⎯ (καὶ) shown to you---what we saw and heard we announce

also to you so that you also may have fellowship with us. ⎯⎯⎯ (καὶ) our

fellowship is with the ⎯⎯⎯ (πατρὸς) ⎯⎯⎯ (καὶ) with his ⎯⎯ (υἱοῦ) ⎯⎯⎯ ('Ιησοῦ) ⎯⎯⎯ (Χριστοῦ).

⎯⎯ (καὶ) these things (we) ⎯⎯⎯⎯⎯ (γράφομεν) so that our joy might be full.

⎯⎯ (καὶ) this is the ⎯⎯⎯⎯⎯ (ἀγγελία) which we heard ⎯⎯⎯⎯ (ἀπ'*) him ⎯⎯⎯ (καὶ)

announce to you: that ⎯⎯⎯ (θεὸς) is ⎯⎯⎯ (φῶς) ⎯⎯⎯ (καὶ) darkness is not in Him at

   *contraction of απο

73

all. If we say that we have fellowship with Him _____ (καὶ) walk ___ (ἐν) darkness,

we lie and do not do the truth. But if we walk ___ (ἐν) the _____ (φωτὶ) as He is

___ (ἐν) the _____ (φωτὶ), we have fellowship with ____ (ἀλλήλων) _____ (καὶ) ____ the _____ (αἷμα)

of _____ (Ἰησοῦ) his _____ (υἱοῦ) cleanses us _____ (ἀπὸ) all sin.

Exercise Six

REVIEWING THE DOUBLED THROAT-LETTERS

1. γγ (English "ng - g")

αγγελος
messenger

Spell in English:

_____

2. γχ (English nch)

αγχυρα

Spell in English:

_____

Also spelled αγκυρα

3. γξ (English nx)

λαρυγξ

Spell in English:

_____

SCRIPTURES

Rejoice as you share in the suffering __ _____ (Χριστοῦ), so that you may also

be glad at the _____ (ἀποκαλύψει) of his _____ (δόξης). 1 Pet. 4:13

My _____ (λόγος) and my _____ (κήρυγμά) was not with enticing _____ (λόγοις)

of _____ (σοφίας) ... 1 Cor. 2:4

They did not find any, though many _____ (ψευδομαρτύρων) came forward.
Matt. 26:60

They ordained _____ (πρεσβυτέρους) in every church. Acts 14:23

_____ (Ἰησοῦς) rebuked it, and the _____ (δαιμόνιον) went out. Matt. 17:18

Which hope we have as an $\overset{\prime}{\alpha}\gamma\kappa\upsilon\rho\alpha\nu$ _____ of the $\psi\upsilon\chi\widehat{\eta}\varsigma$ _____. Heb. 6:19

Their $\lambda\overset{\prime}{\alpha}\rho\upsilon\gamma\xi$ _____ is an open $\tau\overset{\prime}{\alpha}\varphi o\varsigma$ _____. Rom. 3:13

Exercise Seven

CAPITAL LETTERS

Guess which capital letters and small letters go together. Check your answers on the following page.

1. ___ H   a. ρ

2. ___ Θ   b. φ

3. ___ P   c. η

4. ___ Φ   d. θ

5. ___ Λ   e. σ

6. ___ Π   f. δ

7. ___ Σ   g. λ

8. ___ Δ   h. π

9. ___ Ξ   i. ω

10. ___ Υ   j. ξ

11. ___ Ω   k. γ

12. ___ Γ   l. υ

75

THE GREEK LETTERS

CAPS	Small	Name	Sounds like	What each letter was changed to when Greek words were written in English.
A	α	ἄλφα	father	a
B	β	βῆτα	b	b
Γ	γ	γάμμα	hard "g"	both hard and soft g
Δ	δ	δέλτα	d	d
E	ε	ἐ ψιλον	pet	e
Z	ζ	ζῆτα	adz	z
H	η	ῆτα	eight	e or e
Θ	θ	θῆτα	think	th
I	ι	ἰῶτα	pin or machine	i or y or J
K	κ	κάππα	k	k/c, both hard & soft
Λ	λ	λάμβδα	l	l
M	μ	μῦ	m	m
N	ν	νῦ	n	n
Ξ	ξ	ξῖ (ksee)	taxi	x
O	o	ὀ μικρον	log	o
Π	π	πῖ	p	p
P	ρ	ῥῶ	r	r
Σ	σ & ς	σίγμα	s	s
T	τ	ταῦ	t	t
Y	υ	ῦ ψιλον	like German u*	y or v or u
Φ	φ	φῖ	f	ph
X	χ	χῖ	like German ach	ch
Ψ	ψ	ψῖ	ps	ps
Ω	ω	ῶ μεγα	note	o or o

COMBINATIONS: In γγ, γχ, and γκ speak the first γ like "ng".

αυ like cow, ευ like feud, ου like food, υι like wee.

αι like aisle, ει like eight. ACCENTS: ´ ` ⌢ all sound the same.

‛ = breathe hard, like h-sound. ’ = don't make h-sound.

*put lips like oo and say ee

Map of Palestine
For practice with capital letters

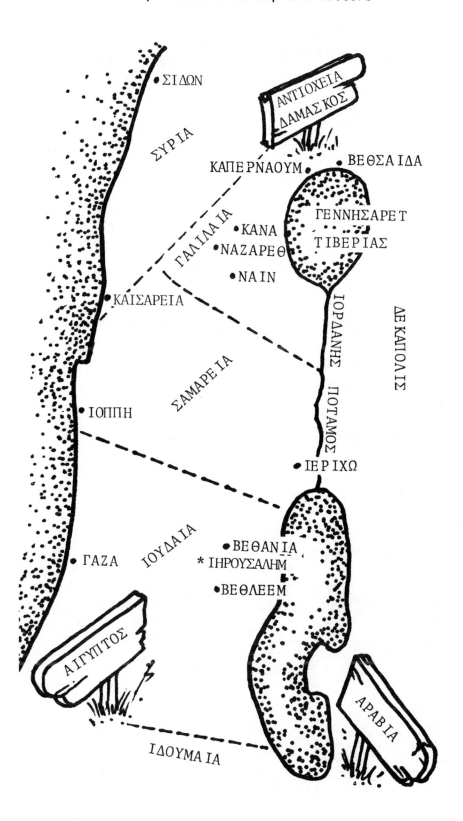

Here are the place-
names in English.
Find them and copy
in Greek small
letters on your own
sheet of paper.

Seas:
Tiberias
Gennesaret

River:
Jordan River

Regions:
Syria
Galilee
Decapolis
Samaria
Judea
Idumaea

Cities:
Jerusalem
Caesarea
Capernaum
Sidon
Antioch
Damascus
Bethsaida

Towns:
Bethlehem
Bethany
Jericho
Cana
Nazareth
Nain
Joppa
Gaza

Countries
Egypt
Arabia

BOOKS OF THE NEW TESTAMENT

For practice with capital letters.
Number them in the order they occur in the Bible. Then write them out using small Greek letters.

I. Gospels and Acts

1. ΚΑΤΑ ΜΑΡΚΟΝ
   _____

2. ΚΑΤΑ ΙΩΑΝΝΗΝ
   _____

3. ΚΑΤΑ ΛΟΥΚΑΝ
   _____

4. ΠΡΑΞΕΙΣ ΑΠΟΣΤΟΛΩΝ
   _____

5. ΚΑΤΑ ΜΑΘΘΑΙΟΝ
   _____

The word κατα means "according to". The word πραξεις reminds me of the word "practices". The word αποστολων means "of apostles".

II. Letters of Paul

1. ΠΡΟΣ ΕΦΕΣΙΟΥΣ
   _____

2. ΠΡΟΣ ΓΑΛΑΤΑΣ
   _____

3. ΠΡΟΣ ΦΙΛΗΜΟΝΑ
   _____

4. ΠΡΟΣ ΡΩΜΑΙΟΥΣ
   _____

5. ΠΡΟΣ ΤΙΤΟΝ
   _____

6. ΠΡΟΣ ΚΟΛΟΣΣΑΕΙΣ
   _____

7. ΠΡΟΣ ΚΟΡΙΝΘΙΟΥΣ Β
   _____

8. ΠΡΟΣ ΤΙΜΟΘΕΟΝ Β
   _____

9. ΠΡΟΣ ΘΕΣΣΑΛΟΝΙΚΕΙΣ Α
   _____

10. ΠΡΟΣ ΤΙΜΟΘΕΟΝ Α
    _____

11. ΠΡΟΣ ΘΕΣΣΑΛΟΝΙΚΕΙΣ Β
    _____

12. ΠΡΟΣ ΚΟΡΙΝΘΙΟΥΣ Α
    _____

13. ΠΡΟΣ ΦΙΛΙΠΠΗΣΙΟΥΣ
    _____

The word προς means "to". The letters α and β are used where we would use I & II.

III. Hebrews to the end

1. ΠΕΤΡΟΥ Α

   _____

2. ΙΩΑΝΝΟΥ Β

   _____

3. ΙΟΥΔΑ

   _____

4. ΙΑΚΩΒΟΥ

   _____

5. ΑΠΟΚΑΛΥΨΙΣ ΙΩΑΝΝΟΥ

   _____

6. ΙΩΑΝΝΟΥ Γ

   _____

7. ΠΡΟΣ ΕΒΡΑΙΟΥΣ

   _____

8. ΙΩΑΝΝΟΥ Α

   _____

9. ΠΕΤΡΟΥ Β

   _____

Note that the breathing marks (ʽ & ʼ) are not used sometimes in capital letter writing, so there is nothing to designate that Hebrews starts with an "h".

Many of these end with -ου, for "of";(Letter) "of James" is the intended meaning.

Remember the 3rd letter of the Greek alphabet is γ.

This is the end of Part I.

You have:

1) become "at home" with the Greek alphabet and pronunciation.*
2) seen dozens of Greek words that remind you of English words.
3) learned a few Greek words that are not like English: και(and), οικος(house), and the prepositions(εν, απο, επι, etc.)
4) seen that Greek words change their endings. In the next part you will find out why and how.
5) seen the derivation of a great many religious and technical terms.

Many additional "cognates" will be found scattered throughout the coming pages.

In Part II you will learn:

1) Endings for nouns which show their purpose in the sentence.
2) How to make the word "the".
3) How to use adjectives and show which nouns they describe.
4) Which endings are to be used after certain prepositions.
5) How to make the present-tense endings of verbs.
6) How to make and translate entire sentences.

But that sounds like grammar!

You have absorbed some Greek grammar already:

1) you have seen that the -ου ending tells you to translate with the word "of" (unless another preposition is already there).
2) you have learned that there is no word for "a" in Greek, but that you can include it in translating at times.
3) you have learned that a small letter ι is found under the last letter of certain words following certain prepositions:

  εν οικῳ   εν λαμπᾳ

*there are a number of systems of pronunciation in use today in various schools. The system used in this book is that used by J. Gresham Machen in his NEW TESTAMENT GREEK FOR BEGINNERS.

PART II

INTRODUCING ENDINGS

In Part II, you will learn:

1. eight endings to put on a verb, and the resulting meanings.

2. eight endings to put on a noun, and the significance of each ending for the noun's place in the sentence.

3. that adjectives and the word "the" make use of these same noun endings.

4. that the words following a preposition make use of these same endings.

5. some of the essential technical terms used in Greek grammar.

6. to use a chart illustrating other noun and adjective endings that perform the same purposes as the eight endings you will actually learn.

7. common pronouns (he, they, etc.)

Since you will be concentrating on endings, this section will use a small number of Greek words, with which you will become very familiar.

Exercise One

A REVIEW OF SOME FAMILIAR TERMS

Match each word in the sentences below to the descriptions found at the right.

1. John lifts stones.

   —   —   —

   a. noun---name of a person, place, or thing.

   b. verb---action word.

2. The man lifts heavy rocks over his

  — — —   —   —   —

head.

  —

   a. noun

   b. verb

   c. adjective---describes a noun.

   d. preposition

   e. pronoun---takes the place of a noun.

   f. Which noun in the sentence above is "plural" (more than one)? _____. Which nouns are singular? _____, _____.

3. John gave Tom a large book.

  _'_   —   _'_   —   _'_

   a. noun

   b. verb

   c. adjective

USES OF NOUNS

   d. subject---who did the action.

   e. direct object---what the action was done to.

   f. indirect object---who received the direct object.

   g. The verb in the sentence is in _____ tense. (present or past or future?)

4. John's friend gave Tom a new book

    —   —   —   —   —

inside the library.

a. preposition

b. prepositional phrase

c. adjective

USES OF NOUNS

d. subject

e. possessive---indicate be-longing to.

f. indirect object

g. direct object

h. the object of the preposi-tion.

RELATED WORDS

(Recognizing similar meanings despite differences in some letters.)

What do these five words have in common:

    GIVE   GAVE   GIFT   GIVER   GIVEN

There isn't a single letter they have in common except the "G", and yet we know they have something in common: they share a single basic meaning. They all have something to do with giving.

The same thing can happen in Greek. The purpose of this page is to open your eyes to some connections between words that might not seem obvious at first. These two words: λεγω and λογος are related to each other, just as GIVE and GIFT are related to each other. In this case, they both have something to do with "speaking". λεγω is a verb, and can be trans-lated "speak" or "say". λογος is a noun, and is usually translated "word". The only letters they have in common are λ and γ, but they share the same general meaning.

Translate the words related to λογος in the following sentences:

Exercise Two

Four of these blanks are for verbs and the other two are for nouns.

λεγω
1. Verily, verily I _____ unto you.

λογος
2. Thy _____ is a lamp unto my feet.

λεγει
3. Now He _____ to us, today is the day of salvation.

λεγεις
4. What do you _____?

5. Jesus answered them, _____λεγων_____, "Take heed to all my _____λογους_____."

Exercise Three

WORDS RELATED TO "καλ"

Words based on the root καλ have something to do with "calling". Fill in the blanks with suitable English translations:

1. I _____καλω_____ unto you.

2. Whoever _____καλει_____ on the name of the Lord shall be saved.

ENDINGS ON VERBS

Greek can say "I call" with only one word: καλω

The ω on the end reveals that the subject of the sentence is "I".

The Greeks also have a word for "I"(εγω) which they can use as an option, for the sake of emphasis.

Therefore, "I call" can be either καλω or εγω καλω.

In a similar way, "you call" can be either καλεις or συ καλεις, and, "he calls" can be either καλει or αυτος καλει.

You have just seen three verb-endings:

> Verbs end with ω when the subject is "I";
>   end with εις when the subject is "you"; and
>   end with ει when the subject is "he, she, or it".

These verb-endings are called "personal endings".

> "I" is called "first person",
> "You" is called "second person", and
> "he, she, and it" are called "third person".

The word καλει is termed the "third person singular" of the verb καλεω.

You have also just seen three pronouns, which you should now add to your dictionary:

> εγω means "I"
> συ means "you"
> αυτος means "he"

When the subject of your sentence is a noun, use the "third person" ending (-ει):

Man calls   = ανθρωπος καλει

Man speaks = ανθρωπος λεγει

God speaks = θεος λεγει

God wills   = θεος θελει

BE SURE THESE WORDS ARE IN YOUR DICTIONARY:

καλω = I call

λεγω = I speak or I say

θελω = I will (or want or wish)

Exercise Four

DRILL ON VERB-ENDINGS

Matching: Match these Greek words with their English translations.

I.   __ 1. θελω   a. you want

     __ 2. θελεις   b. I want

     __ 3. θελει   c. he wants

II. __ 4. λεγω   a. he says

     __ 5. εγω λεγω   b. I say

     __ 6. λεγει

     __ 7. αυτος λεγει

III. __ 8. καλω   a. I want

     __ 9. εγω λεγω   b. he calls

     __10. θελω   c. apostle calls

     __11. καλεις   d. I call

     __12. λεγεις   e. prophet wants

     __13. συ θελεις   f. you say

     __14. αυτος καλει   g. disciple says

     __15. λεγει   h. you want

     __16. θελει   i. I say

     __17. αποστολος καλει j. he wants

     __18. μαθητης λεγει   k. you call

     __19. προφητης θελει   l. he says

PLURAL VERB-ENDINGS

"First person singular" is "I"; therefore,
"First person plural" is "we".(many of us)

"We speak" = λεγομεν

"Second person plural" indicates
"many of you"; if you were from
Texas, you would say "you-all";
In Shakespeare's time, you would
use the word "ye".

"Ye speak" = λεγετε

"Third person plural" is "they".

"They speak" = λεγουσι

(You will learn the pronouns "we", "ye", and "they" on a later page.)

THE PLURAL ENDINGS THEN ARE:

Verbs end with ομεν when the subject is "we";
with ετε when the subject is "ye", and
with ουσι when the subject is "they" or a plural noun.

EXAMPLES WITH PLURAL NOUNS AS SUBJECTS:

Men call =   ανθρωποι καλουσι

Brothers say = αδελφοι λεγουσι

Angels want = αγγελοι θελουσι

Lepers throw = λεπροι βαλλουσι

Apostles write = αποστολοι γραφουσι

(Did you notice that the -οι ending makes a <u>noun</u> into a plural?)

THIS DIAGRAM SHOWS ALL THE ENDINGS

<u>VERB ENDINGS</u>

When subject is	Singular	Plural	
1st Person (I)	-ω	-ομεν	(we)
2nd Person (you)	-εις	-ετε	(You all or ye)
3rd Person (he, she, it)	-ει	-ουσι	(They)

Set aside a few pages in your dictionary to copy the charts of endings, and to list the endings in alphabetical order for quick reference.

A letter ν is often added after the third person endings for smooth connections to the following word.

Exercise Five

PRONUNCIATION CHECK

Match these Greek words with their pronunciations.

__ 1. λογους   a. law-goose   b. low-gauss

__ 2. λεγεις   a. leg-ice   b. leg-ace

__ 3. καλουσι   a. caw-Lucy   b. caw-lousy

__ 4. αυτος   a. ow-toss   b. aw-toce

__ 5. εγω   a. ee-go   b. egg-oh

__ 6. θελομεν   a. Thell-omen   b. Thell-aw-men

MEANING CHECK

Match these Greek words with their translations.

__ 7. αυτος λεγει   c. man says

__ 8. εγω λεγω   d. he says

__ 9. ανθρωπος λεγει   e. we say

__10. ανθρωπος βαλλει   f. I say

__11. καλουσι   g. man throws

__12. λεγομεν   h. they throw

__13. βαλλουσι   i. they call

__14. καλεις   j. you call

__15. θελετε   k. ye want

TWO OTHER ENDINGS:

Another common ending is used when talking about the action in general, without any subject. We do this in English by using two words: "to call". The Greek equivalent is one word: καλειν = to call. This is called the "infinitive". One infinitive ending is -ειν.

One final ending. The "participle" is a complex subject in Greek grammar. For now, add "-ing" to your translation when you come across a Greek verb ending in -ων. Example: λεγων = saying.

SENTENCE ILLUSTRATING SEVERAL VERB FORMS

     θεος   λεγει ,   λεγων ,   θελω   καλειν   ανθρωπους
     God   speaks,   saying,   I want   to call   men.

The example above consists of four(4) verbs and two(2) nouns. Circle the four(4) verbs.

The reason you do not recognize the ending on "men" is that we have not yet talked about noun-endings, only verb-endings.

SCRIPTURES USING THE VERB FORMS YOU KNOW

Pronounce in Greek, translate, and check yourself.

(Jesus fell on his face praying) ____ _____ (καὶ λέγων), my _____ (πάτηρ),

if it is possible, remove this cup _____ (ἀπ') me; nevertheless, not as _____ (ἐγώ)

_____ (θέλω) but as _____ (σύ). Matt. 26:39

If then _____ (Δαυὶδ) _____ (καλεῖ) him _____ (κύριον), how is he his _____ (υἱός)?
                                                                              Matt. 22:45

It is not good to___ take (λαβεῖν) the children's bread _____ __ _____ (καὶ βαλεῖν)

it to the dogs. Mark 7:27

Think not __ _____ (λέγειν) among yourselves, we have (ἔχομεν) _____ (᾿Αβραάμ) as our

_____ (πατέρα), for __ _____ (λέγω) to you that _____ (θεός) is able to raise up (ἐγεῖραι[1])

children of _____ (᾿Αβραάμ) ____ (ἐκ) these _____ (λίθων*). Matt. 3:9

*ων here does not indicate a participle because λίθος is a noun.

(The master of the vineyard answered) "Is it not lawful for me to do (ποιῆσαι[1])

what ___ _____ (θέλω) with my own? Matt. 20:15

_____ (καὶ) no one _____ (βάλλει) _____ (νέον) wine into old wine-skins. Mark 2:22

FOOTNOTES

1. -αι is another "infinitive" ending-- note the word "to" in the translation.

(Pilate answered): Which of the two _θέλετε_[1]_____ that I release unto

you? They said, _Βαραββᾶν_____. _Πιλᾶτος_____ _λέγει_[2]_____, to them, "What

shall I do with _Ἰησοῦν_____ called _χριστόν_____?" _λέγουσιν_[3]___ _____,

"Crucify him."   Matt. 27:21-22

EXAMPLES OF VERB ENDINGS FROM FIRST JOHN

Perfect love _βάλλει_____ out fear. 1 John 4:18

Γράφω

_____ to you, children, because your sins have been forgiven. 2:12

γράφομεν

And _____ these things to you so your joy may be full. 1:4

NEW VERBS ARE INTRODUCED BEFORE SOME OF THE FOLLOWING PASSAGES:

ἔχω = I have.   _ἔχει_
The one who confesses the son _____ the father also. 1 John 2:23

ἔχομεν

If our hearts condemn us, ____ _____ boldness with God. 3:21

ἔχετε

I have written these things to you that ye may know that ___ _____

eternal life. 5:13

FOOTNOTES

1. θελετε is "ye will", but since this is a question, translate as "will
   ye" or "do ye will" (or, "do ye want", or "do ye wish").

2. Your Bible might translate this as a past tense; Matthew uses present
   tense in the original as part of his dramatic style.

3. This is the ending ουσι, and the ν is added at the end just for smoothness in the sentence, as we sometimes say "an" instead of "a".

      ἔχων[1]   ἔχει   ἔχων

The one _____ the Son _____ the life; the one not _____ the

     θεοῦ   ἔχει[2]

Son __ _____ _____ not the life. 5:12

FOOTNOTES

1. Word for word = The one having. A common translation in a case like this would be "He who has" or "the one who has".

2. Word for word = has not the life. You could translate, "does not have the life".

μένω = I remain

                             μένει   ἔχετε

The anointing which you received from him _____ in you, and ___ _____

no need that anyone should teach you. 1 John 2:27

       μένων

Everyone _____ in him does not sin. 3:6

θεὸς   μένων   μένει ἐν θεῷ καὶ

_____ is love, and the one _____ in love ____ ___ _____, _____

θεὸς μένει

_____ _____ in him. 4:16

ποιῶ = I do.

       ποιῶν   ποιεῖ

Everyone _____ sin also _____ lawlessness. 1 John 3:4

                          θέλετε   ποιεῖν

You are of your father the devil and ___ _____ __ ____ the desires of

your father. John 8:44

Pronounce in Greek; translate into English.

μισῶ = I hate.

Do not wonder, brothers, if the _____ κόσμος _____ μισεῖ you. 1 John 3:13

γινώσκω = I know.

Θεὸς _____ is greater than your _____ καρδίας ____ και _____ γινώσκει all.
1 John 3:20

And in this _____ γινώσκομεν that __ _____ μένει in us---he has given us his spirit. 1 John 3:24

In this ____ _____ γινώσκομεν that ____ _____ μένομεν in him and he in us.
1 John 4:13

In this ___ _____ γινώσκετε the Spirit ___ _____ θεοῦ. 1 John 4:2

βλέπω = I see.

_____ _____ βλέπω another law in my members... Rom. 7:23

And why _____ βλέπεις the speck in your brother's eye...? Matt. 7:3

(Remember, there is no special ending for questions, just the question mark. You have to use correct English to make it sound like a question.)

You have used βάλλω, throw. Now put the preposition εκ in front as a prefix:

But the Pharisees said, _____ ἐκβάλλει the demons through the prince of the

δαιμονίων _____. Matt. 9:34

And calling the _____ δώδεκα μαθητὰς _____ to himself, he gave them authority

ἐκβάλλειν _____ unclean spirits. Matt. 10:1

And if ____ ἐγὼ through Beelzebub βεελζεβοὺλ ἐκβάλλω _____ the _____ δαιμόνια, thro

whom do your sons _____ ἐκβάλλουσιν ? Matt. 12:27

VERBS RELATED TO NOUNS AND ADJECTIVES YOU KNOW

Pronounce in Greek; translate into English.

ἀγαπῶ is related to the noun ἀγάπη, love

Remember the comma above the α simply means, "do not make an 'h' sound."

Examples from 1 John:

ἀγαπῶ   θεόν   ἀδελφὸν
If anyone says, ___ _____ _____, and hates his _____, he is a liar.
                                                              1 John 4:20

ἀγαπῶν μένει
The one not _____ _____ in death. 1 John 3:14b

λέγων   μισῶν
The one _____ that he is in the light, and _____ his brother, is in

ἀγαπῶν   ἀδελφὸν μένει
the darkness; the one _____ his _____ _____ in the light.
                                                       1 John 2:9, 10

                                                              ἀγαπῶν
Beloved, love one another, because love is of God, and everyone _____

γινώσκει
is born of God and _____ God. 1 John 4:7

Here is the same sentence showing the nouns used for "beloved" and "love":

Ἀγαπητοί
_____, love one another, because _____ is of God, and everyone

ἀγάπη

ἀγαπῶν
_____ is born of God... 1 John 4:7, 8

The following sentence shows that some verbs change the ο on ομεν to an ω. (More details on these changes in Part V)

γινώσκομεν   ἀγαπῶμεν   θεοῦ
In this ___ _____ that ___ _____ the children (of) _____, when

ἀγαπῶμεν   θεὸν καὶ   ποιῶμεν
___ _____ _____ ___ (___) _____ his commands. 1 John 5:2

The following example shows that some nouns change the vowel at the point where the stem and the ending connect. You would expect the word to end with ετε:

ἀγαπᾶτε
Woe to you Pharisees, because __ _____ the upper seats in the syna-

gogues... Luke 11:43

φιλω = I like or love   (notice resemblance to φιλος, friend, and
                          φιλια, love or friendship)

            φιλεῖ   ποιεῖ
The father _____ the son and shows him everything which ____ ____.
                                                         John 5:20

Exercise One

GUESSING AT RELATED VERBS

Pronounce these Greek words; translate into English

On the blank in front of each scripture, put the letter of the noun or verb from the word list on page 94, which is related to one of the verbs in the quotation.

            μαρτυρῶ   ἔχουσιν
____ 1. For __ _____ about them that __ _____ a zeal for God, but not

        according to knowledge. Rom. 10:2

        (Did you understand the word that ended with ν? It was the
        ουσι ending with ν added)

            ἀποστέλλω
____ 2. Behold, __ _____ you as sheep in the midst of wolves.
                                                      Matt. 10:16

                    πνεῦμα πνεῖ   θέλει   ἀκούεις
____ ____ ____ 3. The _____ ____ wherever __ ____ and __ _____
            φωνην
        the _____ of it. John 3:8

            γινώσκομεν   προφητεύομεν
____ 4. Now __ _____ in part and ____ _____ in part...
                                                      1 Cor. 13:9

93

_____ 5. One and the same $\overset{\text{πνεῦμα}}{\_\_\_\_}$ $\overset{\text{ἐνεργεῖ}}{\_\_\_\_}$ all these things, distributing to each as he wills. 1 Cor. 12:11

_____ 6. You put a lamp on a stand, $\overset{\text{καὶ}}{\_\_\_}$ $\overset{}{\_\_}$ $\overset{\text{λάμπει}}{\_\_\_\_}$ on all those in the $\overset{\text{οἰκίᾳ}}{\_\_\_\_\_}$. Matt. 5:15

_____ 7. Having $\overset{\text{ὀφθαλμοὺς}}{\_\_\_\_\_}$ $\overset{}{\_\_}$ $\overset{\text{βλέπετε}}{\_\_\_\_}$ not, and having ears $\overset{\text{ἀκούετε}}{\_\_\_\_}$ $\overset{}{\_\_\_\_}$ not. Mark 8:18

Word list of related nouns:

a) πνευμα   d) ενεργεια   Verb from Part I

b) λαμπας   e) προφητης   g) "hear"

c) μαρτυρ   f) αποστολος   h) θελημα (will, wish, desire)

VERB POSSIBILITIES SUMMARIZED

Verb construction is complicated and will be explained in Part V. This page will survey the possibilities and introduce the terminology you will need to use a reference book.

I. First there are the six personal endings:

	SINGULAR	PLURAL
1st Person	I throw	we throw
2nd Person	you throw	ye throw
3rd Person	he throws	they throw

These can also be translated: I am throwing, you are throwing, etc.

Remember, each of these is only one word in Greek.

βαλλει = He is throwing.

II. The example above is in PRESENT tense. There is also FUTURE tense (I will throw, you will throw, etc.), and there are four different kinds of past tense. Simplified listing:

IMPERFECT -- I was throwing, etc.
AORIST -- I threw. A simple statement without reference to when it happened. The most common form for past.

PERFECT -- I threw. An act in the past with results still occur-
ring in the present.
(Example: "Jesus died and rose." We would put "died"
in the aorist, because it was a single act; we would
put "rose" in the perfect, because although it happened
in the past, He is still risen.)
PLUPERFECT -- I had thrown, etc.

Multiplying the 6 tenses X the 6 persons = 36 different-
looking verbs, all with a different meaning.

Example: "throw", in third person imperfect = he was throwing.

III. All 6 tenses listed above are in ACTIVE voice. All 36 possibilities can also be found in PASSIVE voice (I am being thrown, etc.)
and in MIDDLE voice (I am throwing myself, etc.), adding up to
108 different constructions.

Example: Second Person singular aorist passive: You were
thrown (one word in Greek!).

IV. All possibilities given so far are in INDICATIVE MOOD.

There are also:

IMPERATIVE mood, for commands: "Throw!"
SUBJUNCTIVE mood. Many uses; one example would be to show
possibility: (if) I should throw.
OPTATIVE mood. Also many possibilities. Example: I would
throw.
INFINITIVE mood. "To throw"

These moods are not found in all tenses, so we don't have to
multiply 108 x 5.

Example: Third Person plural perfect subjunctive: They should
have thrown.

V. PARTICIPLES (such as -en and -ing words) occur in Present, Future,
Aorists, and Perfect. Participles can be used with an adverbial
sense, or less commonly as adjectives or nouns, and each can get
many different endings.

DO NOT try to remember the facts on this page now. This page
was included only to round off the introduction to verb endings,
and to show you what is coming in Part V.

FOUR USES FOR NOUNS

SUBJECTS

Shown in English by coming first in the sentence.
Shown in Greek by having the ending -ος. ανθρωπος λεγει = man says.

> If subject is plural, the ending to use is -οι.
> ανθρωποι λεγουσι = men say.

POSSESSION

Shown in two different ways in English:

1. With an ending (apostrophe s):   God's law = law of God
2. By using the word "of":

Shown in Greek in ONE way: The ending ου. λογος θεου = word of God
                                                           = (God's word)

Exercise One

TRANSLATING

In this workbook, we will always use the word "of" when we see the ου
    ending. Try these:

I.

___ 1. ανθρωπος θεου   a) house of man   If possessor is
                                                   plural, use ending
___ 2. οικος ανθρωπου   b) book of Mark   -ων.
                                                   οικος ανθρωπων
___ 3. βιβλος Μαρκου   c) man of God   = house of men.

(ων looks like the participle ending you learned earlier.
If ων ends a noun, it designates possessive plural; if ων
ends a verb, it designates a participle.)

OBJECT

Shown in English by coming after the verb: Paul helped Mark.
Shown in Greek by the ending ον: Παυλος helped Μαρκον.

II.

   ___ 4.   Παυλος helped ανθρωπον   a) Paul helped Philip

   ___ 5.   Παυλος helped Μαρκον   b) Paul helped Mark

   ___ 6.   Παυλος helped Φιλιππον   c) Paul helped man

   <u>If object is plural, use -ους.   παυλος helped ανθρωπους =</u>
<u>Paul helped men</u>

Since meanings are shown by endings, word order can be mixed up without obscuring the meaning of the sentence:

ανθρωπον helped παυλος   and   ανθρωπον παυλος helped

        both mean, "Paul helped man"

III. Using all three endings

   ___ 7.   ανθρωπος θεου saw Πετρον   a) Man saw house of Peter

   ___ 8.   ανθρωπος saw οικον Πετρου   b) Peter saw house of God

   ___ 9.   Πετρος saw οικον θεου   c) Man of God saw Peter

IV. Using plurals and mixing up word order

   ___ 10.   οικον ανθρωπων saw Πετρος   a) Peter saw houses of man

   ___ 11.   οικους ανθρωπου Πετρος saw   b) Men saw houses of Peter

   ___ 12.   οικους Πετρου ανθρωποι saw   c) Peter saw house of men.

INDIRECT OBJECT

Shown in two ways in English:

   1.   Using the word "to": Peter gave the book TO MARK.
   2.   Using a special word order; putting the word in between the verb and the object: Peter gave MARK the book.

Shown in one way in Greek: The ending ω. We will call this ending the DATIVE ending and we will always translate by using the word "to".

    Πετρος λεγει Μαρκω   =   Peter speaks to Mark

For plural, use οις. ανθρωποις = to men

V. Matching:

____ 13. εγω gave ανθρωπῳ   a) Peter gave to Timothy

____ 14. Τιμοθεος gave Παυλῳ   b) Timothy gave to Paul

____ 15. Πετρος gave Τιμοθεῳ   c) I gave to man

All four endings:

Φιλιππος	gave	βιβλον	Μαρκου	Παυλῳ
Philip		book	of Mark	to Paul
SUBJECT		OBJECT	POSSESSIVE	DATIVE

Exercise Two

CHART OF NOUN ENDINGS

	Singular	Plural
SUBJECT	-ος	-οι
POSSESSIVE (use "of")	-ου	-ων
DATIVE (use "to)	-ῳ	-οις
OBJECT	-ον	-ους

II. Matching. Match these Greek words with their English equivalents

____ 1. θεου   a) to man

____ 2. Μαρκῳ   b) of God

____ 3. Παυλου   c) to men

____ 4. βιβλων   d) of books

____ 5. βιβλοις   e) to Mark

____ 6. ανθρωπῳ   f) of Paul

____ 7. ανθρωποις   g) of men

____ 8. ανθρωπων   h) to books

Words after prepositions use these same endings.

Sentences using singulars and plurals:

ανθρωποι		βιβλους	νομων	λεπροις	εν οικω
men	gave	books	of laws	to lepers	in house
SUBJECT	verb	OBJECT	POSSESSIVE	DATIVE	PREPOSITIONAL PHRASE

Μαρκος	θελει	γραφειν	λογους	νομου	ανθρωποις	θεου.
Mark	wants	to write	words	of law	to men	of God.
SUBJECT	verb	infinitive	OBJECT	POSSESSIVE	DATIVE	POSSESS.

verbs

Exercise Three

PRONUNCIATION CHECK

Match the Greek with its pronunciation:

_____ 1. λογος   a) low-goce   b) law-gawce

_____ 2. λογου   a) log-goo   b) low-go

_____ 3. λογῳ   a) log-go   b) low-go

_____ 4. λογον   a) low-gov   b) log-gone

_____ 5. λογοι   a) log-goo   b) log-goi

_____ 6. λογων   a) law-gone   b) log-own

_____ 7. λογοις   a) log-goose   b) log-oice

_____ 8. λογους   a) log-oce   b) log-goose

MEANINGS OF NOUNS WITH ENDINGS

Match the Greek with the best translation:

_____ 9. λογοις   _____ 17. θεου

_____ 10. λογοι   _____ 18. θεῳ

_____ 11. λογῳ   _____ 19. ανθρωποις

_____ 12. λογος   _____ 20. ανθρωπων

_____ 13. λογου

_____ 14. λογον

_____ 15. λογων

_____ 16. λογους

a) to word
b) to words
c) of words
d) word (subject)
e) word (object)
f) words (subject
g) words (object)
h) of word
i) to men
j) of men
k) to God
l) of God

VERBS PLUS NOUNS

Match the Greek with the best translation:

_____ 21. γραφω λογους   m) to write word

_____ 22. γραφει λογους   n) I write word

_____ 23. γραφω λογον   o) I write words

_____ 24. γραφειν λογον   p) he writes words

_____ 25. λεγει Μαρκῳ   q) to speak words

_____ 26. λεγω Μαρκῳ   r) I speak words

_____ 27. λεγειν λογους   s) I speak to Mark

_____ 28. λεγω λογους   t) he speaks to Mark

Exercise Four

SCRIPTURES USING NOUN ENDINGS

In each set of parentheses, write two letters. First, write a capital
letter indicating whether the ending of the word indicates that the
word is:

        S (subject)   D (dative)

        P (possessive)   O (direct object)

Then write a small s or p to indicate singular or plural.
For smooth English, you may add the words "a" and "the" to the sentences.

1. Follow me and I will make you fishers _____ ἀνθρώπων ( ) . Matt. 4:19

2. Glory _____ θεῷ ( ) in the highest... Luke 2:14

3. If _____ _____ Δαυὶδ καλεῖ him _____ κύριον ( ) , how is he his _____ υἱός ( ) ? Matt. 22:45

4. __ _____ Μαρτυρῶ about them that __ _____ ἔχουσιν _____ ζῆλον ( ) θεοῦ ( ) . Rom. 10:2

5. The Kingdom of heaven is similar _____ ἀνθρώπῳ ( ) who sowed good seed...
                                                Matt. 13:24

6. _____ _____ Ἐχομεν νόμον ( ) and according to our law he ought to die, because

    he made himself _____ _____ υἱὸν ( ) θεοῦ ( ) . John 19:7

7. ὀφθαλμοὶ ( ) Κυρίου ( )
   _____ _____ are upon the righteous. 1 Pet. 3:12

8. Whoever has left houses or ἀδελφοὺς ( ) _____ or sisters or father

   or mother or children or ἀγροὺς ( ) _____ for my name's sake...
   Matt. 19:29

9. While he was still far from the house, the centurion sent

   φίλους ( ) λέγων
   _____, _____ to him... Luke 7:6

10. They ordained πρεσβυτέρους ( ) _____ in every church. Acts. 14:23

11. Ye received it not as λόγον ( ) ἀνθρώπων ( ) _____ _____, but as it is in

    truth: λόγον ( ) θεοῦ ( ) _____ _____. 1 Thess. 2:13

12. Do not lay up for yourselves θησαυροὺς ( ) _____ upon earth. Matt. 6:19

13. He went away from them about the cast λίθου ( ) _____. Luke 22:41

14. Ἰωάννης _____ wore a garment made from hairs καμήλου ( ) _____. Matt. 3:4

Exercise One

SENTENCES WITH NOUN AND VERB ENDINGS

Translate into English on a separate piece of paper, and check answers
on answer page. You'll need to refer to the charts on the previous
pages. After you have completed this, then start with the English
sentences and try to translate the odd-numbered sentences back into
Greek:

A. SUBJECT - VERB - OBJECT

    1. ανθρωποι βαλλουσι λιθους.

    2. αδελφος γραφει λογους.

B. SUBJECT - VERB - DATIVE

    3. θεος λεγει Φιλιππῳ.

    4. αδελφοι λεγουσι λεπροις.

C. PRONOUN SUBJECT - VERB - DATIVE

    5. εγω γραφω Μαρκῳ.

    6. αυτος γραφει Παυλῳ.

D. SUBJECT "understood", - VERB - OBJECT

    7. βαλλω λιθον.

    8. γραφεις λογους.

E. SUBJECT - VERB - OBJECT - POSSESSIVE

    9. αδελφοι γραφουσι νομον θεου.

    10. Μαρκος λεγει λογον ανθρωπων.

F. SUBJECT - VERB - DATIVE - POSSESSIVE
        (slave)
    11. δουλος γραφει ανθρωποις θεου.

    12. λεπροι λεγουσι δουλοις Παυλου.

G. SUBJECT "understood" - VERB - OBJECT - POSSESSIVE - DATIVE

   13. λεγομεν λογους θεου ανθρωποις.

   14. λεγουσι λογον νομου Φιλιππῳ.

H. SUBJECT "understood" - VERB - INFINITE - OBJECT

   15. θελω λεγειν λογους.

   16. διδασκει γραφειν λογους.
      (he teaches)

I. SUBJECT - VERB - OBJECT - PREPOSITIONAL PHRASE

   17. Κορνηλιος γραφει βιβλον εν οικῳ.

   18. Θεος αγαπει ανθρωπους εν κοσμῳ.

J. SUBJECT - VERB - DATIVE - PREPOSITIONAL PHRASE

   19. δουλοι λεγουσι σκορπιῳ επι οικῳ.

   20. Νικοδημος γραφει αδελφῳ επι λιθῳ.

K. SUBJECT - POSSESSIVE - VERB - OBJECT - POSSESSIVE - DATIVE -
POSSESSIVE - PREPOSITIONAL PHRASE - POSSESSIVE

   21. ανθρωποι θεου γραφουσι λογους βιβλου αδελφοις Παυλου

      εν οικῳ προφητων.

   22. αδελφοι λεπρων λεγουσι λογους θεου ανθρωποις θεου εν

      οικῳ θεου.

ADJECTIVES

The adjective gets the same ending as the noun it is describing.

     good man = καλος ανθρωπος

     bad law = κακος νομος

If the noun is plural, the adjective also must have the plural ending.

     good laws = καλοι νομοι

     bad men = κακοι ανθρωποι

If the adjective describes the object of the sentence, it gets the same ending as the object. In this example, it is plural:

     God gives us good things = θεος gives us καλους λογους

A SPECIAL USAGE FOR ADJECTIVES

Sometimes the adjective appears without a noun.

You have to supply a word like "one" or "thing" as you translate:

     good one writes   = καλος γραφει

     good ones speak   = καλοι λεγουσι

     God gives us good things = θεος gives us καλα

The adjective "ἁγιος" means "holy". The backwards comma above the first letter means you are to pronounce an "H" sound, so the word is pronounced "ha-gee-os".

     holy man speaks   = ἁγιος ανθρωπος λεγει

     holy one says   = ἁγιος λεγει

     holy ones write   = ἁγιοι γραφουσι

     God speaks to holy ones = θεος λεγει ἁγιοις

In most English Bible translations, "holy ones" is translated by the word "saints".

EXAMPLES OF THE WAYS ADJECTIVES ARE USED

Pronounce the Greek; translate into English:

                               ἑτερον νόμον

1. Adjective coming before noun: I see _____ _____ in my members...

                                                    Rom. 7:23

2. Adjective after noun: I looked, and behold, _____ _____ ...
                                             ἵππος λευκός
                                                            Rev. 6:2

3. Adjective without noun--you have to add a word, such as "thing":

                                                     χλωρὸν
   They were told not to hurt the earth, nor any _____ ... Rev. 9:4

4. A noun and an adjective on each side of the word "is". Since "is" is treated like an equal sign, both must get a subject ending:

          λόγος   σκληρός
   This _____ is _____. John 6:60

5. "shall be" is a future form of "is": Many of the _____ shall
                                                   πρῶτοι
      ἔσχατοι   ἔσχατοι πρῶτοι
   be _____, and the _____ _____. Matt. 19:30

Exercise One

SCRIPTURES WITH ADJECTIVES

Translate; circle every adjective:

1.   χρυσόν   λίθους
   If anyone builds on the foundation _____ silver _____

     τιμίους
   _____ wood, hay, stubble... 1 Cor. 3:12

2.   μόνῳ σοφῷ θεῷ* διὰ Ἰησοῦ Χριστοῦ. Ἀμήν
   Glory be forever _____ _____ _____ _____ _____ _____. _____.
                                                   Rom 16:27

3. πρῶτοι   ἔσχατοι   ἔσχατοι πρῶτοι
   Many _____ shall be _____ and many _____ _____.
                                                Matt. 19:30

4.   ἑτέρῳ
   He said _____, how much do you owe? Luke 16:7

5. Καὶ ἄλλος ἄγγελος δεύτερος*   λέγων
   _____ _____ _____ _____ followed _____. Rev. 14:8

6.   νεκρῶν ὀστέων
   But inwardly you are full __ _____ _____. Matt. 23:27

*Have you noticed that all the words that go together end the same?
But you only have to say "of" or "to" once for the entire group.

105

7. Among the lamps I saw someone ομοιον υιον ανθρωπου. Rev. 1:13
_____ __ ___ __ _____

Exercise Two

SOME ADJECTIVES WHICH ARE RELATED TO WORDS YOU ALREADY KNOW

In the first blank, write the small letter from the list of Greek
words you know; in the second blank, write the capital letter corresponding to the meaning of the adjective:

ADJECTIVES	WORDS YOU KNOW	ADJECTIVE DEFINITIONS
__ __ 1. λαμπρος	a) ψευδος (lie)	A. wise
__ __ 2. χρυσεος	b) εθνος (nation, Gentile)	B. false
__ __ 3. σοφος	c) ψυχη (the animal self)	C. shining (use twice)
__ __ 4. ψιχικος	d) σοφια (wisdom)	D. psychic (not spiritual)
__ __ 5. εθνικος	e) χρυσος (gold)	E. national, ethnic
__ __ 6. ψευδης	f) λαμπας (lamp)	F. golden
__ __ 7. φανερος	g) φανος (torch)	

THE WORD "THE"

The word "the" is a letter "T" plus the same ending as the noun it is
with:

Θεος λεγει τον λογον = God speaks the word.

EXCEPTION. When "the" appears with the subject, it does not have a
letter "t". "The" with a singular subject is ὁ, pronounced "Haw".
"The" with a plural subject is οἱ, pronounced "Hoi."

ὁ   ανθρωπος   gave   καλους   βιβλους   τῳ   αδελφῳ
The   man   gave   good   books   to the brother.

CAREFUL: τῳ is not the word "to". It is the word "the", with the
dative ending to go with the word αδελφῳ.

106

DIFFERENT CUSTOMS.   The Greeks use the word "the" in places we don't expect, such as before names. When translating, we simply leave out the "the" in conformity with English usage.

ὁ θεος λεγει τῳ Πετρῳ = The God speaks to the Peter. (literal)
= God speaks to Peter. (good translation)

As is the case with adjectives, the word "the" is sometimes used alone, without a noun. You have to add a word like "one" or "thing" so it makes sense.

Examples: With a prepositional phrase:

ὁ εν τῳ οικῳ λεγει   = The one in the house speaks

With a participle:

ὁ λεγων αγαπει   = The one speaking loves; or
                         the speaking one loves; or as a para-
phrase acceptable in translating: He that is speaking loves.

1.   "The" with a noun: God so loved ⎯⎯ τὸν κόσμον .   John 3:16

2.   "The" with an adjective: Paul, apostle of Christ Jesus __ τοῖς ____

ἁγίοις _____ in Ephesus... Eph. 1:1

3.   With the word "is": __ ὁ ἀγρός __ is __ ὁ κόσμος __. Matt. 13:38

A SPECIAL ADJECTIVE PLACEMENT:

A common Greek usage is for an adjective to come after a noun, each with its own word "the" (all endings have to match). When you trans- late, say the word "the" once, then the adjective, then the noun:

ὁ θεος ὁ ἁγιος = The God the holy (word for word)
                 The holy God (translate)

4.   Into the lake burning with fire, which is ὁ θάνατος ὁ δεύτερος ⎯⎯⎯⎯⎯⎯⎯⎯⎯⎯⎯
                                                    Rev. 21:8

The slot after the second "the" can be filled with entire phrases:

5. ὁ ανθρωπος ὁ λεγων λογους μενει εν τῳ οικῳ τῳ μικρῳ.

Word for word:
The man the saying words remains in the house the small.

With adjectives placed correctly in front of nouns:
The saying-words man remains in the small house.

Smooth English:
The man who is saying words remains in the small house.

SCRIPTURES WITH NOUNS AND "THE"

ὁ αγρός   ὁ κόσμος   οἱ υἱοὶ
__ _____ is __ _____; the good seed is ___ ____ of the Kingdom.
                                                    Matt. 13:38

                    τους οφθαλμους
...did not so much as lift ____ _____ into heaven... Luke 18:13

                    τοῦ ἡλίου
...not seeing the brightness __ ___ _____. Acts 26:13

            τοις ανεμοις
He spoke a rebuke __ ___ _____ and to the sea. Matt. 8:26

        τους ιππους   τῶν ιππων
Then I saw ____ _____ in the vision; and the heads __ ___ _____ as

heads of lions. Rev. 9:17

        τον ἡλιον
Because he makes ____ _____ of him rise on the evil and the good.
                                                    Matt. 5:45

                                    τῶν οφθαλμῶν
Everything in the world...lust of flesh, lust ____ _____.
                                                    1 John 2:16

            ὁ χρυσος   τον
Which is greater, __ _____ or the temple that sanctifies ____

χρυσόν
_____? Matt. 23:17

108

Exercise Three

ADJECTIVES AND "THE" -- MATCHING

____ 1. ὁ καλος ανθρωπος   a) The good man (object)

____ 2. οἱ ανθρωποι οἱ καλοι   b) The good men (object)

____ 3. του καλου ανθρωπου   c) to the good men

____ 4. των καλων ανθρωπων   d) The good man (subject)

____ 5. τῳ ανθρωπῳ τῳ καλῳ   e) of the good men

____ 6. τοις καλοις ανθρωποις   f) to the good man

____ 7. τον καλον ανθρωπον   g) of the good man

____ 8. τους καλους ανθρωπους   h) The good men (subject)

FILL IN CORRECT WORD FOR "THE"; then, match to meaning:

____ 9. ἁγιος θεος ____   i) to the holy men

____ 10. κακου ανθρωπου ____   j) to the bad man

____ 11. κακῳ ανθρωπῳ ____   k) of the good men

____ 12. ἁγιον ανθρωπον ____   l) of the bad man

____ 13. κακοι ανθρωποι ____   m) the holy God (subject)

των 14. καλων ανθρωπων k   n) the bad men (object)

____ 15. ἁγιοις ανθρωποις ____   o) the holy man (object)

____ 16. κακους ανθρωπους ____   p) The bad men (subject)

Exercise One

GUESSING MEANINGS

Write the Greek word in the blank:

αριθμοι:

πρωτος   δευτερος   τριτος   αλλος   μεγας   μεσος   μικρος   αλλος

οικος   ναος   αλλος   πληρους   κενος   μεσος   αλλος

ταφος   νεκρος

first	_____	large	_____	temple	_____
second	_____	small	_____	grave	_____
third	_____	other	_____	dead	_____

full	_____	numbers	_____
medium	_____		
empty	_____		

All the words above are adjectives, except three which are nouns.
Write (n) after the nouns.

Exercise Two

Match the Greek with their English equivalents:

VERBS:

____ 1. γραφω   ____ 5. λεγει   a) I throw   e) I call
____ 2. σκοπεω   ____ 6. καλεω   b) to call   f) I see
____ 3. βαλλω   ____ 7. καλειν   c) calling   g) I hear
____ 4. ακουω   ____ 8. καλων   d) I write   h) he says

NOUNS AND ADJECTIVES

____ 9. ἁγιος   ____13. νεκρος   i) grace   m) anointed one

____10. καλος   ____14. αλλος   j) good   n) dead

____11. κακος   ____15. χαρις   k) holy   o) shining

____12. λαμπρος   ____16. χριστος   l) bad   p) other

MATCH meanings to these adjectives. English derivatives given as hints:

____17. ιδιος   q) hidden (cryptic)

____18. ὁμοιος   r) entire (holistic)

____19. εσχατος   s) only (monocle)

____20. χρυσεος   t) young (nepotism)

____21. ἑτερος   u) made of earth or clay (ceramic)

____22. νηπιος   v) other (heterosexual)

____23. κεραμος   w) last (study of last things: exchatology)

____24. κρυπτος   x) golden (chrysalis)

____25. μονος   y) own (idiosyncracy)

____26. ὁλος   z) similar (homogenous)

Exercise Three

SENTENCES WITH ADJECTIVES

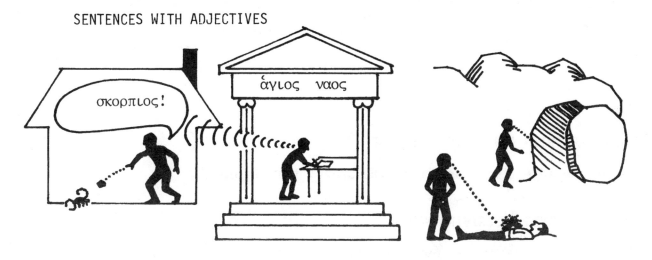

σκορπιος!

ἁγιος ναος

See if you can guess the meaning of the new words through the pictures.
Answers are on page 319.

111

1. ὁ πρωτος ανθρωπος, εν τῳ οικῳ, λεγει λογον.

2. ὁ δευτερος ανθρωπος γραφει λογους εν τῳ ναῳ.

3. ὁ τριτος ανθρωπος σκοπει τον νεκρον ανθρωπον.

4. ὁ πρωτος ανθρωπος βαλλει τον μικρον λιθον εν τῳ οικῳ.

5. ὁ δευτερος ανθρωπος ακουει τον λογον του πρωτου ανθρωπου.

6. ὁ αλλος ανθρωπος σκοπει τον κενον ταφον.

7. οι ανθρωποι βαλλουσι σκληρους λιθους.

8. ὁ αδελφος γραφει σκολιον λογον.

9. Μαρκος λεγει σκληρον λογον του νομου τοις αγιοις αδελφοις.

10. λεγομεν καλους λογους του αγιου θεου τῳ αποστολῳ.

11. λεγουσι νεον λογον θεου τοις σοφοις ανθρωποις.

SCRIPTURES

Pronounce the Greek and translate:

                σκληρός λόγος   ἀκούειν
This is a _____ _____; who is able _____ it? John 6:60b

      ὁ ναὸς τοῦ θεοῦ   ἅγιος
For __ _____ ___ _____ is _____ --and you are that temple!

                                                    1 Cor. 3:17

                λέγων   Ἰησοῦ
The demons cried, _____, "what have you to do with us, _____ of

                              ὁ ἅγιος τοῦ θεοῦ
Nazareth?...I know who you are--__ _____ ___ _____ !" Mark 1:24

Exercise Four

SCRIPTURES WITH ADJECTIVES AND "THE"

Circle the adjectives; pronounce the Greek; translate.

A. ADJECTIVES DESCRIBING NOUNS

                        ἄνθρωπος   τὸν κόσμον
    What shall it profit __ _____ if he should gain ____ _____

ὅλον...
_____   Matt. 16:26

He is a debtor to keep _____ _____ _____. Gal. 5:3..

$$\overset{\smile}{ο}λον \quad \overset{\backprime}{τ}ον \quad ν\acute{ο}μον$$

...which was not made known __ __ _____ ___ _____ as is now

$$τ\hat{ο}\iota ς \quad \overset{\smile}{υ}\iota ο\iota ς \quad τ\hat{ω}ν \quad \overset{\prime}{α}νθρ\acute{ω}πων$$

revealed __ __ _____ _____ of him and prophets in the spirit.
Eph. 3:5

$$τ\hat{ο}\iota ς \quad \overset{\smile}{α}γ\iota ο\iota ς \quad \overset{\prime}{α}ποστ\acute{ο}λο\iota ς$$

In the glory of his father ____ __ __ _____ _____ Luke 9:26

$$κα\overset{\backprime}{\iota} \quad τ\hat{ω}ν \quad \overset{\smile}{α}γ\acute{\iota}ων \quad \overset{\prime}{α}γγ\acute{ε}λων$$

Who can forgive sins if not _____ _____ Luke 5:21

$$μ\acute{ο}νος \quad \overset{\smile}{ο} \quad θε\acute{ο}ς;$$

B. ADJECTIVES WITHOUT NOUNS
Add words like "one" or "thing" if needed to make sense.

You have taken off the old _____ and put on ____ _____.
Col. 3:9, 10

$$\overset{\prime}{α}νθρωπον \qquad \overset{\backprime}{τ}ον \quad ν\acute{ε}ον$$

How are ___ _____ raised up? 1 Cor. 15:35

$$\overset{\smile}{ο}\iota \quad νεκρο\acute{\iota}$$

I know who you are: __ _____ __ __ _____ Mark 1:24

$$\overset{\smile}{ο} \quad \overset{\prime}{α}γ\iota ος \quad τ\hat{ου} \quad θε\hat{ου}$$

_____ __ _____ blew the trumpet. Rev. 8:7

$$κα\overset{\backprime}{\iota} \quad \overset{\smile}{ο} \quad πρ\hat{ω}τος$$

Servants, submit to your masters, not only to the good ones but also

__ ___ _____. 1 Pet. 2:18

$$τ\hat{ο}\iota ς \quad σκολ\iota ο\hat{\iota}ς$$

We believe in God who raises _____ _____. 2 Cor. 1:9

$$τους \quad νεκρο\acute{υ}ς$$

That you ministered __ __ _____ and still minister. Heb. 6:10

$$τ\hat{ο}\iota ς \quad \overset{\smile}{α}γ\acute{\iota}ο\iota ς$$

PRONOUNS

The word "he", (αυτος) changes its endings, like a noun does. If you use the noun endings, you can construct forms like αυτῳ (to him) and αυτου (of him).

    Example: οικος αυτου = house of him (you can say, "his house").

The plural of "he" would be "they"; continuing with the chart, you can make αυτων (of them) and αυτοις (to them).

    Example: οικος αυτων = house of them (their house).

The same possibilities exist for "I", with its plural, "we"; and for "you". These charts show all the possibilities. Notice that you can tell, in Greek, whether you are talking about one "you" or several, which you cannot do in English unless you use a word like "ye" or "you-all".

	I	WE		YOU	
	Singular	Plural		Singular	Plural
SUBJECT	εγώ	ἡμεῖς*	SUBJECT	σύ	ὑμεῖς
POSSESSIVE	μου	ἡμῶν	POSSESSIVE	σοῦ	ὑμῶν
DATIVE	μοι	ἡμῖν	DATIVE	σοί	ὑμῖν
OBJECT	με	ἡμᾶς	OBJECT	σέ	ὑμᾶς

EXAMPLES:

λεγει μοι = he says to me

οικος ημων = house of us = our house.

EXAMPLES:

λεγει σοι = he says to you

οικος ὑμων = house of you = your house

Exercise One

I. MATCHING:

___ 1. ἡμιν   a) to me

___ 2. ἡμεις   b) of me (my)

___ 3. ἡμας   c) we (subject)

___ 4. ἡμων   d) of us

___ 5. μοι   e) to us

___ 6. μου   f) us (object)

II. MATCHING:

___ 7. ὑμεις   a) to you (sing.)

___ 8. συ   b) of you (sing.) (your)

___ 9. σοι   c) you (subject, plural)

___10. ὑμιν   d) of you (plur.)

___11. ὑμων   e) to you (plur.)

___12. σου   f) you (subject, sing.)

* pronounced "hay-mace"

Sometimes you will see the forms starting with μ with an ε in front:
(εμε means the same as με)

III. SCRIPTURES

Pronounce the Greek and translate:

ὑμῖν   ἡμῶν
1. Grace ___ ____ and peace from God the Father __ ____. Eph. 1:2

ὑμᾶς   ὑμῶν
2. And ____, being dead in the trespasses and sins ___ ____...
                                                     Eph. 2:1

Αὐτὸς   ἡμῶν
3. _____ is the peace ___ ____.   Eph. 2:14

αυτος can also mean "self" or "himself":
ὁ θεος αυτος λεγει = God Himself says.

SCRIPTURES USING PRONOUNS

Pronounce the Greek and translate:

ὁ ζῆλος τοῦ οἴκου σου   με
__ zeal __ __ _____ ___ has consumed ___. John 2:17

Παῦλος ἀπόστολος Χριστοῦ Ἰησοῦ διὰ θελήματος   θεοῦ
_____ _____ _____ ____ __ _____ ___ __
                                    will

τοῖς ἁγίοις τοῖς οὖσιν ἐν Ἐφέσῳ καὶ πιστοῖς ἐν Χριστῷ
__ _____ The ones being ___ _____ ___ faithful __ ____

Ἰησοῦ Χάρις ὑμῖν καὶ εἰρήνη ἀπὸ θεοῦ πατρὸς ἡμῶν καὶ κυρίου
_____: ____ ___ ___ _____ ___ ___ _____ ____ ___ _____

Ἰησοῦ Χριστοῦ   ὁ θεὸς καὶ πατὴρ τοῦ κυρίου ἡμῶν
_____ _____. Blessed be __ ___ __ ____ __ _____ ____

Ἰησοῦ Χριστοῦ,   ἡμᾶς ἐν
_____ _____. The one blessing _____ __ every spiritual blessing

ἐν τοῖς   ἐν Χριστῷ καθὼς   ἡμᾶς ἐν αὐτῷ
__ ___ heavenlies __ _____ as he chose _____ __ ____...
                                              Eph. 1:1-4

115

αὐτὸς   ὁ ζατανᾶς   εἰς ἄγγελον

For _____ _____ transforms __ __ _____ of light 2 Cor. 11:14

(Did you consider translating αυτος as "himself"?)

ὁ πατὴρ φιλεῖ τὸν υἱον καὶ   αὐτῷ   αὐτὸς

__ _____ _____ ____ ____ ____   shows __ __ everything which _____

ποιεῖ

_____. John 5:20

In the following two examples, the words under the brackets are being
used as adjectives would be used: following the nouns, and with a
word "the" of their own. Grasp the overall idea, and put the entire
thought into good English.

ὁ υἱος αὐτοῦ ὁ πρεσβύτερος   ἐν ἀγρῷ

_____ was _____. Luke 15:25

       βλέπεις τὸ 1   τὸ 1 ἐν τῷ ὀφθαλμῷ τοῦ αδελφοῦ σου

Why _____ __ splinter _____,

                         ἐν τῷ ἰδίῳ 2 ὀφθαλμῷ

but do not notice the __ __ _____ _____ beam? Luke 6:41

    1 another word for "the"
    2 one's own

             πρὸς με καὶ ἀκούων μου τῶν λόγων καὶ ποιῶν

Everyone coming ____ __ ___ _____ ___ ___ _____ ___ _____

αὐτούς   ὁμοιος

_____ I'll show you what he is _____. Luke 6:47

                τὸν σπορον αὐτοῦ

A sower went out to sow ___ _____ __ ___   Luke 8:5

λέγω σοι   σὺ Πέτρος

____ ___ __ __ that ___ are _____. Matt. 16:18

116

Exercise Two

ENDINGS AFTER PREPOSITIONS

Since there are only eight types of endings, we have to use these same endings when writing a noun after a preposition.

θεῳ = to God, but εν θεῳ = in God, NOT "in to God".

____ 1. εν αδελφῳ	a) to brother
____ 2. αδελφῳ	b) in brother
____ 3. εις αδελφον	c) of brother
____ 4. προς αδελφου	d) towards brother
____ 5. αδελφου	e) into brother
____ 6. λεγει	f) to speak
____ 7. λεγειν	g) he speaks

, N ice that the English word "to" is used for two completely different purposes: if the word is a verb, and ends with ειν, it is an "infinitive", and we use the word "to". If the word is a noun, and ends with ῳ, (or οις for plural), it is the dative or indirect object, and we again use the word "to" with it.

Exercise Three

Some prepositions have more than one meaning.
The meaning is revealed by the ending of the following word. (That word is called the "object" of the preposition.) Example: (see #11, p. 118)

A. μετα ανθρωπου means _____ a man (because of the ου ending.

B. μετα ανθρωπον means _____ a man (because of the ον ending.)

PREPOSITION (with alternate forms)	MEANING IF NEXT WORD-ENDING LOOKS LIKE:		
	POSSESSIVE	DATIVE	DIRECT OBJECT
1. αμφι			around
2. ανα			up
3. αντι	instead of, against		
4. απο (αφ, απ)	from		

PREPOSITION (with alternate forms)	MEANING IF NEXT WORD IS:		
	POSSESSIVE	DATIVE	DIRECT OBJECT
5. δια	through		because of
6. εις			into
7. εν		in	
8. εκ (εξ)	out of, from		
9. επι (εφ, επ)	on	near, on	about against,
10. κατα (καθ)	down from		according to
11. μετα (μεθ)	with		after
12. παρα	from the side	at the side	to the side, compared with
13. περι	concerning		near
14. προ	before		
15. προς	toward	near	towards
16. συν		with	
17. ὑπερ (English hyper)	above		over
18. ὑπο (English hypo)	by	under	during

Exercise Four

ENGLISH WORDS FORMED FROM THE LAST THREE PREPOSITIONS ON THE CHART
Match to the definitions at the right.

____ 1. synergism
____ 2. hypercritical
____ 3. hypodermic
____ 4. synchronize
____ 5. hyperbole
____ 6. hypothermia

a) under the skin (δερμα)

b) work (εργον) along with God

c) under-heated (θερμη is warmth)

d) Checking time (χρονος) with one another

e) over-judging (κριτικος = able to judge; a judge is a κριτης)

f) over-throw: an exaggeration. (βολη is a form of βαλλω.)

118

SCRIPTURES USING PREPOSITIONS

Check the ending of the noun following the preposition in order to
determine which meaning of that preposition to use in your translation.

ὑπὸ ἀνέμου
What did you go out to see? a reed shaken ____ _____? Matt. 11:7

διὰ τὸν στόμαχον   σου
Use a little wine ____ ____ _____ and the frequent ailments ____.
                                                    1 Tim. 5:23

περὶ τῶν χρόνων καὶ τῶν καιρῶν, ἀδελφοί, ἔχετε
____ ____ _____ ____ ____ seasons _____, __ ____ no need that
    ὑμῖν   ἐφ᾽ ἵπποις
I write ___ ____.   1 Thess. 5:1

                              ἐφ᾽ ἵπποις λευκοῖς
And the soldiers of heaven followed him ___ _____ _____. Rev. 19:14

ἐγὼ ἀποστέλλω πρὸς ὑμᾶς προφήτας καὶ σοφοὺς
____ _____ ____ ____ _____ ____ ____ ___. Matt. 23:34

                    εἰς ἕτερον τόπον
And going out they went ____ _____ _____. Acts. 12:17

    ἐξ
Drink ___ it, all of you. Matt. 26:27

        ὑπὸ τοῦ κακοῦ
Do not be overcome ____ ____ _____   Rom. 12:21

        εἰς τὸν τόπον τὸν ἴδιον
Judas went ____ ____ _____ ____ _____. Acts 1:25

        ποταμὸν   λαμπρὸν κρύσταλλον
He showed me __ _____ of the water of life, _____ as _____,

        ἐκ τοῦ θρόνου τοῦ θεοῦ
going __ __ __ _____ ___ ____   Rev. 22:1

LESSON TWENTY-THREE

MEANINGS OF PREPOSITIONS

Why is it that prepositions mean different things in different situations?

Some of these instances can be explained this way: The preposition has to make sense with the relationship that is already suggested by the ending on the noun.

For example, we have been using the word "of" to translate when there is a possessive ending:

ὁ Ἰησους is ὁ υἱος του ανθρωπου.

But what do we mean by this word "of"? We could hardly call it possession in this case--as though the man possessed the son. There is a different relationship there; but a relationship, nonetheless, and our English word "of" seems to cover the situation. (The man "generated" or "begat" the son--grammarians call this sense of the word genitive.)

What would you do with the following sentence?

We are condemned του νομου

There is a relationship expressed here between law and condemnation, but the word "of" doesn't express this relationship adequately. What word would you use?

The Greeks, way back in the formative years of their language, long before Christ, asked themselves the same question. Part of the answer was the development of prepositions to clarify the shades of meaning meant by the noun ending. We could clarify the sentence above by writing:

δια του νομου or ὑπο του νομου

Thousands of years later, when someone set out to make a Greek/English dictionary, he would catch the sense of the entire sentence and then conclude--obviously δια and ὑπο can mean "by" or "through". Greek dictionaries will list a dozen or more words for many prepositions that seem to be the right word at various times. You can often reach the same conclusion just by using common sense.

Language is so complicated that for our purposes it is better just to see what is done, rather than to try to explain it. You will run across two results of the developments we have been describing:

1. You will see endings that don't seem to make sense according to the translating we have done so far:

a. Do not get drunk οινῳ (Eph. 5:18) Here you would supply a preposition as you translate into English, but it won't be the preposition "to".

120

b. Use a little οινῳ for your stomach and frequent ailments.
      (1 Tim. 5:23)   Here you can translate into English without
      using any preposition.

2. You will see prepositions that don't seem to fit their customary
   meaning:

   a. See that no one repay κακὸν ἀντὶ κακοῦ. (1 Thess. 5:15)
   b. If anyone ἐν ὑμῖν should wander from the truth...(James 5:19)

The next section presents some of the many shades of meaning expressed
by noun endings. You are not expected to memorize these possibilities,
or to regard them as rules, but simply to realize that this explains
why some of the endings and prepositions you will see are not translated with their simplest meaning.

MORE ON NOUN CASES -- THE SEVEN CASES

There originally were seven different case endings for seven different
uses of nouns. The endings were simplified to four, but the seven uses
can still be distinguished. In the following examples, the words in
quotes can be stated by one Greek word, just by using the right ending.
In actual usage, a preposition (from, to, under, etc.) is often added--
its function is to strengthen and clarify the tendency that the noun
already has due to its endings.

THE SEVEN CASES

A. Number one is what we have been calling the subject ending:

   1. NOMINATIVE -- subject of sentence

B. The next two use what we have been calling the possessive ending:

   2. GENITIVE -- possible meanings:

      a. possession
      b. relationship, or further definition
           baptism "of repentance" ("in view of repentance")
           the earnest "of (the) spirit"
      c. value. Wheat "for a denarius"
      d. quality. This body "of sin"
      e. The word in the genitive can cause an action to the word
         being modified: obedience "of faith" (ie., faith produces
         obedience)
      f. On the other hand, the main noun can cause action to the
         noun in the genitive: blasphemy "of the Spirit".

   3. ABLATIVE -- main idea: source, separation
      (Answers the question "from where"? Also used for comparisons.)

Examples:

> I will give him "of (the) manna" (a part of all the manna)
> (Rev. 2:17)
> All of you, drink "of it" (a part of it). (Matt. 26:27)

The phrase, Church "of God", makes sense whether regarded as a genitive (God's possession) or as an ablative (the church's) source is God).

C. The next three use what we have been calling the dative ending:

4. LOCATIVE   (compare English word "location") -- Answers the questions "Where?" "In what?"

Examples:

> "In (the) boat";   Poor "in spirit";   Baptized "in the Jordan".

ALSO used to express time: "On the (first) day"

5. DATIVE -- usually used about people who receive the action of the sentence. Varieties of meaning:

a. Indirect Object
b. Object of such verbs as TRUST.
c. possessing something. The promise is "to you"
f. reference. We died "to sin." (we died so far as sin is concerned.)
g. personal interest. It is "to (the) advantage" of you that I go away. (John 16:7)

6. INSTRUMENTAL (what "instrument" or tool is used to bring about the action of the sentence) -- Answers the questions "How?" "With what method?"

Examples:

> Partake "with thanks"; bound "with fetters"; killed "with (the) sword"; purchased "by blood".

ALSO association: They followed "him"
ALSO time: "about 400 years"

D. This one is the one we have been calling the direct object.

7. ACCUSATIVE -- Answers questions like "To what extent?" "In what direction?" "How long?" "To what purpose?"

There is also an 8th usage, called VOCATIVE, used in speaking directly to someone. Example in English: <u>Father</u>, may I go out?

Example in Greek: (Jesus is speaking to the Father): πάτερ δίκαιε,...
(translate: "righteous father,...")   (John 17:25)

These 8 usages were found in the language which was ancestral to the Greek language (see Charts on page 238 for more information).

Examples taken from LIGHT FROM THE GREEK NEW TESTAMENT by Boyce W. Blackwelder. Anderson, Indiana. 1958

EXAMPLES OF POSSESSIVE AND DATIVE ENDINGS

This first set of examples is from Ephesians Chapter One.

Words with Possessive endings

1. Genitive use:

Blessed be the God and Father τοῦ κυρίου ἡμῶν Ἰησοῦ Χριστοῦ.
Eph. 1:3

2. Ablative use:

God made known to you the mystery τοῦ θελήματος αὐτοῦ.
Eph. 1:9

   (The ending ατος is another type of possessive ending: θεληματος means "of will". The meaning here is that the source of the mystery is in God's will. The word αυτου is back to genitive meaning: It is His will.)

Words with Dative endings

1. Dative use:

Paul is writing τοῖς ἁγίοις (to the saints). Eph. 1:1

2. Locative use (place) with the usage strengthened by the preposition εν:

Paul is writing to the saints ἐν Ἐφέσῳ. Eph. 1:1

3. Instrumental use ("how" or "with what"). Here again the word εν is used, but our English word "in" doesn't begin to do justice to the relationship expressed:

God predestined us ἐν ἀγάπῃ. Eph. 1:4

Some additional uses of datives:

1. Certain words regularly are followed by datives rather than direct objects (accusatives). One of these words is "believed":

Abraham believed _θεῷ_. Rom. 4:3

If you do not believe _τοῖς_ _λόγοις_ _μου_ Luke 1:20

"Believe" is also often followed by a prepositional phrase:

I believe _εἰς_ _τὸν_ _θεόν_.

2. A dative is sometimes used to tell when something happened:

Jesus healed _τῷ_ _σαββάτῳ_. Luke 13:14

These many uses of noun endings will jump out at you as you look at actual scripture passages. A college text or course will go into much more detail, specifying these variations.

EXAMPLES OF PREPOSITIONS WITH VARIOUS MEANINGS

And be not drunk with wine, but be filled _ἐν_ _πνεύματι_. Eph. 5:18

Lest you dash _πρὸς_ _λίθον_ _τὸν_ _πόδα_ _σου_. Matt. 4:6

Σίμων answered, pray _ὑμεῖς_ _ὑπὲρ_ _ἐμοῦ_ _πρὸς_ _τὸν_ _κύριον_ that what

you said will not happen _ἐπ'_ _ἐμὲ_. Acts. 8:24

Christ also suffered _περὶ_ sin, the righteous _ὑπὲρ_ the unrighteous.
1 Pet. 3:18

The one who has blessed us _ἐν_ every spiritual blessing... Eph. 1:3

Simeon said _πρὸς_ Mary... Luke 2:34

The one conquering shall not be hurt ἐκ τοῦ θανάτου τοῦ δευτέρου ___ ___ _____ ___

Rev. 2:11

and if ____ __ _____ _____ _____ ἐγὼ ἐν βεελζεβοὺλ ἐκβάλλω δαιμόνια, οἱ υἱοὶ ὑμῶν ἐν __ ___ ___ ___ ___

whom _____ ἐκβάλλουσιν; Matt. 12:27

We announce __ __ the eternal ____ which was ___ ___ _____ ὑμῖν ζωὴν πρὸς τὸν πατέρα

1 John 1:2

_____ __ ___ if anyone ___ ____ should wander from the truth and Ἀδελφοί μου ἐν ὑμῖν

someone brings him back.   James 5:19

THE NOUN ENDINGS -- SIMPLIFIED LISTING

You have learned eight endings for nouns, corresponding to four uses
of nouns in a sentence, with singular and plural variations. The
endings you have learned are only one of three different sets of endings.
These sets of endings are called "declensions". You have learned the
noun endings for the second declension (Roman numeral II on the chart
below).

The words in capital letters at the left are the abbreviations for the
correct terms for the four possible uses of nouns in a sentence.

What we have been calling

"subject"	is termed	NOMINATIVE CASE
"possessive"	is	GENITIVE CASE
"dative"	is	DATIVE CASE
"direct object"	is	ACCUSATIVE CASE

Singular:	I*	II	III
NOM.	α or η or ης or ας	ος or ον	----**
GEN.	ας or ης or ου	ου	ος or ως or ους
DAT.	ᾳ or ῃ	ῳ	ι
ACC.	αν or ην	ον	α or ν or ος or like NOM.

Plural:	I*	II	III
NOM.	αι	οι or α	ες or εις or α
GEN.	ων	ων	ων
DAT.	αις	οις	σι
ACC.	ας	ους or α	ας or εις or η or ιν or α

*   technical name: "first declension"
**   no particular ending: words like φως, πατηρ

We are NOT going to learn all the details for how to attach these endings on to words. These details would be covered in a college course in Greek. We are going to learn how to use the chart to understand sentences in the Greek New Testament.

Let's begin by looking a little closer at Column II. Three endings are given as alternates. These are used when the noun is listed in the dictionary as "neuter".

For example, δενδρον happens to be a neuter noun. Its ending, ον, shows us that it is a second declension noun--it uses the endings from Column II. If we want to say "trees", the form would be δενρδα. If we want to say "of a tree", there is no alternative listing, so we write δενδρου. If you ask, "How can you tell the difference between Nominative and Accusative with a second-declension neuter word?", the answer is "You can't". You have to determine it from the context of the sentence.

> EXAMPLE: The word εγρον (work) is a second declension neuter
> noun.
>
>
> What does it profit if a man says he has faith, but has not
> εργα
> _____? James 2:14

With the ending "α", εργα must be either nominative plural (subject) or accusative plural (direct object).

Since the subject of the sentence is "man", the word "works" must be the direct object (accusative), since that is the only other alternative.

It is a general principle about neuter words, of any declension, that the NOM and ACC will be the same, and their plurals will end with α.

EXAMINING THE NOUN-ENDING CHART

Δbout the Chart as a Whole

One simplifying factor is that the genitive plural endings (ων) are the same in all three declensions. Unfortunately, ων is also the ending you learned as a participle ending:

λεγων   ανθρωπων
Jesus spoke, _____, I do not require the approval _____ _____.

You know you cannot translate ανθρωπων with an "ing" because it is a noun.

Another simplifying factor is that all the dative endings have a letter "ι" -- either full-size or small.

About the Third Declension

The following example uses a third declension word you know:

$$λέγω \qquad ὑμῖν \qquad\qquad\qquad ἐν \ τῷ \ φωτί$$

What ____ ____ ___ ____ in darkness, speak out ___ __ι ____. Matt. 10:27

Most of the third declension words appear in a short version in the nominative singular, so that the real "stem" of the word appears only in the other forms. A dictionary will give you this information, by showing you what the word looks like in both nominative and genitive forms.

For example, "light" in the dictionary is listed as φως, ωτος n (the n tells us it is a neuter word). This means the genitive form of φως is φωτος, and the stem is φωτ (you find the stem by taking off the genitive ending). All the rest of the endings are to be hooked on to the stem. In the scripture example above, the dative ending ι was therefore hooked on to the stem φωτ, not on to φως or φω.

An Exception

In the following example, "light" is a direct object, so you would expect it to have one of the accusative endings:

...but on a lampstand, so those coming in may see the ____φῶς. Luke 8:16

The reason it does not end as you would expect is that NEUTER WORDS ARE WRITTEN THE SAME IN BOTH NOMINATIVE AND ACCUSATIVE.

Another Exception

The σ in the dative plural ending σι interacts with the stem of the word in a way that results in some of the stem letters being changed. This is no problem for you, however, since as soon as you see the ι at the end, you know you are dealing with a dative ending. (The ending ουσι would only be found on verbs, and the nominative plural endings are usually obvious just from the sense of the sentence.)

THIRD DECLENSION SCRIPTURE EXAMPLES

Dictionary entry: πατηρ, πατρος m father (therefore stem is πατρ)

...pray $\underline{\smash{\tau\tilde{\omega}}}$ $\underline{\smash{\pi\alpha\tau\rho\acute{\iota}}}$ $\underline{\smash{\sigma\text{ou}}}$ $\boxed{\tau\tilde{\omega}\ \dot{\epsilon}\text{v}\ \tau\tilde{\omega}\ \kappa\rho\upsilon\pi\tau\tilde{\omega},}$ $\underline{\smash{\kappa\alpha\grave{\iota}}}$ $\underline{\smash{\dot{o}}}$ $\underline{\smash{\pi\alpha\tau\acute{\eta}\rho}}$ $\underline{\smash{\sigma\text{ou}}}$

βλέπων ἐν τῷ κρυπτῷ

seeing ___ ___ _____ will give a reward ___ ___ (σοι). Matt. 6:6

> The part in the box is an entire phrase which is used as an adjective.
>
> Word-for-word: to the father of you to the in the secret
> Placed in adjective position: to the in-the-secret father of you
> Smooth English: to your father in secret

The next example shows how the Greeks may add or change letters as they make connections between stem and endings: (the η of πατηρ changed to ε)

καὶ τὸν πατέρα αὐτῶν

They left the boat ____ ____ _____ __ ____ and followed him. Matt. 4:22

This book will NOT go into all the rules about connecting stems and endings. That is a major subject for a full college course.

Dictionary entry: παῖς, παιδός m & f, child or slave

(m and f means the word can be used to designate either a boy or a girl; the word is sometimes translated "child", sometimes as "slave".)

τοὺς παῖδας

Then Herod slew all _____ _____ in Bethlehem... Matt. 2:16

All you need to notice is that one of the accusative plural endings was placed on the stem, which is shown in the second word of the dictionary ending to be παιδ. As a reconfirmation, the form of the word "the" used also indicates accusative plural.

τῶν παίδων

The elder son called one ____ ___ _____ and asked what this might mean.
Luke 15:26

A Word About Cognates

Many of our English words which came from Greek are based on the stem of the word rather than on the nominative form. Our word "pedagogue" is made from the stem παιδ plus the word αγω (lead). So "pedagogue" means one who leads a child--a teacher.

The Greeks had already formed this particular word. Example:

$$\overset{(}{ο} \quad \overset{/}{νόμος} \quad \overset{\backslash}{παιδαγωγὸς} \quad \overset{(\frown}{ἡμῶν} \qquad\qquad\qquad \overset{\rangle}{εἰς} \quad Χριστόν$$

Therefore __ _____ _____ __ __ was constituted ____
_____ Gal. 3:24

$$\overset{(\backslash}{ὑπὸ} \quad \overset{/}{παιδαγωγόν}$$

...now that faith has come, no longer ____ _____ are we...
Gal. 3:25

The word "constituted" is treated like the word "is", with the nouns
on both sides of it receiving nominative endings. When you translate,
move the expression "was constituted" in between the word "law" and
the word "pedagogue."

By the way, what declension is the word παιδαγωγος? (second)

Another example: The Greek dictionary entry for "foot" is πους, ποδος.
We did not make our word "podiatrist" from the nominative (πους) but
rather from the stem (ποδ).

EXAMINING COLUMN I - FIRST DECLENSION

Before you react to how complicated this column looks, look at the
bottom half--at least there are no alternatives for the plural endings.
Notice that the genitive plural ending is the same as all the others,
that the dative plural has an "ι" in it (but notice that the nominative
plural does also), and that the accusative plural is the same as the
first alternative listed for genitive singular (ας).

What about all those alternatives? All you need to know is that a word
will not jump from one column to another. If the nominative form (found
in the dictionary) ends with α, the other endings needed will be listed
under the α.

But what if the nominative ends with ης? A dictionary will tell you how
to make the genitive. From that point on there are no additional alternatives. Since there was an η in the nominative form, continue to use
endings with η in them in dative and accusative.

| Dictionary entry: μαθητης, ου   m,   disciple, pupil, follower |

$$\overset{/}{λέγει} \quad \overset{\frown}{τῷ} \quad \overset{\frown}{μαθητῇ} \qquad\qquad \overset{/}{μήτηρ} \quad σου$$

Then ____ ___ _____: behold the mother ___ ___ _____.

$$\overset{\rangle}{ἀπ'} \quad \overset{/}{ὥρας} \quad \overset{(}{ὁ} \quad \overset{\backslash}{μαθητὴς}$$

And ___ that _____ __ _____ took her as his own. John 19:27, 28

(Dictionary entry for "hour" is ὥρα, ας. In our example it

takes the genitive ending because it comes after the word
απο.)

Then ___ _____ _____ _____ _____ ___ _____... Matt. 9:37

λέγει   τοῖς   μαθηταῖς   αὐτοῦ

A simplifying factor about the first declension: the stem is found in all forms, even in the nominative.

Dictionary entry: γη, γης   f, earth

Other (seed) fell on rocky ground where it had not much ____, and dried

γῆν

up ____ not having much depth ___ _____. Mark 4:5

διὰ   γῆς

Thy will be done, as in heaven, so ____ _____. Matt. 6:10

ἐπὶ γῆς

Dictionary entry: ζωη, ζωης   life   (ζωον was animal) from which we get English word zoo.

Here is the word with the genitive ending, ης.

The hope ___ ____ eternal, which God who cannot lie has announced ____

ζωῆς   αἰωνίου   πρὸ

χρόνων αἰωνίων
_____ _____.   Titus 1:2

ALL THE FORMS OF "THE"

SINGULAR	Masculine	Feminine	Neuter
NOMINATIVE (subject)	ὁ	ἡ	το
GENITIVE (possessive)	του	της	του
DATIVE	τῳ	τῃ	τῳ
ACCUSATIVE (object)	τον	την	το
PLURAL			
NOMINATIVE	οἱ	αἱ	τα
GENITIVE	των	των	των
DATIVE	τοις	ταις	τοις
ACCUSATIVE	τους	τας	τα

So far you have learned the "masculine" column. Those endings are second declension endings, except for the nominative singular, which is special.

The neuter column is the same as the masculine column, except that:

1. the nominatives are special, and
2. the accusatives are the same as the nominatives.

This corresponds to the endings listed as neuter alternatives in the second declension column, except that the nominatives and accusatives end with ον for nouns, but with ο for "the".

EXAMPLES WITH A NEUTER NOUN, εργον.

Τιμόθεος   τὸ ἔργον Κυρίου
If _____ comes accept him for he does ___ ____ ___ _____.
                                                              1 Cor. 16:10

        ὁ υἱὸς τοῦ θεοῦ   τὰ ἔργα
For this __ ____ ___ ____ was manifested, to destroy ___ ____

τοῦ διαβόλου
__ __ _____.   1 John 3:8

132

The feminine endings are taken directly from the first declension column.

ὁ θησαυρός σου   ἡ καρδία σου
For where __ _____ __ _____ is, there also __ _____ __ ___

shall be. Matt. 6:21

> (Note that the word "the" and the noun will not necessarily
> rhyme, but they must correspond; they must be the right
> "gender" (masculine, feminine or neuter) and the right "case"
> (nominative, genitive, etc.)

> Dictionary entry: στομα, τος   n, mouth. It is the subject of the
sentence below.

τῆς   καρδίας τὸ στόμα
For out of the fulness __ ___ _____ __ _____ speaks. Matt. 12:34

τὸ ἔργον τοῦ νόμου   ἐν ταῖς καρδίαις
Which show __ _____ ___ ___ ____ written __ ____ _____

αὐτῶν
__ ____. Rom. 2:15

Some dictionaries use the word "the" to indicate the gender of a noun,
instead of the initials m, f, or n.

A dictionary entry for "love" is αγαπη, ης, ἡ. This indicates:

1. the genitive of αγαπη is αγαπης.
2. it is a feminine noun, because ἡ is the feminine form of "the".

ADJECTIVE ENDINGS

Adjectives also use the endings on the noun ending chart. Each adjective
needs to use three sets of endings, so it can describe a masculine,
feminine, or neuter noun. A Greek dictionary will indicate which columns
(i.e., which declensions) to use with a given adjective by listing the
NOMINATIVE SINGULAR ending for all three possibilities.

For example, "new" in the dictionary is listed as follows: νεος, α, ον.

This means that a new man would be a νεος man, that a new woman would
be a νεα woman, and that a new temple would be a ναον temple. In the
case of this particular word, the masculine and neuter endings are from
column II, and the feminine endings are to be taken from column I. If
you want to say, "to new women", you would have to use the dative plural
ending from column I, and write: to νεαις women. If you wanted to say
"new temples" as the subject of your sentence, you would use the neuter
variation from column II (the letter α) and write: νεα temples.

133

Repent and do ___ _____ _____. Rev. 2:5

τὰ πρῶτα ἔργα

The dictionary entry for "city" is πολις, εως, ἡ, which shows you it is a third declension feminine noun. The entry for "holy" is ἁγιος, α, ον, which shows you it is an adjective, and the feminine forms of the adjective will use endings from the α column of first declension. I have left the following scripture in its original word order:

ὁ διάβολος εἰς τὴν ἁγίαν πόλιν

Then takes him __ _____ ____ ____ _____ _____. Matt. 4:5

The last three words go together. Although they do not rhyme, they are all ACCUSATIVE endings, as required following the preposition εις.

Dictionary entry: πνευμα, πνευματος, το (=neuter) spirit

ἑπτὰ ἕτερα πνεύματα

then goes and brings along _____ _____ _____ worse than himself.
Matt. 12:45

In the next example, the adjective follows the noun, with its own word "the". The noun is feminine, so must take a feminine "the" and a feminine adjective. The dictionary entry for "good" is καλος, η, ον, showing us that the feminine endings will be from the η column. Finally, the preposition εις requires that the words following it have accusative case endings.

And other (seed) fell εις τὴν γῆν τὴν καλήν Mark 4:8

Word-for-word: ___ ___ _____ ___ _____

Smooth English: _____

Do not greive τὸ πνεῦμα τὸ ἅγιον τοῦ θεοῦ. Eph. 4:30

Word-for-word: ___ _____ __ _____ ___ __ ____.

Smooth English: _____

In the next example, there is an adjective with no verb; it is neuter plural, so add "things"

τὰ κρυπτά τῶν ἀνθρώπων

In the day that God judges ___ ___ ____ _____ _____. Rom. 2:16

SCRIPTURES WITH FIRST AND THIRD DECLENSION ENDINGS

Remember that "he" was the word αυτος. In order to say "she", use the feminine endings of the word "the", making sure that each word starts with αυτ (αυτη, αυτης...etc.)

And his mother kept all these words $\underset{\text{εν}}{\rule{1.5em}{0.4pt}}\ \underset{\text{τῇ}}{\rule{1.5em}{0.4pt}}\ \underset{\text{καρδίᾳ}}{\rule{3em}{0.4pt}}\ \underset{\text{αὐτῆς}}{\rule{2em}{0.4pt}}$. Luke 2:51

("The heart" has the dative endings because it comes after "εν". αυτης is genitive: of her.)

I gave $\underset{\text{αὐτῇ}}{\rule{2em}{0.4pt}}$ time to repent, but she does not wish to repent of the

fornications $\underset{\text{αὐτῆς}}{\rule{2em}{0.4pt}}$. Rev. 2:21

The same approach is used for neuter. To say "it", put αυ in front of the neuter endings on the "the" chart (p. 132).

If words go together, as in the following example, they will all be in the same case, even if they might be in different declensions. In the example, both words are genitive, but the first word is third declension, so ends with "ος", while the second word is second declension, and ends with "ου":

Andrew, the brother $\underset{\text{Σίμωνος}}{\rule{3em}{0.4pt}}\ \underset{\text{Πέτρου}}{\rule{3em}{0.4pt}}$ John 1:40

σαρξ, σαρκος = flesh. (cognate to English <u>sarcophagus</u> when added to φαγος = eat)

Since therefore $\underset{\text{τα}}{\rule{1.5em}{0.4pt}}\ \underset{\text{παιδία}}{\rule{3em}{0.4pt}}$ share $\underset{\text{αιματος}}{\rule{3em}{0.4pt}}\ \underset{\text{καὶ}}{\rule{1.5em}{0.4pt}}\ \underset{\text{σαρκός}}{\rule{3em}{0.4pt}}$ he partook of the

same...   Heb. 2:14

The adjective μεγας (large, great) is an example of an irregular adjective.

The dictionary entry is μεγας, μεγαλη, μεγα. The accusative neuter is the same as the nominative μεγα; the masculine accusative is μεγαν. All the rest of the forms make use of the extra λ, as you see it in the feminine form. For example, the masculine genitive is μεγαλου.

In this example, the words are feminine, in accusative case:

φωνὴν μεγάλην

And I heard behind me _____ _____ as a trumpet... Rev. 1:10

Here the words are in dative, and tell "how" Jesus cried:

μεγάλῃ φωνῇ, λέγων

Jesus cried _____ _____ _____ Matt. 27:46

The following are masculine, accusative:

λίθον μέγαν

And rolled _____ _____ to the door of the tomb. Matt. 27:60

Two adjective examples using first declension:

τὴν ἰδίαν

And seeking to establish ____ _____ righteousness... Rom. 10:3

τὴν ἄλλην

If anyone strikes you on the cheek, turn to him also ____ _____.

Matt. 5:39

FORMS OF THE VERB "TO BE"

Αυτος εστι means "he is".

Remove the αυτος, and εστι alone would still be translated "he is".

Put a noun before it, and the word εστι will be translated "is".

ὁ αποστολος εστι means "The apostle is"

Think of the word "is" as an equal sign. The word on the right side of the equal sign is not the direct object, but is the equivalent of the subject of the sentence. The word on the right side of the word "is" will have a nominative ending.

ὁ ανθρωπος εστι δουλος.　　The man is a servant.
　　　　　　　　　　　　　　　(noun with nominative ending)

ὁ ανθρωπος εστι καλος.　　The man is good.
　　　　　　　　　　　　　　　(adjective with nominative ending)

Sometimes the letter ν will be added to εστι in order to make a smooth connection to the word that follows:

ὁ ανθρωπος εστιν αποστολος.　The man is an apostle.

Sometimes the word order will be different from English:

ὁ ανθρωπος δουλος εστιν.　　The man is a servant.

Check the following examples in your Bible:

ὁ θεὸς φῶς ἐστὶν
_____ _____ _____.　　1 John 1:5

ὁ θεὸς ἀγάπη ἐστίν
_____ _____ _____　　1 John 4:8

The word with "ὁ" is the subject, and should begin the English version:

Κύριος ἐστιν τοῦ σαββάτου ὁ υἱὸς τοῦ ἀνθρώπου
_____ _____ _____ _____ _____ _____ _____ _____.　Matt. 12:8

Εγω ειμι means "I am".

Ἐγώ εἰμι ὁ πρῶτος καὶ ὁ ἐσχατος
_____ _____ _____ _____ _____ __ _____　　Rev. 1:17

137

If you remove the word εγω, you have to supply the word "I".

Ειμι καλος = I am good.

In the following example, the word order is not like English:

υἱὸς τοῦ θεοῦ εἰμι

_____ ____ _____ __ ___. John 10:36

This chart shows the forms of the verb "to be" in the present tense:

Persons:	Singular	Plural	Infinitive
1	ειμι	εσμεν	ειναι
2	εις or ει	εστε	
3	εστι	εισι	

ENGLISH EQUIVALENT

(I) am	(we) are	to be
(you) are	(you) are	
(he) is	(they) are	

(ν sometimes added to third person)

MATCHING, to see if you can follow the chart

____ 1. ειναι   a) he is

____ 2. εσμεν   b) to be

____ 3. εστιν   c) I am

____ 4. ειμι   d) we are

SCRIPTURE EXAMPLES:

σοι λέγω   σὺ εἶ Πέτρος
And I also __ __ _____ that ___ ___ _____ and upon this rock I will

build my church. Matt. 16:18

Εγὼ καὶ ὁ πατὴρ   ἐσμεν
_____ ____ __ _____ one _____. John 10:30

θέλω ὑμᾶς σοφοὺς   εἶναι   εἰς* τὸ κακόν
__ ___ _____ __ _____ to the good, but innocent ____ __ _____.
                                                              Rom. 16:19

              ὑμεῖς ἐστέ   ἐγὼ   εἰμί
(Jesus said): _____ _____ from this world; ____ not _____ from this

world. John 8:23

*This is the preposition "to", not the 2nd person of "to be".

138

In the next example, the last word is an adjective with a third declension ending, genitive case to match the word "God" which it is describing.

Σίμων Πέτρος   Σὺ εἶ ὁ χριστὸς ὁ υἱὸς τοῦ θεοῦ τοῦ

_____ _____ said, ___ ___ ___ _____ __ ____ ___ ____ ____

ζῶντος

_____ . Matt. 16:16

Some samples of Greek word order that seem unusual to us:

                        σκληρὸς εἶ ἄνθρωπος

Lord, I know that you _____ __ _____ .   Matt. 25:24

σκληρός ἐστιν ὁ λόγος

_____ _____ __ ____ this.   John 6:60

SOME NEW VOCABULARY

Find the meanings of these nouns by looking up the Bible passages.

Ἐγω ειμι ἡ ἀνάστασις καὶ ἡ ζωή

_____ _____ __ _____ _____ __ ___   John 11:25

The word "the" is ἡ because the nouns are feminine. The noun chart shows that -η is a nominative ending in first declension. But the ending -ις is not found on the chart. The word happens to be third declension, in which nominatives end in various ways.

Ἐγω ειμι ὁ ἄρτος τῆς ζωῆς

_____ _____ __ _____ _____ _____   John 6:35

The third and fourth words have nominative endings, but the word της is a genitive (possessive) form of "the", and the noun chart shows us that -ης is a genitive ending in the first declension. The literal translation of the last two words would be "of the life". Since we don't commonly use the word "the" with the word "life" in a sentence like this, we may omit the word "the" in the translation.

Ἐγω ειμι ὁ ποιμὴν ὁ καλός

_____ _____ __ _____ .   John 10:11

An example of a noun and an adjective, each with its own word "the". We rearrange the words to make good English. Word for word, it says "I am the shepherd the good".

ὁ θεὸς ἀληθής ἐστιν

_____ _____ _____.   John 3:33

SUPPLYING THE FORM OF "TO BE" WHEN IT IS LACKING

The word εστι is sometimes omitted, and the meaning has to be added by the translator:

θεος εστι ἁγιος and θεος ἁγιος both mean "God is holy".

The problem is that with only two words -- θεος & ἁγιος -- you might not know whether to translate "God is holy" or "holy is God." To the rescue comes the word ὁ (the). It is used to point out which word is the subject. You can put the words in any order, and you will still know which one is the subject: the one with ὁ.

ὁ θεος ἁγιος and ἁγιος ὁ θεος both mean "God is holy".

ὁ ἁγιος θεος εστι καλος and ὁ ἁγιος θεος καλος
both mean "The Holy God is good".

It will still mean the same if we mix up the word order, as long as we put ὁ in the right place: καλος ὁ ἁγιος θεος

In the following scriptures, begin your translation with the word that has a form of "the".

πνεῦμα ὁ θεός

_____.   John 4:24   (pneuma means "spirit")

ὁ νόμος ἁγιος
So that, on the one hand, __ _____ _____. Rom. 7:12

καλὸς ὁ νόμος
We know that _____ __ _____ if anyone uses it lawfully. 1 Tim. 1:8

τάφος ὁ λάρυγξ αὐτῶν
An opened _____ __ _____ _____   Rom. 3:13

140

SPECIAL PLACEMENT OF ADJECTIVES REVIEWED

This handy use of the word ὁ is complicated by the fact that there are two ways to place adjectives in a Greek sentence:

1. The adjective can go before the noun as we do in English.

    ὁ ἁγιος θεος = the holy God

2. The adjective can come after the noun--but in this case, each word must have its own ὁ.

    ὁ θεος ὁ ἁγιος = the God the holy = the holy God

    (If you would leave out that second ὁ, you would have "God is holy.")

Adjectives can be placed in that manner anywhere in the sentence. For example, here the object of the sentence has an adjective:

Μαρκος γραφει τον ἁγιον λογον and Μαρκος γραφει τον λογον τον ἁγιον both mean "Mark writes the holy word."

In actual scriptural examples, you will find cases where the adjective is placed after the noun, without those extra "the's". You will usually not get mixed up if you look at the sense of the entire sentence. If the sentence already has a verb, then you would know you cannot add the verb "is". Also, anytime "is" would be required, the main word on both sides of the word "is" both have to have the "subject" endings.

MATCHING

Match these Greek phrases with their English equivalents:

_____ 1. ὁ θεος ἁγιος

_____ 2. ὁ ἁγιος θεος

_____ 3. θεος εστι ἁγιος

_____ 4. ἁγιος ὁ θεος

_____ 5. ὁ θεος ὁ ἁγιος

_____ 6. θεος ἁγιος

_____ 7. ὁ ἁγιος θεος εστι

_____ 8. ὁ θεος ἁγιος εστι

_____ 9. ὁ θεος ὁ ἁγιος εστι

_____ 10. ἁγιος ὁ θεος εστι

_____ 11. Εστι ὁ θεος ἁγιος

_____ 12. Εστι ὁ θεος ὁ ἁγιος

_____ 13. ὁ θεος ὁ ἁγιος εστι;

_____ 14. ὁ θεος εστι ἁγιος;

a) The holy God is.

b) The holy God

c) Is the Holy God?

d) God is Holy.

e) Is the God Holy?

141

The following sentence is a common form for a blessing, and translators have customarily inserted the word "be" rather than "is".

Check your Bible for the meaning of the first word.

Εὐλογητὸς   ὁ   θεὸς   καὶ   πατὴρ   τοῦ   κυρίου   ἡμῶν...

_____ __ ____ ____ ____ ____ _____ __ __   Eph. 1:3

LESSON TWENTY-SEVEN

Exercise One

EXAMPLES using plural

οἱ ανθρωποι εισι καλοι and οἱ ανθρωποι καλοι both mean
"the men are good".

Remember that when two parts of a sentence are connected by a form of
"be", such as "is" or "are", both parts of the sentence have the nominative ending. If the subject is plural, the word after "is" will also
have to have a plural ending.

ὁ Πετρος και ὁ Ιωαννης αποστολοι = Peter and John are apostles.

MATCHING

Match these Greek sentences with their English equivalents.

____ 1. οἱ αδελφοι καλοι.

____ 2. ὁ Πετρος και ὁ Παυλος αποστολοι.

____ 3. οἱ καλοι αδελφοι ἁγιοι.

____ 4. καλοι οἱ ἁγιοι αδελφοι.

a) The good brothers
   are holy.
b) The brothers are
   good.
c) The holy brothers
   are good.
d) Peter and Paul are
   apostles.

EXAMPLES using "he" and "they"

____ 5. ἁγιοι καλοι.

____ 6. αὐτοι καλοι.

____ 7. αὐτος εστι καλος.

____ 8. καλος ὁ θεος.

____ 9. ὁ θεος αυτος καλος.

e) God is good.
f) God Himself is
   good.
g) The holy ones are
   good.
h) He is good.
i) They are good.

FIRST JOHN, CHAPTER ONE

What you do NOT know are the connecting words like "as", which will be
covered in Part III; the past tenses of the verbs, which will be explained
in Part V; the words for the important religious concepts, which will be
the subject matter of Part IV; and some additional vocabulary, which you
would have to look up in a lexicon. (This is the word we should be using,
rather than "dictionary", for a Greek/English reference book.) Now let's
find out what you do know:

ἀπ' ἀρχῆς
That which was ___ _____, which we heard, which we saw

τοῖς[1] ὀφθαλμοῖς ἡμῶν,   καὶ αἱ χεῖρες ἡμῶν
_____, what we beheld ____ __ _____ __ ___ touched

143

περὶ τοῦ λόγου τῆς ζωῆς--καὶ ἡ ζωὴ ____ καὶ ____ καὶ ____
____ ____ ____ ____ ____ appeared, ____ we saw ____

μαρτυροῦμεν καὶ ____ ὑμῖν τὴν ζωὴν τὴν² αἰώνιον³
____ ____ announce ____ ____ ____ ____ ____ which was

πρὸς τὸν πατέρα καὶ ____ ἡμῖν
____ ____ ____ ____ shown ____ ____ .

What we saw and heard we announce also __ ___ so that also _____ may

κοινωνίαν⁵ μεθ᾽ ἡμῶν. καὶ ἡ κοινωνία ____ 4 μετὰ τοῦ
have _____ ____ ____. ____ ____ of ours ____ ____

πατρὸς καὶ μετὰ τοῦ υἱοῦ αὐτοῦ Ἰησοῦ Χριστοῦ Καὶ
____ ____ ____ ____ ____ ____ ____ ____ . ____ these things

γράφομεν ἡμεῖς ____ ἡμῶν ____ καὶ
____ ____ so that the joy __ ___ might be full. ____ this

ἔστιν ἡ ἀγγελία ____ ἀπ᾽ αὐτοῦ καὶ ____ ὑμῖν
____ ____ ____ which we heard ____ ____ announce __ ___ that

ὁ θεὸς φῶς ἔστιν καὶ ____ ἐν αὐτῷ ἔστιν
____ ____ ____ ____ darkness __ ___ not ____ at all. If we

κοινωνίαν ἔχομεν μετ᾽ αὐτοῦ καὶ ἐν τῷ
say that _____ ____ ____ ____ ____ ____ darkness walk,

____ ποιοῦμεν τὴν ἀλήθειαν ____ ἐν τῷ φωτὶ
we lie and not __ ____ ____ ____ . But if __ ___ ____ we

αὐτὸς ἔστιν ἐν τῷ φωτί, κοινωνίαν ἔχομεν μετ᾽ ἀλλήλων⁶
walk as ____ ____ ____ ____ ____ ____ ____ ____

καὶ τὸ αἷμα Ἰησοῦ τοῦ υἱοῦ αὐτοῦ ____ ἡμᾶς ἀπὸ
____ ____ ____ ____ ____ ____ ____ cleanses ____ ____ all sin.

NOTES

1. Dative ending with instrumental use: answers the question "with what?"
2. The adjective coming after the noun, each with its own word "the".
3. eternal. Cognate to "eon".
4. Add the word "is".
5. This word means "fellowship", from the word κοινον common: having
     something in common. Some churches have "koinonia" groups. A
     related word is κοινη -- that is used for the "common" Greek of
     the world at the time of Christ, as opposed to the "classical"
     Greek in which the masterpieces of the 400's B.C. were written.
6. related to αλλος, other; translate: each other.

PART III

THOSE SMALL WORDS

The purpose of this section is that you become so familiar and fluent with the common small words of Greek that when you look at a sentence you will be able to grasp the basic flow of it, and only have to look up the verb and possibly a few of the nouns in a dictionary.

In Part III, you will learn:

1. More uses for the words "and" and "to".

2. The common negative words like "no" and "not".

3. Common connectives like for, but, and therefore.

4. Common adverbs such as "badly".

5. Adding "more" and "most" to adjectives.

6. More pronouns used as adjectives: This, that, who, etc.

MORE USES FOR THE WORD καὶ (and)

1. Also.

   Surely ὶκαὶ _____ you are one of them...Matt. 26:73

   Since the children share in blood and flesh, he καὶ _____ partook of

   the same... Heb. 2:14

2. even

3. yet, but nevertheless

4. very, truly, in fact

5. indeed

6. καὶ...καὶ = both...and

   καὶ _____ the tabernacle καὶ _____ all the utensils of worship he sprinkled

   with blood. Heb. 9:21

7. καὶ + εγω = καγω: and I

   κἀγὼ   σοι λέγω   σὺ εἶ   Πέτρος
   ___ _____   __ __ __ __ that __ __   _____   Matt. 16:18

MORE USES FOR THE WORD αυτος (he)

1. "self" when used without its own word "the":

   God himself = ὁ θεος αυτος or αυτος ὁ θεος

        αὐτὸς Δαυιδ λέγει ἐν βίβλῳ ψαλμῶν
   For _____ _____ _____ __ _____ __ ____   Luke 20:42

2. "same" when used with its own word "the":

   The same God = ὁ αυτος θεος or ὁ θεος ὁ αυτος

   And here it's used without a noun:

   Since the children share in blood and flesh, he καὶ ____ partook τῶν ___ ___

   αὐτῶν.   Heb. 2:14

   _____

The entire scripture:

Ἐπεὶ   οὖν   τὰ   παιδία   κεκοινώνηκεν   αἵματος[1]
Since therefore _____ ___ _____ shared _____ _____

καὶ   σαρκός   καὶ   αὐτὸς   παραπλησίως[3]   μετέσχεν[2]   τῶν
___ _____ ___ _____   likewise   partook   __ ___

αὐτῶν
_____. Heb. 2:14

1   genitive ending with the sense of "having a portion".
2   This verb was made from μετα in the sense of "with", plus εχω "have".
3   This is an adverb, saying something about the verb "partook".

Exercise One

A great many Greek adverbs are adjectives with an ως ending; this ending
then does not change. Can you guess the meaning of the following adverbs,
which are related to adjectives you know:

__ 1.   αλλως   a)   well

__ 2.   καλως   b)   in the same way, likewise

__ 3.   κακως   c)   at all, wholly

__ 4.   ὁλως   d)   for the first time

__ 5.   ὁμοιως   e)   otherwise

__ 6.   προτως   f)   wrongly, badly

THE WORD NOT

The two words commonly used are ου and μη. There are definite rules about
when to use one or the other: ου is used with a verb which is making an
ordinary statement of fact, and μη is used for verbs with other shades
of meaning, and with infinitives and participles.

                                                   οὐ
More joy over one repenting sinner than over ninety-nine others who _____

     ἐχουσιν
need _____ of repenting. Luke 15:7

My children, __ _____ these things __ ____ so that ___ ye may sin.
γράφω these things ὑμῖν so that μὴ ye may sin.

1 John 2:1

You can see that it's going to take creativity on your part
to translate these Greek sentences with negatives in them
into English.

In the following sentence, the verb κρινω, "judge", is used. In its
first appearance it is giving a command. In its last appearance, it is
passive: ye may be judged.

Μὴ κρίνετε   μὴ κριθῆτε
_____ so that _____. Matt. 7:1

The next example uses a participle: loving-one. The "the" goes with
the participle, to produce "the loving-one". Then the negative is stuck
between them:

ὁ μὴ ἀγαπῶν   μένει ἐν τῷ θανάτῳ
_____ ____ __ _____. 1 John 3:14

Check your Bible to get an idea of how translators have
needed many English words to bring out what is meant in
cases like this.

Using two negative words in a sentence does not change the meaning to
a positive, as it does in English; rather, it just adds emphasis:

                        οὐ βλέπετε   ἀμὴν λέγω
Jesus answered his disciples: _____ all these? ____ __ ___

ὑμῖν, οὐ μὴ   λίθος ἐπὶ λίθον   οὐ
__ __ ___ shall be left here ____ ____ _____ which ___ shall be

cast down. Matt. 24:2

The preceding scripture also gave you a chance to translate
a question. Check your Bible.

Letters are added to the basic negative words when they come before
vowels in order to provide smoothness in sound. The point is that whatever may be added, those little words οὐ and μη are noticeable, and
always indicate something negative.

                οὐ βλέπετε καὶ   οὐκ ἀκούετε;
Having eyes _____ ___ having ears _____; Mark 8:18

        οὐχ   τοῦ θεοῦ
They _____ submitted to the righteousness ___ ____. Rom. 10:3

148

Many different words combine with the negative words to produce very specific shades of meaning. Some samples to guess at:

οὐκέτι

So then you are _____ strangers and sojourners, but fellow-citizens...
Eph. 2:19

οὐδὲν   τοῖς   ἐν Χριστῷ

There is therefore now _____ condemnation __ ___ __ __ _____

Ἰησοῦ

_____. Rom. 8:1

THOSE LITTLE INDEFINITE WORDS

Have you ever said, "I just want to praise the Lord?" What did you mean by the word "just"? Certainly you weren't referring to "justice", but you did add a certain flavor to your meaning.

Greek also has these little words. Two of them are γε and τε. Sometimes they're not even translated:

For τε I had not known lust, if the law had not said "Don't covet".
Rom. 7:7

These little words combine with other words, as well. In the next example, τε has combined with "not" to provide one of the many words used in Greek for either...or and neither...nor situations.

But whoever should speak against the Holy Spirit, it shall not be for-

οὔτε   οὔτε

given to him, _____ in this age _____ in the age to come. Matt. 12:32

A word with a little more weight, but still hard to translate, is μεν. In the next translation example it is in a sentence that has just summed up a paragraph, and means something like "on the one hand, then". Again, it is often left untranslated.

ὁ μὲν νόμος ἅγιος   ἁγία

So __ ___ _____ _____ and the commandment is _____ and just and good.
Rom. 7:12

The word αρα is still a little stronger, and usually gets translated, with the sense of "then, consequently, so".

ἄρα   οὐκέτι

_____ therefore you are _____ strangers and foreigners... Eph. 2:19

ἄρα

Now _____ no condemnation to those in Christ Jesus.   Rom. 8:1

(you have to add the word "is" in this sentence.)

This brings us to the two most common "little" words you will be coming across: γαρ and δε.

One thing that is unusual about them is their placement in the sentence; they always come second (even if they have to split up a noun from its word "the"), but when you translate, you always say them first.

MEANING: γαρ (which is γε + αρα) means "for"

δε can mean and, but, and various other shades of meaning, depending on how the sentence it is in is related to the preceding sentence.

Οὐ γὰρ   γὰρ θεοῦ ἐστιν
___ ____ am I ashamed of the gospel, power ___ __ __ _____ unto

salvation. Rom. 1:16

Αὐτὸς γὰρ Δαυὶδ λέγει ἐν βίβλῳ ψαλμῶν...
_____ ____ _____ _____ ___ _____ _____... Luke 20:42

                                                        δὲ τῷ θεῷ
Who shall rescue me from the body of this death? Thanks ___ ___ ___

δια Ιησοῦ χριστοῦ τοῦ κυριοῦ ἡμῶν   ἄρα   αὐτὸς ἐγὼ
___ _____ _____ ___ _____ ____ ___. ___ therefore _____ ___

μεν*   νόμῳ θεοῦ, τῇ δὲ* σαρκι νόμῳ
_____ in my mind serve ____ _____ ___ ___ flesh ___ of sin. Rom. 7:25

* μεν...δε used for "on the one hand...on the other hand".

COMMON MAJOR CONNECTING WORDS

> ἵνα = in order that

Τίμα   ἵνα   σοι
_____ your father and mother, ____ it may be well __ ___ Eph. 6:2, 3

                    γράφω   ἵνα
My children, __ ____ these things to you ____ ye may not sin. 1 John 2:1

                                  ἵνα
He is faithful and righteous ____ he may forgive our sins and cleanse

us...   1 John 1:9

> ὅτι = that, because

              ὅτι   οὐκ   ἔχομεν
If we say ____ ____ __ ___ sin, we deceive ourselves... 1 John 1:8

              ὅτι   υἱὸν   θεοῦ
He ought to die, ____ he made himself ____ __ ___   John 19:7

Κἀγὼ   δέ   σοι   λέγω   ὅτι   σὺ   εἶ   Πέτρος
__ __ ___ ___ __ __ __ ___   Matt. 16:18

              ὅτι   ἐκ τοῦ θανάτου εἰς τὴν ζωὴν ὅτι
We know ____ we have passed __ __ _____ ___ ___ ____ ___ __

ἀγαπῶμεν   τοὺς   ἀδελφούς
__ _____ __ _____   1 John 3:14

> ἀλλά = but

                                                        ἵνα
God so loved the world that he sent his only son, ____ everyone believing

                    ἀλλὰ   ζωὴν αἰώνιον
in him should not perish, _____ have _____ _____   John 3:16

                                    ἀλλὰ   σοφοί
Look carefully how you walk: not as unwise ____ as _____   Eph. 5:15

> οὖν = therefore

              οὖν
Everyone ____ who hears my words and keeps them is like a man...
                                                          Matt. 7:24
ἄρα οὖν οὐκέτι ἐστὲ
__ __ _____ __ ___ strangers and foreigners... Eph. 2:19

Ἐπεὶ οὖν τὰ παιδία   καὶ αὐτὸς

Since ____ ___ _____ share in flesh and blood, ____ _____ partook

τῶν αὐτῶν ἵνα διὰ τοῦ θανάτου   τὸν ἔχοντα

___ _____ ___ ___ ___ _____ he might destroy the one ____ ing

τοῦ θανάτου...

the power ____ _____ ... Heb. 2:14

> ὡς = as

Forgive us our trespasses, _{ὡς} ___ we forgive those who trespass against

us. Matt. 6:12

         ὡς αὐτός ἐστιν ἐν τῷ φωτί

If we walk in the light ___ _____ _____ __ __ _____ 1 John 1:7

       ὑμῶν διάβολος ὡς λέων

The adversary __ ___ _____ __ ___ _____ roaring walks about seeking

someone to devour. 1 Peter 5:8

       ἀστὴρ μέγας   ὡς λαμπάς

And there fell from heaven _____ _____ burning ___ _____ Rev. 8:10

> καθώς = as (κατα + ὡς)

           καθὼς   ἁγίοις

Let not greediness be named among you, _____ is fitting _____

                                          Eph. 5:3

      ὅτι   λόγον*   παρ᾽

We thank God constantly, ____ having received _____ you heard ___

ἡμῶν τοῦ θεοῦ*   οὐ λόγον ἀνθρώπων ἀλλὰ καθώς

_____ _____ you received ___ _____ _____ ____ _____

ἐστὶν   λόγον θεοῦ.

___ in truth: _____ ___ ____ 1 Thess. 2:13

*These words go together in the English translation.

> ὥστε = so as, that (made from ὡς + τε)

The son of perdition sets himself up against everything called God or

      ὥστε   εἰς τὸν ναὸν τοῦ θεοῦ   ὅτι

worshipful, _____ to sit ___ ___ _____ ___ _____ claiming ____

ἔστιν θεός

___ ___ ____ 2 Thess. 2:4

152

God so loved the world _____ (ὥστε) he gave his only son... John 3:16

| οὕτως = so, thus |

As a sheep before his shearers is dumb, _____ (οὕτως) he opened not __ _____ (τὸ στόμα) __ __ (αὐτοῦ) Acts 8:32

Οὕτως γὰρ _____ _____ loved _____ ____ ____ _____ ____ _____ (ὁ θεὸς τὸν κόσμον, ὥστε τὸν υἱὸν) the only-begotten he gave, ____ (ἵνα) everyone believing ____ __ ____ (εἰς αὐτὸν) would not perish _____ (ἀλλὰ) have eternal life. John 3:16

| ἤ = or, than |

Let none of you suffer ___ (ὡς) murderer __ (ἤ) thief __ (ἤ) evildoer... 1 Pet. 4:15

There will be more joy in heaven over one sinner repenting __ (ἤ) over ninety-nine righteous... Luke 15:7

 Distinguish ἤ (or) from ἡ (the, feminine) by the direction of the breathing mark. The word for "the" starts with an h-sound.
 ἤ...ἤ is another way to say "either...or".

| εἰ = if |

Save yourself, __ ___ __ ___ ____ _____ (εἰ υἱὸς εἶ θεοῦ) Matt. 27:40

 (Distinguish "if" from "are" by the accent, found only on "are".)

εἰ τὸ ἔργον
____ _____ of anyone which he has built _____, (μενεῖ) he'll receive a reward. 1 Cor. 3:14

καὶ εἰ ἐγὼ ἐν βεελζεβοὺλ ἐκβάλλω τὰ δαιμόνια, οἱ υἱοὶ

___ ___ ___ ___ ___ ___ ___ ___

ὑμῶν ἐν ἐκβάλλουσιν ;

___ ___ ___ whom _____ Matt. 12:27

εἰ with μὴ = "except" (if not)

        εἰ μὴ

A prophet is not without honor _____ in his own country. Matt. 13:57

ἐάν = if

    ἐάν   λόγον κατὰ τοῦ υἱοῦ τοῦ ἀνθρώπου

Whoever ____ he should speak ____ ____ ____ ____ ____ ____

it will be forgiven him.   Matt. 12:32

Ἀγαπητοί, ἐὰν ἡ καρδία μὴ   ἔχομεν πρὸς τὸν
Beloved, ___ __ _____ ___ condemn us, boldness ___ ___ _____ ___

θεόν
_____.   1 John 3:21

A shorter version, ἄν lends an "iffy" meaning to a sentence: (translated often by using the word "would")

        οὐκ ἂν

Lord, if you had been here, ____ ____ have died my brother.   John 11:21

κἄν = "and if" (καὶ + ἐαν)

λέγει αὐτῷ ὁ Πέτρος, κἂν   με σὺν σοί
_____ __ _____ __ ___ it should behoove __ ____ ____ to die,

οὐ μή σε
_____ ___ I will forsake! Matt. 26:35

νῦν = now. Also spelled νυνι

οὐδὲν ἄρα νῦν   τοῖς ἐν Χριστῷ Ἰησοῦ
_____ ____ ____ condemnation __ ____ __ _____ _____.   Rom. 8:1

PRONOUN/ADJECTIVE COMBINATION: "this"

οὑτος = this

Use the endings on the noun chart

	masculine	feminine	neuter
NOM:	οὑτος	αὑτη	τουτο
	etc.	etc.	etc.

1. The difference between αὑτη (feminine form of "this") and αὐτη (femi-
    nine form of αὐτος translated "she") is found in the breathing mark.
    The word we are now learning has an h-sound; the word for "she" does
    not.

2. The plurals are   οὑτοι   αὑται   ταυτα   = "these"

3. Remember that in all neuters, the ACCUSATIVE forms are the same as
    the NOMINATIVE forms. All the other neuter forms, (that is,
    GENITIVE and DATIVE), are the same as the masculine forms.

4. All the masculine and feminine forms, except the nominatives, which
    were described above, start with a τ . So for example, the masculine
    genitive will be τουτου; the feminine genitive (since it uses first
    declension endings) is ταυτης.

The word can be used to describe a noun: μυστηριον τουτο = this mystery;
or without a noun, as in the following neuter plural: ταυτα = these
things.

Exercise One

MATCHING

The genders are mixed together here; identify the meaning of each Greek
phrase.

___ 1. ταυτης   a) to these

___ 2. τουτῳ   b) this one (speaking of a man)

___ 3. τουτων   c) to this

___ 4. ταυταις   d) this thing

___ 5. τουτο   e) of this

___ 6. ταυτα   f) this one (of a woman)

___ 7. αὑτη   g) these things

___ 8. οὑτος   h) of these

SCRIPTURE EXAMPLES

τὸ   μυστήριον   τοῦτο

I do not want you to be ignorant about _____ _____ .   Rom. 11:25

Ἔχομεν   τὸν   θησαυρὸν   τοῦτον

___ ____ ____ _____ _____ in earthen vessels.   2 Cor. 4:7

σὺ   εἶ   Πέτρος,   καὶ   ἐπὶ   ταύτῃ   τῇ   πέτρᾳ

____ ___ _____ _____ ____ _____ ___ _____

μου
I will build __ __ the church.   Matt. 16:18

οὔτε   ἐν   τούτῳ   τῷ   αἰῶνι   οὔτε   ἐν
It shall not be forgiven him, _____ __ _____ __ _____ _____ __

τῷ
__ coming age.   Matt. 12:32

μου   ταῦτα γράφω ὑμῖν ἵνα μὴ
Children __ ___, __ __ __ __ __ __ ___ __ ye may sin.   1 John 2:1

καὶ   ἔστιν   αὐτὴν   ἡ   ἀγγελία
____ _____ _____ __ _____ which we heard from him.   1 John 1:5

    ("This" has to be feminine to match "message")

τοῦ   θανάτου,   τοῦτ᾽
That he might destroy the one having the power ____ _____ _____

ἐστιν   τὸν   διάβολον
_____ ____ _____ .   Heb. 2:14

WHY IS THE WORD "THIS" IMPORTANT?

In Ephesians 2:8, where it says "by grace are ye saved through faith,
and that not of yourselves...", the word "that" is a form of the word we
have just studied, οὗτος.

It is given in its neuter form, τοῦτο.   In Greek, the passage goes:

τῇ   γὰρ   χάριτί* ἐστε   σεσῳσμένοι   διὰ   πίστεως   καὶ   τοῦτο
__ ___ _____ ____ "having been saved" ___ _____ ; __ ___

οὐκ   ἐξ   ὑμῶν
___ __ ____

*Dative endings in the "instrumental" sense -- i.e., "by what method?"

156

The question is, does the word τοῦτο refer to the word grace, the word saved, or the word faith? It has to refer to something "neuter".

The word faith happens to be feminine, so the sentence does not say that the "faith" is not of yourselves (although other scriptures may teach God as the author of faith); the word "grace" also happens to be feminine. The sense of the sentence is then that the entire process of salvation is not "of you", but is a gift of God.

NUMBERS

The number One is completely different in the three genders:

	masculine	feminine	neuter
NOM	εἱς	μια	ἑν
GEN	ἑνος	μιας	ἑνος
DAT	ἑνι	μια	ἑνι
ACC	ἑνα	μιαν	ἑν

NOMINATIVES are differentiated from the prepositions εἰς and εν because the number one has the h-sound.

The following sentence uses all three genders:

ἑν σῶμα καὶ ἑν πνεῦμα, καθὼς καὶ

For there is ___ ____ ___ __ ____ _____ ___ you were called

ἐν μιᾷ   εἰς κύριος, μια   ἑν βάπτισμα,

___ ___ hope of your calling; ___ ____ ___ faith,___ _____

εἰς θεος καὶ πατηρ πάντων, ὁ* ἐπὶ πάντων καὶ δια πάντων καὶ

___ ____ ___ ___ ____ ___ ___ ____ ___ ___ _____ ___

ἐν πᾶσιν.
___ _____   Eph. 4:4, 5

* this is an example of the word "the" without a noun; translate "the one".

Ἐγὼ καὶ ὁ πατηρ ἑν ἐσμεν
___ ___ __ ____ __ _____   John 10:30

τοῦ ἑνὸς ἀνθρώπου
Through the disobedience __ __ ____ _____ many were made sinners
                                                    Rom. 5:19

There is no "a" or "an" in Greek; when they felt a need for a word like that, they would use number one.

It is interesting to note how some of the words that mean "no" are combinations of the basic negative words with number one, as if to mean: not one! Example: ουδεις, ουδεν.

TWO   δυο or δυω   in NOM and ACC

         δυσιν or δυσι   in GEN and DAT

Οὐδεὶς   δυσὶ κυρίοις   ἢ γὰρ τὸν ἕνα   καὶ τὸν
___ ___ can ____ _____ serve; __ ___ ___ ____ he'll hate ___ ____

ἕτερον   ἢ ἑνὸς   καὶ τοῦ ἑτέρου
_____ love, __ ____ be devoted to ___ ___ _____ despise. Matt. 6:24

   THREE   τρεις   in NOM and ACC   (τρια for neuter)

             τριων   in GEN

             τρισι   in DAT

                                              ἐν τρισὶν
You who cast down the temple and rebuild in ___ _____ days, save

yourself... Matt. 27:40

                                              Τριῶν ταβερνῶν
The brethren came as far as the Appian Forum and _____ _____

                                                      Acts 28:15

ALL

παν is cognate with a phrase like "Pan-American Highway"--a road that goes all through North and South America.

Here are the forms for each gender:

	masculine	feminine	neuter
NOM	πας	πασα	παν
GEN	παντος	πασης	παντος

The genitive shows you the stem, which the rest of the endings are attached to. You can see that the masculine is using third declension endings, and it will use that ντ in all the rest of its forms. For example, the dative will be παντι.

158

Something unusual happens in third declension words when you get to the dative plural. The οι ending from the noun chart interacts with the stem and changes it. In this case, the dative plural turns out to be πασι.

Exercise Two

MATCHING (all genders and numbers mixed together)

Match these various forms of "παν" with their respective meanings. Refer to the chart on page 126.

__ 1. πασης   __ 5. παντος   a) to all

__ 2. παντων   __ 6. πασων   b) of all

__ 3. παση   __ 7. παντι

__ 4. πασι   __ 8. πασαις

SCRIPTURES

                    ἵνα   πᾶς
God...sent his son ____ ____ believing in him would not perish...
                                                        John 3:16
            μυστήρια   πάντα
If I know _____ _____   1 Cor. 13:2

                    ἐν παντὶ φόβῳ τοῖς δεσπόταις
Slaves, submit ___ _____ ____ ____ _____   1 Pet. 2:18
ὁ γὰρ πατὴρ φιλεῖ τον υἱον καὶ πάντα
__ ___ _____ _____ ___ ____ ___ _____ shows ___ ____ what _____
ποιεῖ
_____   John 5:20

                            ἐν πάσῃ
Blessed be God...who has blessed us . _____ spiritual blessing.
                                                        Eph. 1:3
                        ἡμᾶς ἀπὸ πάσης
He'll forgive our sins and cleanse _____ ___ _____ unrighteousness.
                                                        1 John 1:9

There are seven related adverbs, all of which start with παντ.
Example: παντως by all means
                        ἵνα παντως
I have become all things to all men, ____ _____ I might save some.
                                                        1 Cor. 9:22

Same sentence, including two forms from the top of the page:

τοῖς πᾶσιν   πάντα   ἵνα   πάντως

____ _____ I have become _____ , ____ _____ I might save some.

The adjective πολυς, much, gets endings similar to μεγας given in Part II.

The lexicon entries are: πολυς   πολλη   πολυ

γῆν πολλήν

Some fell on the rocks where they did not have ____ _____ and dried

up.   Matt. 13:5

A related adverb is πολλακις frequently.

SELF

"I myself" would be ἐγώ αὐτός. If a girl was talking, ἐγώ αὐτή. For the other cases, these two words combine to make a new word.

GEN: εμου + αυτου = εμαυτου "of myself"

This new word appears in all genders in all the remaining cases:

	masculine	feminine	neuter
GEN	εμαυτου	εμαυτης	εμαυτου
etc.			

The same treatment is given to σεαυτου (yourself) and ἑαυτου (himself)

The one speaking in tongues builds up _____ ἑαυτόν 1 Cor. 14:4

You who cast down the temple and rebuild in three days, save _____ σεαυτόν.
Matt. 27:40

If I rebuild the things I tore down, I make _____ ἐμαυτόν a transgressor.
Gal. 2:18

According to our law he ought to die ____ ____ ____ _____ ὅτι υἱόν θεοῦ ἑαυτόν he made.
John 19:7

If we say we have no sin, we deceive _____ ἑαυτούς 1 John 1:8

This example is in the accusative plural, "themselves", though to make sense in English we translate it as "ourselves".

A DIFFERENT WORD MEANING "OUR"

	masculine	feminine	neuter
NOM	ἡμετερος	ἡμετερα	ἡμετερον
	etc.	etc.	etc.
	2nd declension	1st declension	2nd declension

And _____ ἡμετέρα fellowship is with the father. (Feminine to match "fellowship")

Same sentence: (you have to add the word "is")

Καὶ ἡ κοινονία ἡ ἡμετέρα   μετὰ τοῦ πατρὸς

____ __ _____ __ _____ __ _____ _____.   1 John 1:3

ἐκεῖνος = that. An adjective.

	masculine	feminine	neuter
NOM	ἐκεῖνος	ἐκείνη	ἐκεῖνο

                                                ἔχει   τον
(The man who finds the treasure) goes, sells all ____ and buys ____

ἀγρὸν ἐκεῖνον
_____ _____.   Matt. 13:44

                          ἀπὸ τῆς ὥρας ἐκείνης
And the woman was saved ____ _____ _____.   Matt. 9:22

Related adverbs: ἐκεῖ there; ἐκεῖθεν from there (thence);
                  ἐκεῖσε to there

ASKING QUESTIONS

The English word "who" can have two meanings:
1) to start a question, as in "Who did this?"
2) to relate one part of a sentence to another, as in "The man who did this is not here."

These two uses are expressed by two totally different words in Greek. The second use is called a "relative pronoun", and will be taken up on the next page. The first use--the word used for asking a question--is the topic of this page.

The endings are all third declension, and they are all identical except for the usual neuter exceptions:

	singular		plural	
	masculine & feminine	neuter	masculine & feminine	neuter
NOM	τίς	τί	τίνες	τίνα
GEN	τίνος	same	τίνων	same
DAT	τίνι	same	τίσι	same
ACC	τίνα	τί	τίνας	τίνα

SCRIPTURES:

The man with an unclean spirit cried, λέγων, τί ἡμῖν καὶ σοί,*
___ ___ ___ ___ ___ ___ ___

Ἰησοῦ Ναζαρηνέ; Have you come to destroy us? I know σε τίς εἶ, ὁ
___ ___ ___ ___ ___ ___

ἅγιος τοῦ θεοῦ . Mark 1:24
___ ___ ___ ___

* Literally, "What to us and to you, Jesus Nazarene?"
It is interesting to see how translators have tried to turn that phrase
into something that makes sense in English.

Τί δὲ βλέπεις τὸ   τὸ ἐν τῷ ὀφθαλμῷ τοῦ ἀδελφοῦ σου,
___ ___ ___ ___ splinter ___ ___ ___ ___ ___

τὴν δὲ ἐν τῷ σῷ ὀφθαλμῷ   οὐ
___ ___ ___ ___ your ___ beam ___ notice? Matt. 7:3

INDEFINITE PRONOUN

...has the same forms as τίς, above, except without any accents.
Translate as: some, a certain, anyone, someone, etc.

Ἀδελφοί μου, ἐάν τις ἐν ὑμῖν
___ ___ ___ ___ ___ ___ ___ should wander from the truth and

τις
___ bring him back... James 5:19

                ὑμῶν διάβολος ὡς λέων   τινα
The enemy __ ___ _____ ___ ____ roaring walks seeking ____ to

devour. 1 Pet. 5:8

THE RELATIVE PRONOUN

ὅς. It relates one word of a complete sentence to another, explanatory
portion.

ENGLISH EXAMPLE: The relative pronoun is underlined twice.

    The man who hears words stays in the house.

The entire part underlined can be removed, and you'll still have a complete sentence.
The part underlined is called the "dependent clause".

SAME SENTENCE IN GREEK:

ὁ ανθρωπος ὃς ακουει λογους μενει εν τω οικω

The relative pronoun must have masculine, feminine, and neuter forms to
go with the noun it follows, and must exist in all cases so it can fill
a function in its part of the sentence. Almost all the forms look like
the word "the" without any τ. The only way you can differentiate from
"the" in its feminine form is through the accent:

the ἡ (no accent)   who ἥ (the same thing happens in NOM
                                 plurals)

The neuter is easy to differentiate because the neuter "the" has a τ,
but the neuter relative pronoun does not (ὅ). The masculine form was
given in the first Greek example, above (ὃς). Notice it is like the
noun endings you learned at the beginning of Part II.

In the following example, the word for "who" is masculine, to fit the
subject of the sentence, but it is in the ACCUSATIVE case, so it can be
the direct object in its own part of the sentence, the part underlined.
The subject of the part underlined is "you":

ὁ ανθρωπος ὅν ακουεις μενει εν τω οικω

The correct translation of the double underlined word is "whom". The
man whom you hear stays in the house.

λιθος ὅν the builders rejected has become the cornerstone.

Matt. 21:42

If the relative pronoun refers to a word which is neuter in English,
translate with "which" or "that", as in the example above.

This basic rule of thumb about case for the relative pronoun has exceptions. Sometimes the relative pronoun is in the same case as the word
it is relating to:

The man speaks to the apostle whom you hear

ὁ ανθρωπος λεγει τω αποστολω ᾧ ακουσεις

Sometimes the noun is missing, and so the relative pronoun has to be
translated:

ὅς he who   ἥ she who   or for neuter, ὅ that which

EXAMPLE

Ὅ was from the beginning, ὅ we have heard, ὅ we have seen with our eyes,

ὅ we beheld and our hands touched, regarding the word of life...

1 John 1:1

164

Καὶ ὃς ἐὰν   λόγον κατὰ τοῦ υἱοῦ τοῦ ἀνθρώπου
___ ___ shall speak ___ ___ ___ ___ ___ ___

                    αὐτῷ ὃς δ'   κατὰ τοῦ
it shall be forgiven ___ ; ___ ___ should speak ___ ___

πνεύματος τοῦ ἁγίου   αὐτῷ , οὔτε ἐν
___ ___ ___ , it shall not be forgiven __ ___ ___ ___

τούτῳ τῷ αἰῶνι οὔτε ἐν τῷ
___ ___ age ___ ___ ___ coming one.   Matt. 12:32

SCRIPTURES WITH RELATIVE PRONOUNS

Draw a line under the relative pronoun, and a box around its part of
the sentence.

Ὁ γὰρ πατὴρ φιλεῖ τὸν υἱον καὶ πάντα   αὐτῷ ἃ αὐτὸς
__ ___ ___ ___ ___ ___ ___ ___ shows ___ __ ___

ποιεῖ
___ .   John 5:20

The relative pronoun is neuter plural to match πάντα ("all things")

Εἰ τινος τὸ ἔργον μενεῖ ὃ
__ ___ __ ___ ___ ___ __ he has built, he'll receive a reward.
                                                        1 Cor. 3:14
Neuter singular to go with "work" (εργον)

GENITIVE EXAMPLE:

                                                    ὧν
Transforming themselves into ministers of righteousness, __ __ the end

       κατὰ   τὰ ἔργα αὐτῶν
shall be ___ __ __ ___ __ ___   2 Cor. 11:15

        ἣν
The hope of life eternal, ___ God who cannot lie announced... Titus 1:2

Feminine accusative, not because it has anything to do with
women, but because the word "life", which the ην has to go
with, happens to be a feminine noun. But English doesn't
consider it feminine, so translate ην as "which".

Εἰ δὲ ὃ οὐ θέλω τοῦτο ποιῶ ,   τῷ νόμῳ ὅτι καλός
__ __ __ __ __ ___ ___ ___ I agree ___ ___ __ ___ .
                                                    Rom. 7:16
(Did you add the word "is"?)

ὃ
ο = There is no noun for it to relate to, so add the word
"that": "That which"

RELATIVE PRONOUNS--WHY ARE THEY IMPORTANT?

Titus 3:5 ...(He saved us) by his own mercy through the washing λουτροῦ

παλιγγενεσίας ἀνακαινώσεως   πνεύματος οὗ
of rebirth and "making-new again" of the Holy Spirit, ___ he shed upon

us bounteously through Jesus Christ...

The question is, "What did he shed upon us bounteously? The washing?
The rebirth? The renewal? The Spirit?

The relative pronoun could be masculine or neuter, so that leaves out
rebirth and renewal, which happen to be feminine. Washing and Spirit
are both neuter, so either one could be the answer; the translator
would probably pick Spirit, since it is closer to the relative pronoun.
Notice also that the relative pronoun is genitive, with the sense of
"of whom" or "of which", just as in English we use the word "of" when
we are talking about a "portion" of something: (I would like a glass
of water).

The passage then could be translated: "...washing of rebirth and
renewal of the Holy Spirit, "of whom" he shed upon us richly through
Jesus Christ..." That is, Jesus has shed upon us a portion of the
Holy Spirit.

ANOTHER RELATIVE PRONOUN

Combine the one you just learned (ὅς) with the word τις and you get
ὅστις, "whoever" or "whatever".

Πᾶς οὖν ὅστις ἀκούει μου τοὺς λόγους τούτους καὶ ποιεῖ

____ ____ _____ _____ ___ ____ _____ _____ ___ _____

αὐτούς   ὅστις   αὐτοῦ τὴν οἰκίαν ἐπὶ τὴν
_____ is like a wise man _____ built _____ ___ _____ ___ ___

πέτραν
_____ . Matt. 7:24

As you form this word in the various cases, actually combine the correct
case of ὅς with the right form of τις. For example, genitive would be
οὗ + τινος = οὗτινος. Plural would be οἱ + τινες = οἵτινες.

There shall be more joy in heaven over one sinner repenting than over

οἵτινες
ninety-nine righteous _____ have no need of repentence. Luke 15:7

166

Feminine, ἡ + τις to go with the feminine word "life" in the following sentence:

                                                    ἥτις
We announce to you the eternal life _____ was with the father.

1 John 1:2

In Greek:

ὑμῖν   τὴν   ζωὴν   τὴν   αἰώνιον   ἥτις   πρὸς   τὸν
We announce __ __ ____ ____   _____ _____ was ____ ____

πατέρα
_____ .   1 John 1:2

SOME, MORE, MOST. COMPARING ADJECTIVES.

σοφος means "wise". It can receive endings to fit masculine, feminine, and neuter in all cases:

	masculine	feminine	neuter
NOM	σοφος λογος	σοφα κεφαλη "head"	σοφον δωρον "gift"
GEN	σοφου λογου	σοφας κεφαλης	σοφου δωρου

etc.

To change to "wiser", add τερ + the case ending

	masculine	feminine	neuter
NOM	σοφωτερος λογος	σοφωτερα κεφαλη	σοφωτερον δωρον
GEN	σοφωτερου λογου	σοφωτερας κεφαλης	σοφωτερου δωρου

etc.

1 Cor. 1:25   ὅτι τὸ μωρὸν τοῦ θεοῦ σοφώτερον τῶν ανθρώπων εστίν.

To change to "wisest", add τατ + the case ending

	masculine	feminine	neuter
NOM	σοφωτατος λογος	σοφωτατα κεφαλη	σοφωτατον δωρον
GEN	σοφωτατου λογου	σοφωτατας κεφαλης	σοφωτατου δωρον

Jude 20   Build yourselves up on your ἁγιωτάτῃ faith.

Other types of adjectives are found which use -ιων for the -er ending and -ιστος for the -est ending.

EXAMPLE: κακος, bad.   κακιων, worse.   κακιστος, worst.

(words that end in ων use "TYPE III" noun endings--see chart, page 126.)

Luke 1:3 The dedication of the book of Luke, to write to you, κράτιστε

θεόφιλε.

(κρατος = strength, used here as a common word of greeting. The ε ending is used when talking directly to someone.)

There are also expressions which have the word "more" in them:

ποσω μαλλον = how much more (literally by how much, rather)

Εἰ οὖν ὑμεῖς

___ ___ ___ know how to give good gifts to your children,

ποσῳ μᾶλλον ὁ πατὴρ ὑμῶν

_____ _____ in heaven will give good things to those

αὐτόν
asking _____ . Matt. 7:11

Exercise One

ENGLISH WORDS WITH VARIED MEANINGS

I. Four uses for the English word "that"

Match the sentence to the explanation at the right.

__ 1. I came that they might
       have life.

__ 2. I wrote that book.

__ __ 3. The man that came
          to our door entered.

a) A relative pronoun--which
    "relates" an explanatory
    group of words to a noun.
    Greek ὅς and its forms.

b) As a connective between two
    complete sentences; Greek
    words like ἱνα, in order
    that.

c) A pronoun used to point out
    a certain noun. Greek:
    εκεινος.

d) A round-about way to trans-
    late a Greek participle.

    Literally: the saying man

    Smooth English: The man
    that is speaking.

II. Three uses for the word "to".

__ 4. I came to church.

__ 5. I spoke to Peter.

__ 6. I want to go home.

e) Infinitive--a verb form with
    no subject ending. Greek
    endings ειν or αι.

f) A preposition, such as
    προς or εις.

g) Indirect object; Greek
    Dative.

These are just two examples of ways that Greek can be very precise.
Greek verb structures also lead to precision, as we will be seeing in
Part V. Here's just one example:

"You shall come"

In English, you wouldn't know whether I meant you were going
to come in the future, or whether I was commanding you to
come. In Greek, the difference would be obvious because two
different endings would be used.

FIRST JOHN, CHAPTER ONE

The connecting words and the rest of the pronouns you have learned are
now included:

Ὁ 1   ἀπ᾽ ἀρχῆς,   ὃ   ὃ   τοῖς ὀφθαλμοῖς 5 ἡμῶν,
__ __ was ____ _____ we heard, __ __ we saw _____

ὃ   καὶ αἱ χεῖρες ἡμῶν   περὶ τοῦ λόγου τῆς
__ __ we beheld ____ _____ _____ touched ____ ____ _____ ____

ζωῆς - καὶ ἡ ζωὴ   καὶ   καὶ μαρτυροῦμεν καὶ
_____ ____ __ ____ appeared ____ we saw ____ _____ announce

ὑμῖν τὴν ζωὴν τὴν αἰώνιον ἥτις   πρὸς τὸν πατέρα καὶ
____ ___ ____ ___ _____ ____ was ____ ____ _____ appeared

ἡμῖν - ὃ   καὶ   καὶ ὑμῖν, ἵνα καὶ ὑμεῖς
____ __ we saw ____ heard we announce ____ ____ ____ _____

κοινωνίαν   μεθ᾽ ἡμῶν   καὶ ἡ κοινωνία δὲ ἡ ἡμετέρα μετὰ
_____ may have _____ ____ . ____ __ _____ __ __ _____ ____

τοῦ πατρὸς καὶ μετὰ τοῦ υἱοῦ αὐτοῦ Ἰησοῦ Χριστοῦ. Καὶ ταῦτα

γράφομεν ἡμεῖς ἵνα ἡ χαρὰ2 ἡμῶν   καὶ ἔστιν αὐτη
_____ _____ ____ __ _____ _____ might be full. ____ _____ ____

ἡ ἀγγελία ἦν   ἀπ᾽ αὐτοῦ καὶ   ὑμῖν ὅτι ὁ θεὸς
__ _____ ___ we heard ____ ____ ___ announce ____ ___ __ ____

φῶς ἔστιν καὶ σκοτία3 ἐν αὐτῷ οὐκ ἔστιν οὐδεμία.4 Ἐὰν
___ _____ ___ _____ __ ____ ___ _____ _____ we say

ὅτι κοινωνίαν ἔχομεν μετ᾽ αὐτοῦ καὶ ἐν τῷ σκότει
___ _____ _____ ____ ____ ___ __ __ _____ walk, we lie

καὶ οὐ ποιοῦμεν τὴν ἀλήθειαν. Ἐὰν δὲ ἐν τῷ φωτὶ   ὡς
___ __ _____ ___ _____ . ____ __ __ __ ____ we walk __

αὐτὸς ἔστιν ἐν τῶ φωτί, κοινωνίαν ἔχομεν μετ᾽ ἀλλήλων, καὶ τὸ

____ ____ ____ ____ ____ ____ ____ ____

αἱμα Ἰησοῦ τοῦ υἱοῦ αὐτοῦ   ἡμᾶς ἀπὸ πάσης   Ἐαν

____ ____ ____ ____ ____ cleans ____ ____ ____ sin. ____ we

         ὅτι   οὐκ ἔχομεν, ἑαυτοὺς   καὶ ἡ ἀλήθεια οὐκ

say ____ sin ____ ____   we deceive ____ ____ ____ ____

ἔστιν ἐν ἡμῖν Ἐαν   ἡμῶν,   ἔστιν καὶ

____ ____ ____ .   ____ we confess the sins __ ____ faithful ____ ____

              ἵνα   ἡμῖν   καὶ   ἡμᾶς ἀπὸ

righteous ____ he may forgive __ ___ the sins ____ clean ____ ____

πάσης   Ἐαν   ὅτι οὐχ   ψεύστην

_____ unrighteousness. ____ we say ____ we have sinned, _____

ποιοῦμεν αὐτὸν καὶ ὁ λόγος αὐτοῦ οὐκ ἔστιν ἐν ἡμῖν.

____ ____ ____ ____ ____ ____ ____ ____ ____ ____ ____ .

1. Relative pronoun, neuter: That which
2. Joy
3. Darkness
4. ου + δε + μια (one) = not even once
5. Dative in "instrumental" sense = what we saw with

PART IV

WORD STUDIES

After completing Part IV, you will

1. be familiar with dozens of the most important religious
   terms used in the Greek New Testament.

2. see connections between English words that are based on
   the same Greek word.

3. understand basic meanings of religious terms through
   seeing the Greek words from which they are derived.

HOW TO USE PART IV

In order to introduce you to many new words used in context in Bible passages, I have included words with endings that you do not know. I do not expect you to understand these endings, but simply to fill in the blanks with the basic meaning of each word. You will be able to tell, from the context, whether to translate it as a verb or a noun, etc.

The word studies are purposely included before you know more about endings and word-changes so that you will not translate them as academic exercises, but rather catch the general meaning and think of it immediately in terms of its English meaning. Being able to decipher endings is important, but it can wait. The first goal is a feel for the language.

On the other hand, when I use endings you do know, I expect you to translate them fully; so that, if two English words are needed to translate the Greek word, I have put two blanks there to remind you:

εστιν
he is

When dealing with a complicated verb ending, I have sometimes added extra words in the blank to give you a hint;

αμαρτητε   σωθησομαι
ye may   .   shall be   -ed
      (sin)   (saved)

but if I felt you could fill in the right word because the passage was familiar, I did not give any hints.

The purpose of Part IV is to show you how translators struggle to put concepts into smooth English. Typically, I will give you the general meaning of a word, then give you a sentence that has that word in it. After you have tried to express the overall meaning in your own words, I expect you to look up the passage in a Bible and see what the translator did there. I intend that you be surprised as you do this, for you will find cases where you put a concept into ordinary, down-to-earth English, and then discover that a translator has used a more technical term or a lesser known word.

For example, you are going to be exploring some words based on οικος. Along the line, you'll find yourself translating a word based on οικος as "up-building, or building-up". When you look up this passage in a Bible, and find that the translator there chose to use the word "edify", I want you to exclaim to yourself--"Oh. So that's what 'edify' means."

In this fashion, I hope to lead you through many important New Testament religious concepts. Feel free to guess; don't worry about endings you don't know, and compare your efforts with a Bible.

Exercise One

WORDS RELATED TO "καλ"

Words based on the root καλ have something to do with "calling".

Fill in the blanks with suitable English translations:

καλω
1. I _____ unto you.

WORD LIST

καλει
2. Whoever _____ on the name of the Lord shall
be saved.

called

call

(In the next word, the α is omitted between the
κ and the λ, similar to our process of contract-
ing)

calls

called one

calling

καλητης
3. Many are _____, but few are chosen.

caller

(The ε in front of the next word makes it past
tense, and the θ makes it "passive")

εκληθητε
4. You <u>were   </u>-ed by God. (I put "were"

on the line because the one Greek word needs
two words to be translated fully into English.)

κλησις
5. God gave us a _____ to be holy.

κλητος
6. Paul was the _____, specially selected by God

to preach to the non-Jews.

Exercise Two

You translated successfully above, through guesswork, without having to
know the rules about the endings you saw or whether the forms you were
dealing with were different words or the same words with different endings. This is the way we will proceed throughout Part IV; in Part V,
we'll actually learn the endings.

Here are the words you translated, as they would be listed in an analytical lexicon, which lists all related words together:

(see below for abbreviations)

__ 1. καλεω   fut. -εσω pass. aor. εκληθην   to call, send for

__ 2. κλησις, εως,   fut. a calling, an invitation

__ 3. κλητος, η, ον   called, invited.

In the short blanks above, indicate whether each word listed is a
a) noun   b) adjective   c) verb.

Abbreviations used:

fut. = future
pass. = passive (when the action is done to the subject)
aor. = aorist, (a type of past tense)

Now try these scriptures:

ἐν τῇ κλήσει   ἐκλήθη
Let each one remain ___ __ _____ in which he was _____.

Δοῦλος   ἐκλήθης;
_____ were you _____; don't let it matter to you.   1 Cor. 7:20-21

                              καλέσαντος   κλήσει
(God, who is the one) saving us and _____ (with a) holy _____,

not according to our works but according to his purpose.   2 Tim. 1:9

Exercise Three

COMBINING καλ WITH THE PREPOSITION εκ (out-of)

The result is a new word, εκκαλεω, meaning call-out or summon-forth.

                εκκαλεω
As a verb: A. I _____ the swimmers from the pool.

                εκκαλει
           B. God _____ believers from this sinful world.

BUT when Greek changes this word into a noun, we don't have an English word that would make a good translation:

                        εκκλησια
           I belong to those _____.

"Callees" would be awkward. We could use a phrase like "called out ones" or "who have been called out". Unfortunately, even though this noun is so awkward to translate, it occurs often in the New Testament.

Check your translation for these passages:

ἐκκλησίαν
1. Upon this rock I will build my _____. Matt. 16:18

(also used to refer to Old Testament believers)

ἐκκλησίᾳ
2. Moses was in the _____ in the wilderness. Acts 7:38

(also used to refer to secular gatherings)

ἐκκλησίαν
3. And having said this, he dismissed the _____. Acts 19:41

The English word _____ comes from this word.

Bible translators then have chosen to translate the word that means, "called out ones" or "gathering" by the word "church".

Exercise Four

What follows is the background of the English word "church":

Remember the word κυριος? If you are acquainted with the traditional liturgy, you might remember that the name for the first major "song" in the liturgy is _____ from the phrase "Lord have mercy": κυριε, ελεισον.

A related noun is κυριοτης lordship, ruling authority, as in the sentence:

ἀρχῆς
Seated at His right hand in the heavenlies, above all chief-ship and

δυνάμεως κυριότητος
authority and power and _____ and every name that is named...
Eph. 1:21

The adjective related to κυριος is κυριακος, η, ον "pertaining to the Lord", as in

κυριακῇ
    I was in the spirit on the _____ day. Rev. 1:10

By a long process of language change, generalized here, let's see what generations of Anglo-Saxon and English believers did to that word.

start with <u>κυριακος</u>

1. Remove the ending (ος) and you get

   _____

2. Contract by removing the ια and you get
   (if you respell this word with i instead
   of u, you get a word used in Scotland)

   _____

   _____

3. Soften the k's to ch's, and the result
   is

   _____

COMBINING καλ WITH THE PREPOSITION παρα

An example of a concept that is difficult to translate.

παρα means "next to" or "alongside". The resulting word, παρακαλεω, is very common in the New Testament, but there is no single English word that translates it adequately. The basic meaning obviously is "call-alongside", but what would you do with a sentence like

"I παρακαλω you to be careful."

A Greek dictionary lists words like "urge, beg, appeal". You could think of the concept as "call alongside to help, or as a friend."

This passage from Ephesians 4:1 uses the new word, as well as forms of the word call, from the previous pages:

παρακαλῶ
I therefore, the prisoner of the Lord, _____ you to walk worthily

κλήσεως   ἐκλήθητε
of the _____ with which <u>you have been _____</u>.

In the following passage, the word is best translated "comfort":

παρακληθήσονται
Blessed are those that mourn, for they <u>shall be _____</u>. Matt. 5:4

NOW try putting the idea into a NOUN:

παρακλήσεως   παρακαλῶν
...blessed be the God of all _____, the one who's _____ us

παρακαλεῖν
in all our affliction, so we are able <u>to _____</u> those in any afflic-

παρακλήσεως
tion with the same _____ with which we ourselves were

177

```
┌─────────────────────────────┐
│        παρακαλούμεθα          │
└─────────────────────────────┘
_____ by God.    2 Cor. 1:3,4
```

The Greeks used another form of this word for "someone who brought help in legal matters": a "lawyer".

    Before you put me in jail, let me call my παράκλητον.

    Because He helps me, I can correctly call Jesus my παράκλητος.

In John 14:16, Jesus tells His disciples He'll be going away. Then He adds,

                                                παράκλητον

I will ask the Father, and He will give you another _____ to

be with you forever, even the Holy Spirit.

Put together all these ideas of "being alongside in a helpful way", of "comforting and appealing", and of "standing in for us in the sense that a lawyer would", and you begin to see what a good choice of words it was for Jesus to call the Holy Spirit a παράκλητος--and also how difficult to put this term into English. You will find the English form of this word, paraclete, in theological writings and hymns about the Holy Spirit.

WORD FAMILY ἅγιος (holy)

A. Originally meant something "set apart" just for God--like the special cup set aside for use at communion.

θεός   ἁγίαις
1. ...as _____ promised in the _____ scriptures. Rom. 1:2

2. God said to Moses, "Loosen your sandals, you're standing on

ἁγία
_____ ground."   Acts 7:33

Exercise One

In the two examples above ἅγιος is used as what: (noun, verb, adjective).

In the next two examples, ἅγιος is still an adjective, but there is no noun for it to describe--you have to make one up-- such as "person", "ones", "things", or "place"--that would make sense.

ἅγιον
3. Do not give _____ to dogs. Matt. 7:6

4. In the Old Testament, the blood of animals was brought into the

ἅγια
_____ by the high priest as a sacrifice for sin

Χριστός   ἅγια
(Heb. 13:11); but _____ went into the _____ (the real one

in heaven, not the copy on earth), not with the blood of

animals, but with his own blood, to get eternal redemption for

us. (Heb. 9:11,12)

B. Later, the same word ἅγιος was used to describe the character of God himself--for He is "set apart" from everything else. He is better, He is more special.

ἅγιοι   ἐγὼ   ἅγιος
5. God says, "Ye shall be _____, for ____ am _____. 1 Pet. 1:16

ἅγιε πάτηρ

6. Jesus prayed, _____ _____, (keep my disciples safe).
John 17:11

This characteristic of God naturally applies to Jesus, too:

7. Signs and wonders were performed through the name of thy

ἁγίου   Ἰησοῦ

_____ servant _____.   Acts 4:30

8. The demons cried, "what have you to do with us, _____ of

Ἰησοῦ

Nazareth? Have you come to destroy us? I know who you are--

ὁ ἅγιος   θεοῦ

__ _____ _____ ___ _____· Luke 4:34

The same word ἅγιος is used to describe the Spirit (πνευμα means
both wind and spirit)

9. If even you evil people know how to give good gifts to your

πάτηρ

children, how much more will the _____ in heaven give the

ἅγιον πνεῦμα

_____ _____ to those that ask Him?   Luke 11:13

καρδίαις

10. The love of God has been poured into our _____ by the

ἁγίου πνεύματος

_____ _____ which was given to us.   Rom. 5:5

C. The same word ἅγιος is used in worshipping God--telling Him that we
know He is really special, "set apart" from all others:

11. Day and night (the creatures in heaven) never cease to sing,

ἅγιος ἅγιος ἅγιος κύριος θεὸς

"_____ _____ _____ _____ _____ Almighty."   Rev. 4:8

180

Now try turning ἁγιος into a verb--that is, "be holy".

12. Our _____ in heaven, _____ Thy name. Matt. 6:9
      πατηρ   αγιασθητω

Did you recognize this as the beginning of the Lord's prayer, and write the word "hallowed"? Or did you try to say it in your own words? If so, you might have discovered that you would have to write words both in front of and behind the words "thy name" in order to translate that one Greek word into good English--you might have come up with something like "let your name be holy".

Besides "holy" and "hallowed", there are lots of other words that translators have used to try to get across the meaning of ἁγιος. A few examples: consecrated, sanctified, saintly, sacred. These words might help as you try to do the rest of this sheet.

13. Don't be afraid when people harm you for doing good; just
    αγιασατε

    _____ Christ as Lord in your hearts.
                                  1 Pet. 3:14,15

(the meaning is "consider as being holy". The word "hallow" would fit here. Some translations use the word "reverence".)

D. Jesus followed God's will by "setting himself apart" for the special task of being crucified. He knew the end result would be that we would then be set apart in a special way as God's children:

          εγω αγιαζω
14. Jesus prayed, ____ _____ myself in behalf of my follow-
                                 ηγιασμενοι
ers, so that they also <u>may be</u> _____-ed in truth.
                                            John 17:19

(You might have written, "I set apart myself", and that would be good translating. Many translators used the word "sanctify", since it means the same thing.)

(The η at the beginning of the last word is a substitute for α, and makes it into a past tense.)

E. As a result of Christ's death, God looks at us in a new way:

15. Jesus made peace between you and God through his death, in

181

ἁγίους

order to present you _____ before him, if you continue in

the faith.   Col. 1:22

ἁγίους

16. God chose us before the world began, to be _____ and pure

before him.   Eph. 1:4

F. Besides looking at us as holy (set apart) just for Him and His
Kingdom, God also works His characteristics of holiness into our
behavior.

ἡγιάσθητε

17. You were evil, but you were washed, you were _____-ed, you

Ἰησοῦ   πνεύματι

were justified in the name of _____ and by the _____

θεοῦ

__ ____ .   1 Cor. 6:11

18. God disciplines us for our profit, so we may share his

ἁγιότητος

_____.   Heb. 12:10

θεοῦ   ἅγιος

19. For the temple __ _____ is _____ --and you are that temple.
1 Cor. 3:17

ἅγιος

Here the word ἅγιος is turned into a noun:

θεοῦ   ἁγιασμός

20. This is the will __ ____, your _____.   1 Thess. 4:3

(Most translators try to put it into one word, like
"holiness" or "sanctification".)

G. God wants us to submit to His plan of building His holiness in us:

21. I beseech you, by the mercies of God, present your bodies as

ἁγίαν

a living sacrifice, _____ and well-pleasing to God.   Rom. 12:1

The end result is a type of person who is a blessing to others:

182

22. Paul writing to a young person named Timothy: "Be a pattern

to the believers in speech, love, faith, and _____.
ἁγνείᾳ
1 Tim. 4:12

(this happens to be a different word but meaning is similar.)

H. Because God looks at us as holy (special, set apart just for Him)--
and works holiness in us--the Bible calls believers "holy ones".
That is just one word in Greek--the word ἅγιος with no noun of its
own. You have to add in the word "ones".

Paul opens one of his letters:

ἡγιασμένοις εν Χριστοῦ Ἰησοῦ
23. Paul, to those who have been _____

ἁγίοις
who are now called _____ _____.   1 Cor. 1:1,2

Translators customarily translate "holy ones" or "set-apart ones"
as one word: SAINTS.

Try the beginning of another letter:

Παῦλος, ἀπόστολος   Χριστοῦ Ἰησοῦ διὰ
24. _____, _____ ___ _____ _____ ____ the will

θεοῦ   τοῖς   ἁγίοις   εν Ἐφέσῳ καὶ
__ _____, to the _____ who are ___ _____ ____ who are

εν Χριστοῦ Ἰησοῦ   καὶ   ἀπὸ
faithful ___ _____ _____, grace to you ____ peace ____

θεοῦ   πατρὸς καὶ   κυρίου Ἰησοῦ Χριστοῦ
_____ our _____ ___ the _____ _____ _____.
                                              Eph. 1:1-2

Exercise Two

SUMMARY

Six of the words below are good words to use in translating words
related to ἅγιος. Cross out the ones that are NOT.

Holiness	Peace	Sanctification	Lord
Love	Saint	Word	Sanctify
Consecrated	Faith	Apostle	Holy

LESSON THIRTY-FIVE

THE πνεῦμα WORD FAMILY

πνεῦμα means both "wind" and "spirit". In the next sentence, it is used both ways:

                                 πνεῦμα πνεῖ

1. Jesus said to Nicodemus, "The _____ blows wherever it wants to--so

                                       πνεύματος

    it is with everyone who is born of the _____". John 3:8

In the King James translation, the word πνεῦμα was translated "ghost":

                                  βαπτίζοντες

2. Jesus said, "Go and disciple all nations, _____ them in the

        τοῦ πατρὸς καὶ τοῦ υἱοῦ καὶ τοῦ ἁγίου πνεύματος

    name of ___ _____ ___ ___ ___ ___ ___ _____ _____.

The same word, πνεῦμα, might also refer to an evil spirit, or demon. In the following sentence the word ἀκαθαρσις is from καθαρσις which means "clean". The α in front turns it into its opposite.

                          δαιμόνιον

3. After Christ casts out a demon____ the crowd cries, "What a mes-

                                      ἀκαθάρτοις

    sage!" With authority and power, he commands the _____

  πνεύμασιν

  _____ and they come out!" Luke 4:36

Now combine θεος (God) with πνευμα and you get a word meaning "wind coming from God", or "God-breathed":

                θεόπνευστος, καὶ

4. All scripture is _____ ____ profitable for teaching...
                                              2 Tim. 3:16

Every human being is made up of spirit and body. When these two are separated, the result is death. Ezekiel wrote, "the body returns to dust, and the spirit returns to Him who gave it." The apostle James referred to this in the following passage:

                        πνεύματος   πίστις

5. For just as the body without the _____ is dead, so also faith ___

    without works is dead. James 2:26

THE πιστις WORD FAMILY

Select a word-family that would make sense in all three sentences:

    1. I would like more πιστιν   (noun)

    2. God is πιστος   (adjective)

    3. I πιστευω in Jesus   (verb)

Translators have used the following English words to translate πιστις: believe; belief; faith; faithful; trust; put trust; rely on.

As a noun:

        εγω   πιστιν εω θεω
    1. ____ have _____ ___ ____

As a verb:

            πιστευει
    2. Whoever _____ and is baptized shall be saved.

        εγω   πιστευω   εις Ιησου
    3. ____ _____ into _____

As an adjective:

        θεος   πιστος
    4. ____ is _____ He won't let you be tempted beyond your

strength.

GOING DEEPER

The BASIC WORD in the family that πιστις comes from is πειθω which means "persuade". The forms in the following blanks are based on this word:

    5. Jesus said, "If they don't hear Moses and the prophets, neither

           πεισθησονται
will they be _____ if someone were to rise from the dead
                                       Luke 16:31
           πεπεισμαι
    6. Paul said, "I am _____ that nothing can separate us from

the love of God.   Rom. 8:38

(Other translations use the word "convinced" for the passages above.)

7. Paul writes, "We are the true people of God, who worship God

right from the spirit, and having put no πεποιθότες _____ in the flesh

(our own ways). Phil. 3:3

(Other translations use the word "confidence" to translate this passage.)

8. Paul said, "God allowed us to suffer so we would not be putting

πεποιθότες
_____ in ourselves, but in Him.   2 Cor. 1:9

9. How difficult for them that πεποιθότες _____ in riches to enter the

Kingdom of heaven, thought the disciples. Mark 10:24

(Other translations use the word "trust" for these passages.)

Why would the Greeks pick a word for faith that is in a word family that
means persuasion? This suggests to us that we don't believe because of
"blind faith", but the Holy Spirit has actually persuaded us inside that
God is real and that Jesus has died for our sins.

SOME WORDS BASED ON οἶκος

Those who live in one are called οἰκεῖοι

"You are fellow-citizens with the saints

    οἰκεῖοι θεοῦ
and _____ __ ____." Eph. 2:19

(This word is an adjective: οἰκειος, -εια, -ειαν. "belonging to a house".
You could translate "family member".) Another example:

                                                              οἰκείων
If anyone does not care for his own, and especially his _____ he has

denied the faith. 1 Tim. 5:8

(Another word, οικετης, means a household slave, domestic servant):

οἱ οἰκέται   ἐν παντὶ φόβῳ τοῖς δεσπόταις
_____ , submit ___ _____ ____ ___ __ _____   1 Pet. 2:18

Now combine παρα plus οικος
    (alongside)

             παροικοι
You are no longer _____, but fellow citizens with the saints and

οἰκεῖοι θεοῦ
_____ __ ____.   Eph. 2:19

Παροικοι are those who are not part of the household--neighbor, sojourner,
visitor, temporary resident, stranger. Here is the corresponding verb:

                               Σὺ μόνος παροικεῖς
(on the road to Emmaus) Cleopas said to him, "___ _____ _____ in

Jerusalem and do not know what has happened in these past days?
                                                  Luke 24:18

Now combine κατα plus οικος
    (down, inside)

             κατοικῆσαι
...that Christ (may_____) in your hearts by faith. Eph. 3:17

The corresponding noun form:

                             κατοικητήριον
In Christ you are built together into an _____ of God.
                                               Eph. 2:22
    (You could translate: an "indwelling-place")

          οἶκος
Now combine οικος plus νεμω (administer) = οικονομος   "manager"

(from the parable of the unjust steward):

ὁ οἰκονόμος
__ _____ said to himself, "What shall I do? My Lord wants to take

             οἰκονομίαν
away the _____ from me?" Luke 16:3

That latter word is hard to translate without being awkward--you could
say administration, stewardship, management. In the next passage, the
word is applied to God as the one who manages the entire universe, who
runs it, and keeps it in order and on schedule:

            μυστήριον   οἰκονομίαν
God made known the _____ of His will, for an _____ of the ful-
                                    Χριστῷ.
ness of time, to head up all things in _____ Eph. 1:9-10

Exercise One

ENGLISH DERIVATIVE

If you can respell the word οικονομια cleverly enough, you'll come up
with the word we use to apply to the financial order. Hint: replace
the first two letters with an "e".

A related Greek Word,
_____ οικουμενικος which means re- _____
lated to the inhabited world,
became the English word we use
when talking about the "world-
wide" unity of church bodies.

Now combine οικος plus δομω (build)

λιθον ον οι οικοδομουντες
_____ ___ ___ _____ rejected has become the head of the corner.
                                                        Matt. 21:42

    (The reason for the longer ending is that this example
    happens to be a participle: translate "those building".)

                                                    τον ναον και εν
(to Christ on the cross): You, the one casting down ____ _____ ____ ___

τρισιν   οικοδομων   σεαυτον, ει υιος ει του θεου
_____ days _____ -ing, save ____ ____ ____ ____ ____
                                                        Matt. 27:40

                            οικοδομει εαυτον
He that speaks in tongues _____ _____. 1 Cor. 14:4

    (A common translation of the term is "edify". The fact that
    that word means "build up" can be seen if you notice the
    resemblance to the word "edifice", which means a building.)

Here's the corresponding noun, referring to the act of building:

                        οικοδομην
God gave gifts for the _____ of the body of Christ.

    (This can be translated "edification", that is, "up-building".)

Now combine together επι + οικος + δομω

                        εποικοδομηθεντες
You are the family of God, _____ on the foundation of the

apostles and prophets... Eph 2:20

188

(This is a past participle: having been built like a house upon.)

Here's the same passage in fuller form:

(You are) _____ ___ ____ _____ ___ __ foundation
οἰκεῖοι τοῦ θεοῦ, ἐποικοδομηθέντες ἐπὶ τῷ

τῶν ἀποστόλων καὶ προφητῶν
__ ___ _____ ____ _____... Eph. 2:19, 20

Now combine συν plus οικος plus δομω. "Built together with"

συνοικοδομεῖσθε
In whom also you _____ into a dwelling place of God in

Spirit. Eph. 2:22

Same passage in fuller form:

ἐν ᾧ καὶ ὑμεῖς συνοικοδομεῖσθε εἰς κατοικητήριον τοῦ θεοῦ ἐν
___ __ ___ _____ _____ ___ _____ ___ ____ __

πνεύματι
_____.

At this point, let's put all the words we've seen based on οικος into a complete passage. Eph. 2:19-22:

ἄρα οὖν οὐκέτι ἐστὲ ξένοι[1] καὶ πάροικοι, ἀλλὰ ἐστὲ
___ ___ _____ ____ ____ ___ _____ ____ ____

συμπολῖται[2] τῶν ἁγίων καὶ οἰκεῖοι τοῦ θεοῦ, ἐποικοδομηθέντες
_____ ___ ____ ___ _____ ___ ____ _____

ἐπὶ τῷ θεμελίῳ[3] τῶν ἀποστόλων καὶ προφητῶν, ὄντος[4]
___ __ _____ ___ _____ ___ _____ ____

ἀκρογωνιαίου[5] αὐτοῦ[6] Χριστοῦ Ἰησοῦ, ·ἐν ᾧ πᾶσα οἰκοδομὴ
_____ ____ _____ ____ __ _ ____ _____ being

εἰς ναὸν ἅγιον ἐν κυρίω
fitted-together, grows ___ ___ ___ __ ____

   (the rest of the passage is already quoted in full at the top of the page.)

NOTES

1. Every hear of xenophobia? (hatred of foreigners)
2. You probably know that a Greek city was called a πολις. Those who

189

lived there would be called πολιται. The word συμ (with) has been put in front to indicate that you are city-members along with those who were there before you. Literal: "with-citizens."

3. Foundation
4. This is a participle of "is": translate "being".
5. Cornerstone
6. Of it

Exercise One

PUTTING THE LETTER α IN FRONT OF A WORD...

changes it to its opposite (just like "im" does in English: possible becomes "impossible").

INSTRUCTIONS

Below are listed some real Greek words, with their meanings. Then the same Greek words, but with the letter "α" in front, are listed. Match to the English translations listed.

I. γνωσις -- knowledge   θεος -- God

   τομος -- "can be divided-up"   σβεστος -- can be put out if on fire

___ 1. αθεος   ___ 3. ασβεστος

___ 2. ατομος   ___ 4. αγνωστος

A. A fireproof material

B. Someone who is without God; compare our word "atheist".

C. At one time scientists thought they had found a particle so small it couldn't be divided any further, so they called it an "atom"; in scripture, it's used for a small moment of time.

D. Someone who says he doesn't know whether there is a God-- "agnostic". In New Testament times, the "Gnostics" claimed to have superior knowledge about how to make contact with the divine, over and above that which the ordinary person would know (and over and above that revealed in the life and message of Jesus Christ).

II. σοφος -- wise   συμφωνος -- in harmony (cf. Eng. "symphony")

   τιμος -- honored   μαρτυρος -- witness (cf. Eng. "martyr")

___ 5. αμαρτυρος   E. ignorant

___ 6. ατιμος   F. dishonored

___ 7. ασοφος   G. clashing

___ 8. ασυμφωνος   H. without witness

III. σιτος -- food, wheat   μετρος -- measure

    φοβος -- fear   γραμμα -- letter, learning (a "scribe"
                                          in New Testament was called
                                          a γραμματευς)

  ___ 9. αφοβως   I. starving or fasting

  ___ 10. αγραμματος   J. uneducated

  ___ 11. αμετρος   K. brave

  ___ 12. ασιτος   L. infinite, boundless

IV. κακος -- evil   φωνος -- sound

    καρπος -- fruit   νους -- mind (dative is νοι)

  ___ 13. ανοια   M. unfruitful

  ___ 14. ακακος   N. thoughtless, insane

  ___ 15. αφωνος   O. silent

  ___ 16. ακαρπος   P. good

V. πιστις -- faith   ψυχος -- soul

    ψευδης -- lie   λογος -- word

  ___ 17. αψυχος   Q. truth

  ___ 18. αλογος   R. unbelieving

  ___ 19 απιστος   S. cold-hearted

  ___ 20. αψευδης   T. speechless

VI. θανατος -- death   γαμος -- married (cf. Eng. "monogamous)

    ορατος -- visible   δυνατος -- powerful, able (cf. Eng.
                                            "dynamite")

  ___ 21. αγαμος   U. invisible

  ___ 22. αδυνατος   V. impossible

  ___ 23. αορατος   W. single

  ___ 24. αθανασια   X. immortality

VII. In the following examples, an ν is placed after the α to make a smoother transition into the main word.

ὕδωρ   -- water (cf. Eng. "hydraulics")

ὑποκριτης -- one who pretends to be what he is not (cf. Eng. "hypocrite")

αιτιον   -- cause, guilt

ωφελεω   -- be useful

ἅλς, ἁλός -- salt

αξιος   -- worthy

___ 25. ανυποκριτος
___ 26 ανυδρος
___ 27. ανωφελης
___ 28. αναξιος
___ 29. αναιτιος
___ 30. αναλος

Y. sincere, genuine

Z. useless (this is the scientific name of the mosquito that caused trouble during the building of the Panama Canal)

AA. dry, desert

BB. innocent

CC. saltless, insipid

DD. unworthy

Exercise Two

CAUTION

Do not confuse words that start with αν with those that start with ανα, which means "from above" or "again". Examples of such words include:

1. ανα + γενναω (give birth to) = ___ αναγενναω   a. sit up

2. ανα + καθεδρα (chair) = ___ ανακαθιζω   b. refresh

3. ανα + κεφαλη (head) = ___ ανακεφαλαιοω   c. reborn

4. ανα + ψυχη (soul) = ___ αναψυχω   d. sum up

5. ανα + μνεια (mention) = ___ αναμνησις   e. recall

This last word when spelled in English, is the technical term used to refer to the part of a communion prayer in which the first Lord's Supper is remembered: _____.

SCRIPTURES USING WORDS THAT START WITH α

When they saw the boldness _____ _____ ____ _____ _____ perceived
τοῦ Πέτρου καὶ Ἰωάννου καὶ

ὅτι ἄνθρωποι ἀγράμματοί εἰσιν καὶ ἰδιῶται
____ _____ _____ ___ __ ____ _____, they wondered.
                                                            Acts. 4:13

He will clear his threshing floor and gather ____ _____ __ ___ ____
τὸν σῖτον αὐτοῦ εἰς

τὴν ἀποθήκην,   πυρὶ ἀσβέστῳ
____ storehouse, but the chaff he will burn with fire _____.
                                                            Matt. 3:12

Exercise Three

Note two more English cognates to words used above:

_____ : One who operates a storehouse for drugs,
                      "drugstore"'
_____ : Add -maniac and you get a person who likes to
                      set fires.

βλέπετε οὖν   μὴ ὡς ἄσοφοι ἀλλ' ὡς σοφοί
_____ ___ carefully how you walk, ___ ___ _____ _____...
                                                     Eph. 5:15

Οὐκ ἔστιν προφήτης ἄτιμος εἰ μὴ
___ ____ _____ _____ __ ___ in his own country... Matt. 13:57

        ζωῆς αἰωνίου ἣν   ὁ ἀψευδὴς θεὸς πρὸ
...the hope __ _____ eternal, ___ announced _____ ___

χρόνων αἰωνίων
_____ _____.   Titus 1:2

Καὶ ὡς   ἄφωνος οὕτως οὐκ
____ ___ a lamb before his shearers (is) _____ _____ ____ opened

τὸ στόμα αὐτοῦ
__ _____ __ _____.   Acts 8:32

                    ἀμάρτυρον
Yet God did not leave himself ____ _____.   Acts 14:17

                         ἀσύμφωνοι δὲ   πρὸς
Some were convinced, some disbelieved; ___ _____ being among

ἀλλήλους
themselves they departed.   Acts 28:24-25

194

Καλὸν τὸ ἅλας ἐὰν δὲ τὸ ἅλας ἅναλον

_____ __ _____; ___ ___ _____ _____ becomes, how shall you

season it?   Mark 9:50

And if you are to judge ὁ   κόσμος, ἀνάξιοι   ἐστε of lesser
___ _____ _____ ____ ____

κριτηρίων;
judgements? 1 Cor. 6:2

Having purified τὰς ψυχὰς ὑμῶν by obedience to the truth εἰς
____ _____ __ ____ ____

φιλαδελφίαν ἀνυπόκριτον...
_____ _____.   1 Pet. 1:22

(Christ), ὅς ἐστιν εἰκὼν τοῦ θεοῦ τοῦ ἀοράτου firstborn πάσης
___ _____ _____ ___ _____ __ ___

creation, ὅτι ἐν αὐτῷ τὰ πάντα ἐν τοῖς καὶ
___ ___ ___ were created _____ __ ____ heavens ___

ἐπὶ τῆς γῆς, τὰ ὁρατὰ καὶ τὰ ἀόρατα εἴτε θρόνοι εἴτε
___ ___ ___ __ _____ ___ __ _____ whether _____ or

κυριοτητες εἴτε ἀρχαὶ εἴτε
"lord-ships" _____ "chief-ships" _____ authorities... Col. 1:15-16

δίκαιος AND RELATED FORMS

This word is one of the most important in the Bible, and one of the richest in meaning. Rather than give a definition, you will gradually see the concepts contained in this word as you guess at meanings in the following scriptures:

δίκαιον

(Boss to workers): "I'll pay you whatever is _____." Matt. 20:4

    (Basic meaning is fair, just right)

The following sentence refers to the "just right" result of unbelief:

δίκην

Those who reject the gospel will pay the _____ of eternal destruc-

tion. Jude 7

    (This "just right" result would be a penalty, or a just result.)

This characteristic of being "just right" is descriptive of God Himself:

πατὴρ δίκαιε

Jesus, addressing the Father in prayer: _____, the world has

not known Thee... John 17:25

δίκαιος

Centurion, seeing Jesus die, said "Surely, this man was _____.

Luke 23:47

    (Some use the word "righteous" to translate this characteristic)

The word δίκαιος was used a lot in courtrooms. In God's courtroom, all of us have to admit:

δίκαιος

There is not a _____ man, no, not one. Rom. 3:10

Some people may try to appear okay on the outside, but that doesn't fool God:

δικαιοῦντες

You may _____ yourself before men, but God knows your heart.

Luke 16:15

    (You may have translated "seem righteous" or "pretend to be okay"; a common translation of the verb form of our word is "justify".)

No matter what we've done, we'll be guilty in God's courtroom:

δικαιωθήσεται
No one will be _____ by works of the law. Gal. 2:16

So God came up with another plan:

δικαιοσύνη
But now, apart from law, the _____ of God has been shown...

though all have sinned and fall short of the glory of God, they

δικαιούμενοι
are _____ as a gift by grace through the redemption which is

in Christ Jesus. Rom. 3:21, 24

For example, Abraham was a sinner; but:

Abraham believed God, and it (his believing) was reckoned to him as

δικαιοσύνην
_____. Rom. 4:3

This is for all of us:

δικαιοσύνη
Blessed is the man to whom God reckons _____ without works.
                                                      Rom. 4:6

This quality is something we do not possess in and of ourselves; it
has to be reckoned to us by God. That is why the verb forms which
describe this concept are placed in the "passive" voice, which
expresses action being done to the subject.

δικαιοῦσθαι
We reckon a man to have been _____ by faith without works.
                                                      Rom. 3:28

The believer who has been put right with God also sees this characteristic of "rightness" come forth in his life and can be described
with this term:

δικαίου
The earnest prayer of a _____ man has great results. James 5:16

For the Christian, it takes a definite purpose to bring the "rightness" which God has declared about you into the experiences of daily living:

Flee youthful passions, and pursue δικαιοσύνην _____, faith, love, and

peace...   2 Tim. 2:22

Exercise One

SUMMARY

Six of the following words have something to do with translating the δικαιος word family. Cross out the six that do NOT:

just	faith	righteousness
holy	justify	lordship
fair	saint	believe
love	right	justification

DICTIONARY references:

δικη, ης (Feminine)	-- noun: justice, judgement
δικαιος, αια, αιον	--adjective: just, righteous, fair
δικαιως	--adverb: justly, fit, proper
δικαιοσυνη, ης (Feminine)	-- noun: justice, rightness
δικαιοω	-- verb: to make right, to justify
δικαιωμα, ατος (Neuter)	-- noun: an act of justice, a sentence, a decree
δικαιωσις, εως (Feminine)	-- noun: a declaration of justice
δικαστης, ου (Masculine)	-- noun: a judge

Two verses from Romans 10:

γὰρ τὴν τοῦ θεοῦ δικαιοσύνην, καὶ τὴν ἰδίαν

3.   Not knowing ____ ____ ____ ____ _____ ____ ____ _____

δικαιοσύνην   τῇ δικαιοσύνῃ τοῦ θεοῦ
_____ seeking to establish, __ ___ _____ ___ ___

οὐχ
____ did submit;

4. end γὰρ νόμου ____ ____ ____ (__) Χριστὸς εἰς δικαοσύνην παντὶ τῷ
____ ____ ____ _____ ____ _____ ____ __

πιστευόντι
believing ones.

NOTES

Under the bracket, the first "the" goes with "righteousness".
In verse 4, you have to add the word "is".

WORDS RELATED TO δικαιος

Remember that the letter α in front of a word changes it to its
opposite.

δίκαιος
If we confess our sins He is faithful and _____ to forgive our sins

ἀδικίας
and cleanse us from all _____ . 1 John 1:9

δίκαιος   ἀδίκων
For Christ died, _____ for _____ . 1 Pet. 3:18

ἀδικίαν
God's wrath is revealed against the _____ of men who suppress the

ἀδικίᾳ
truth in _____ . Rom. 1:18

The words that start with κ in the following scriptures are all
related to the concept "judge".

κρίνω
Jesus said, I do nothing on my own; as I hear, ___ _____ , and my

κρίσις   δικαία
_____ is _____ . John 5:30

κρίνειν   δικαιοσύνη
God has set a day ___ _____ the earth in _____ . Acts 17:31

Christ didn't revile in return, but put the whole matter into the hands

           κρίνοντι   δικαίως

of the one _____ -ing _____ -ly . 1 Pet. 2:23

Μὴ κρίνετε, ἵνα μὴ   κριθῆτε   ἐν ᾧ γὰρ κρίματι

__ __ ____ __ __ ye may be _____ ; __ __ ____ __ _____ -ment

κρίνετε   κριθήσεσθε   καὶ ἐν ᾧ μέτρῳ μετρεῖτε

__ _____ , ye shall be ____ -ed, ___ __ __ _____ __ _____ ,

     μετρηθήσεται   ὑμῖν

it shall be _____ -ed __ ___ . Matt. 7:1-2

Here's κρίνω and δικαιος combined into one word:

(Those who sin) are treasuring up wrath for the day of wrath and of

                  δικαιοκρισίας

the revelation of the _____ of God. Rom. 2:5

ἢ οὐκ   ὅτι οἱ ἅγιοι τὸν κόσμον   κρινοῦσιν;   καὶ

__ ____ you know ____ __ _____ ___ _____ will _____ ? ____

εἰ ἐν ὑμῖν   κρίνεται   ὁ κόσμος,   ἐστε

___ __ _____ will be ____ -ed __ _____ unworthy ___ __ of lesser

κριτηρίων

_____ ? 1 Cor. 6:2

Exercise Two

English cognate of last word in the verse above: _____

Exercise Three

                    κριτικός

The word of God is alive and active...and _____ the thoughts and

intentions of the heart. Heb. 4:12

English cognate of the word above: _____

Combining εκ with δικαιος yields the notion of "avenging":

ἀδικίας κριτής, ἐκδίκησόν
The widow said to the <u>unrighteous judge</u> _____ me from my

opponent...

ἐκδίκησιν
Jesus concluded, "Won't God perform _____ for his chosen ones?
                                                          Luke 18:3,7

ἐκδικοῦντες
Beloved, don't be _____-ing yourselves, but give place to wrath;

ἐκδίκησις
for it is written, "mine is _____, I will repay, saith the Lord.
                                                          Rom. 12:19

Combining δικαιος plus κατα = condemnation.
                        (down)
                                                          καταδίκην
The chief priests gave information against Paul, asking _____

against him.   Acts 25:15

κρίνετε   κριθῆτε   καταδικάζετε
Don't _____ and you won't be _____ ; don't _____ and you

καταδικασθῆτε
won't be _____ .   Luke 6:37

Exercise One

WORDS ABOUT SIN

These are some of the New Testament words, each with a different shade of meaning, that illustrate the depth and meaning of sin.

First, words that have the letter σ in front:

Root words: δικαιος - righteous   σεβασμα - object of
             καθαρσια - clean   worship
             πειθω - obey (be   νομος - law
                    persuaded)   πιστις - faith

Resulting words: (match to English descriptions)

___ 1. ασεβης   a) unrighteous

___ 2. αδικια   b) uncleanness

___ 3. ακαθαρσια   c) law-breaker

___ 4. ανομος   d) disobey

___ 5. απειθω   e) against what is worthy of worship

___ 6. απιστος   f) unbeliever

SOME SCRIPTURE QUOTES

πορνεία δε και ακαθαρσια πασα η   μηδε
_____ ___ __ _____ __ ___ greediness _____ let be named

εν υμιν καθως   αγιοις
__ ____ _____ is fitting __ _____ . Eph. 5:3

...ο ανθρωπος της ανομίας, ο υιος της
___ _____ ___ _____, _ ___ ___ perdition, setting himself

          πάντα λεγομενον   θεον η σεβασμα ωστε αυτον εις
up against _____ called   ___ _ _____ ____ _____ ___

τον ναον του θεου καθίσαι   εαυτον οτι εστιν θεος
___ ____ ___ ____ to sit claiming _____ ___ _____ ____ .
                                                  2 Thess. 2:3,4
                              απιστοις
Do not be unequally yoked together _____ _____ . 2 Cor. 6:14

Ο πιστευων εις τον υιον εχει ζωην αιωνιον: ο
The one   -ing ___ ___ ____ ____ ____ eternal; __

δε απειθων τω υιω ουκ   ζωήν...
__ _____ __ ___ ___ shall see _____ ... John 3:36

Exercise Two

The following word is the one usually translated by the word "sin" in the New Testament. The general meaning has to do with "missing the mark". Here are the forms used:

a) Verb: ἁμαρτάνω   "miss the mark"

b) Noun: ἁμαρτία   "a missing of the mark"

c) Noun: ἁμαρτωλός   "one who misses the mark"

On the blank at the end of each scripture reference, write "a", "b", or "c" to indicate which of the forms given above was used in that scripture.

Ἐὰν   ὅτι   ἁμαρτίαν   οὐκ   ἔχομεν,   ἑαυτοὺς   πλανῶμεν
____ we say ____ _____ _____ _____ we deceive _____

καὶ   ἡ   οὐκ   ἔστιν   ἐν   ἡμῖν
____ __ truth ____ _____ __ _____ . 1 John 1:8   (1)_____

ὅτι   καὶ   Χριστὸς   περὶ   ἁμαρτιῶν   δίκαιος   ὑπὲρ
___ ___ _____ once ____ _____ suffered-_____ ____

ἀδίκων
_____ . 1 Pet. 3:18   (2)_____

                τοῦ   ἑνὸς   ἀνθρώπου...οἱ πολλοί
Through the disobedience __ ___ _____ ___ ___ _____ were made

ἁμαρτωλοί
_____ . Rom. 5:19   (3)_____

         ταῦτα   γράφω   ὑμῖν   ἵνα   μὴ   ἁμάρτητε
My children, _____ __ ___ ___ ___ ___ ___ ye may _____ .

                                    1 John 2:1   (4)_____

       τοῦτο,   ὅτι   δικαίῳ   νόμος   οὐ   ἀνόμοις   δὲ
Knowing _____ ___ _____ _____ __ is laid down, _____ __

καὶ   ἀσεβέσι   καὶ   ἁμαρτωλοῖς
___ unruly, _____ ___ _____   1 Tim. 1:9   (5)_____

SIN-WORDS THAT START WITH παρα

παρα (alongside) + πτωμα (fall) = παραπτωμα (usually translated "trespass")

καὶ   ὑμᾶς   νεκροὺς   τοῖς   παραπτώμασιν   καὶ   ταῖς
___ ___ being ___ (in regard) __ ___ _____ ___ ___

ἁμαρτίαις ὑμῶν

_____ __ ____. Eph. 2:1   (6)_____

Note that by the choice of words, this sentence includes
both aspects of the nature of sin:
1) missing the mark--not doing what you should have done.
2) trespassing--doing what you were not supposed to do.

παρα (alongside) + βαινω (go) = words about deviating, transgres-
sing.

    Verb: παραβαινω - transgress

    Noun: παραβασις - transgression

    Noun: παραβατης - transgressor, violator

εἰ γὰρ   οἰκοδομῶ, παραβάτην
___ ____ those things I tore down, again __ _____ _____

ἐμαυτόν
_____ I establish. Gal. 2:18

παρα (alongside) + ακουω (hear) = not hear, fail to listen,
neglect to obey

    Verb: παρακουω - disobey

    Noun: παρακοη - disobedience

καὶ πᾶσα παράβασις καὶ παρακοὴ
____ ____ _____ ____ _____ received a just payment.
                                              Heb. 2:2

ὀφειλω = owe, incur a debt

Used in a secular sense:
                                              ὀφείλεις
(The dishonest steward said to the first debtor): How much _____

τῷ κυρίῳ μου;
_____?   Luke 16:5

    Verb: οφειλω   - owe

    Noun: οφειλημα - debt

    Noun: οφειλητης - The one who owes a debt: the "debtor"

                      καὶ   ἡμῖν τὰ ὀφειλήματα ἡμῶν,
In the Lord's prayer: ____ forgive __ __ ___ _____ __ ____

ὡς καὶ ἡμεῖς   τοῖς ὀφειλέταις ἡμῶν
___ ___ _____ forgive _____ _____ __ ____ . Matt. 6:12

κακος (evil) + ποιω (do) = do evil

   Verb: κακοποιω - do evil

   Noun: κακοποιος - evil-doer

Μὴ γάρ τις ὑμῶν   ὡς   ἢ κλέπτης ἢ κακοποιὸς
___ ___ ___ _____ let suffer ___ murderer __ _____ __ _____

ἢ ὡς
__ ___ mischief-maker. 1 Pet. 4:15

Finally, put the α in front of ἁμαρτωλός to get the opposite of
sinner: (v included for smoothness)

           ἀναμάρτητος
Let him who is _____ among you cast the first stone.
                                         John 8:7

CONFESSION AND REPENTANCE

Words based on ὁμος have to do with likeness, similarity:

                              ἀκούων   ποιῶν
I will tell you what the man _____-ing and _____-ing my words is

      ὅμοιος ἐστιν ἀνθρώπῳ   οἰκοδομοῦντι οἰκίαν ὃς
like: _____ _____ _____ __ _____ -ing _____ ___ dug

                              ἐπι την πέτραν
and deepened and laid a foundation ____ ____ _____. Luke 6:47,48

The following word refers to the "communicating" that goes on among
associates (those of <u>like</u> interests):

κακαι ὁμιλίαι
_____ _____ _____ corrupt good morals.   1 Cor. 15:33

Exercise One

ENGLISH DERIVATIVE

The short talk given to a religious gathering is based on the word
above.
Take off the ιαι and add y:_____

Combining ὁμο and λογος = "say the same", that is, profess something to be true which someone else has told you is true.

The Sadducees say there are no angels, resurrection, or spirit:

Φαρισαῖοι   δε ὁμολογοῦσιν
_____ ___ _____ both. Acts 23:8

This word is often used in professing the truth of something God has
said:

                ὁμολογήσῃς   στόματι κύριον   Ἰησοῦν
That if you <u>should</u> _____ with your _____ _____ (___) _____

και πιστεύσῃς   ἐν τῇ καρδίᾳ σου ὅτι ὁ θεος   αὐτον
and <u>should</u> _____ ___ __ _____ ___ ___ _ ____ _____ raised _____

ἐκ νεκρῶν
___ __ _____ you shall be saved. Rom. 10:9

We have become accustomed to using the word mainly to profess something negative:

ἐὰν ὁμολογῶμεν τὰς ἁμαρτίας ἡμῶν, πιστός ἐστιν καὶ δίκαιος
——— —— ——— ———— ———— ——— ——— ——— —— —————— to

ἡμῖν τὰς ἁμαρτίας   ἀπὸ πάσης ἀδικίας
forgive __ ___ ____ _____ and cleanse us ___ _____ _____ .
                                                           1 John 1:9

But in scripture passages, it is usually used to profess something
positive:

ὃς ἐὰν – ὁμολογήσῃ   ὅτι Ἰησοῦς ἐστιν ὁ υἱὸς τοῦ θεοῦ,
Whoever should _____ ____ _____ ____ _ ___ ___ ____

ὁ θεὸς ἐν αὐτῷ μένει καὶ αὐτὸς ἐν τῷ θεῷ
_____ ___ ____ _____ ___ _____ __ __ ___ .   1 John 4:15

That's why the word "confess" is used not only about sin, but for
claiming the promises of God (confessing the truth), in talking about
creeds ("let us confess our faith") and doctrinal writings (Augsburg
Confession, Westminster Confession). If I say the same thing God
says on a certain subject, I have "confessed."

The word also appears with the prefix ἐξ : Every knee shall bow
and every tongue εξομολογησηται that Jesus Christ is Lord. Phil. 2:11

You have used the preposition μετα to mean "with" and "after". In
the following words, it is used as a prefix, with the idea of "change."

μετα + μορφη (form) = change form

                                     μεταμορφοῦσθε
Don't be conformed to this world, but be ye _____ by the

renewing of your minds.   Rom. 12:2

Exercise Two

ENGLISH DERIVATIVE

The process of a caterpillar changing into a butterfly:_____.

μετα + σχημα (form, plan) = English _____ (replace
the final α with an e)

207

These are _____ ψευδαπόστολοι, evil workers, _____ μετασχηματιζόμενοι ___ εἰς

ἀποστόλους Χριστοῦ. _____. And no wonder: ___ ___ αὐτὸς γὰρ ὁ σατανᾶς ___

μετασχηματίζεται εἰς ἄγγελον φωτός, οὐ μέγα οὖν εἰ καὶ οἱ
_____ _____ _____ ___ ___ ___ ___ ___

διάκονοι αὐτοῦ μετασχηματίζονται ὡς διάκονοι δικαιοσύνης, ὧν
servants ___ ___ _____ ___ servants ___ _____ ___

τὸ τέλος κατὰ τὰ ἔργα αὐτῶν
___ end shall be ___ ___ ___ ___ . 2 Cor. 11:13-15

We return to our subject by introducing the word for "mind": νους

Genitive example: I see another law striving against ___ τῷ νόμῳ ___

τοῦ νοός μου
_____ . Rom. 7:23

Dative example: With my ___ νοΐ I am subject ___ τῷ ___ νόμῳ ___ θεοῦ ...
                                                                    Rom. 7:25

Now combine μετα plus νους = a change of mind

As a noun: μετανοια

I did not come to _____ καλέσαι δικαίους _____ ἀλλὰ _____ ἁμαρτωλοὺς ___ εἰς

μετανοιαν
_____ . Luke 5:32

...not knowing that the kindness of God leads you to _____ μετάνοιαν .
                                                                    Rom. 2:4

As a verb: μετανοεω
___ καὶ ___ ἐὰν your brother should _____ ἁμαρτήσῃ seven times a day and should

turn ___ πρὸς ___ σὲ _____ λέγων, ___ μετανοῶ, _____ forgive him.   Luke 17:4

τοῖς ἀνθρώποις   μετανοεῖν

Now God calls ____ _____ everywhere ____ _____. Acts 17:30

λέγω   ὑμῖν   ὅτι   ἐπὶ   ἑνὶ

____ ____ ____ ____ ____ there shall be more joy in heaven ____ ____

ἁμαρτωλῷ μετανοοῦντι   ἢ   ἐπὶ   δικαίοις οἵτινες   οὐ

____ _____ -ing __ ____ ninety-nine _____ _____ _____

ἔχουσιν μετανοίας

need _____ __ _____. Luke 15:7

αὐτῇ   χρόνον   ἵνα   μετανοήσῃ   καὶ   οὐ θέλει

I gave ____ _____ __ ____ she might ᶜ ____ ____ ____

μετανοῆσαι   ἐκ   τῆς   πορνείας   αὐτῆς

to _____ ____ ____ _____ ____. Rev. 2:21

Seeing repentance as a "change of mind" helps us avoid two extremes:
If a person expresses sorrow, but is not yet willing to call what he's
done a sin in God's sight, he hasn't really "changed his mind" about
what he's done; on the other hand, if a person truly changes his
attitude toward his sin, and hates it as God does, he has repented, even
if later he should fall into the same sin again.

The following word combines μετα and μελω (care about). It is translated with the word "repent" in the King James version, but it does
not refer to repenting in the religious sense, but simply to a change
of mind. Using the word "regret" to translate it is one way to bring
out its difference from "repent":

οὐ μεταμέλομαι   εἰ καὶ

If I grieved you in the letter, I do not _____ ____ ____

μετεμελόμην

I _____ -ed (for I see the letter brought you sorrow), I rejoice

εἰς μετάνοιαν   ἐργάζεται

that you grieved ____ _____...for grief towards God works _____

μετάνοιαν εἰς   ἀμεταμέλητον

_____ ____ salvation (which is) _____. 2 Cor. 7:8-10

Words based on στρεφω (turn) are often found in conjunction with words
about repenting. The following examples show that these words have both
secular and sacred meanings:

στρέψον[1] αὐτῷ   καὶ   τὴν   ἄλλην

Whoever hits you on the right cheek, _____ __ ____ ____ _____.

Matt. 5:39

ʼΑμὴν λέγω ὑμῖν, ἐὰν μὴ στραφῆτε[2] καὶ ὡς τὰ παιδία,
_____ _____ _____ except ye _____ ___ become ___ _____

you may not enter into the kingdom of heaven.   Matt. 18:3

In the following examples the prefix επι is put in front of στρεφω,
resulting in "turn upon" or "return".

Then (the demon) λέγει, εἰς τὸν οἶκον μου   ἐπιστρέψω[3]
_____ _____ ___ ___ _____ __ ___ I will _____ whence

I came.   Matt. 12:44

                                                 μετανοεῖν καὶ
(Paul said he kept telling everyone, even Gentiles)...___ _____ ___

ἐπιστρέφειν ἐπὶ τὸν θεόν   ἔργα   τῆς μετανοίας
__ _____ __ ___ _____ doing ___ worthy ___ _____.
                                                 Acts 26:20

ʼΑδελφοί μου, ἐάν τις ἐν ὑμῖν   πλανηθῇ
_____ ___ ___ ___ __ ____ should wander from the truth,

καὶ ἐπιστρέψῃ τις αὐτόν γινώσκετε ὅτι ὁ ἐπιστρέψας
___ _____ ___ _____ know ___ ___ the-one-_____ -ing

ἁμαρτωλὸν ἐκ πλάνης ὁδοῦ αὐτοῦ σώσει ψυχὴν αὐτοῦ ἐκ
_____ __ wandering __ ___ _____ shall save ____ __ ___ __

θανάτου καὶ καλύψει   ἁμαρτιῶν
_____ ___ shall cover a multitude __ _____.   James 5:19-20

FOOTNOTES

1. Spelling change, φ to ψ because it is a command
2. Spelling change, ε to η because it is conditional
3. Spelling change, φ to ψ because it is future

Exercise Three

SUMMARY

On the long blanks, write the two Greek words each of the given words
was constructed from. On the short blanks, write the letters of the
two selections from the right-hand column that correspond to each word.

1. ___ ___ επιστρεφω _____ + _____   a) say the same thing
2. ___ ___ μετανοια _____ + _____   b) repent
3. ___ ___ ομολογεω _____ + _____   c) turn
                                          d) confess
                                          e) change mind
                                          f) be converted

Exercise Four

REVIEW

Each Greek word below has related forms which correspond to the English
meanings in the column at the right.

___ ___ ___ 1. ἁγιος   a) justify   h) sin
___ ___ ___ 2. πιστις   b) spirit   i) sanctify
    ___ ___ 3. πνευμα   c) saint   j) faith
    ___ ___ 4. οικος   d) belief   k) edify
    ___ ___ 5. δικαιος   e) family   l) missing the mark
    ___ ___ 6. ἁμαρτια   f) wind   m) righteousness
                              g) holy   n) being persuaded

Final example with α in front:

                        ἀμετανόητον καρδίαν
Because of your hardness and _____ _____, you're storing up

wrath for yourself.   Rom. 2:5

BLESSING AND THANKSGIVING

Remember the word ευ (good) which we added to αγγελ (angel or messenger) to make words that had to do with evangelism--telling the good message?

It is important that you practice your pronunciation in these scripture sections.

ἵνα   εὖ   σοι
(Honor your father and mother) ___ ___ ___ it may be...   Eph. 6:3

ἐγὼ ἀποστέλλω τὸν ἀγγελόν μου
Behold, ___ _____ ____ _____ before your face... Matt. 11:10

οὐ γὰρ   τὸ εὐαγγέλιον
___ ___ am I ashamed of ___ _____...   Rom. 1:16

COMBINING ευ with λογος = "good words"

1. As a verb: ευλογεω

    εὐλογεῖτε   ὑμᾶς
    _____ those who curse _____.   Luke 6:28

    καὶ Συμεὼν εὐλόγησεν αὐτοὺς καὶ   πρὸς Μαριὰμ τὴν
    ___ _____ _____ _____ ___ said ____ _____ ___

    μητέρα αὐτοῦ...
    _____.   Luke 2:34

2. As a noun: ευλογια, ας, f

    ἵνα ἡ εὐλογία τοῦ Ἀβραὰμ   εἰς τὰ ἔθνη
    ___ __ _____ ___ _____ might come ___ __ _____.   Gal. 3:14

3. As an adjective: ευλογητος, η, ον

                  ὅς ἐστιν εὐλογητὸς   Ἀμήν
    ...the creator, ___ _____ _____ forever. _____.   Rom. 1:25

A sentence with all three uses:

    Εὐλογητὸς   ὁ θεὸς καὶ πατὴρ   κυρίου Ἰησοῦ Χριστοῦ
    _____ be __ ____ ___ _____ of our _____ ____ _____,

            εὐλογήσας   πνευματικῇ εὐλογία
    who has _____ us in every _____ _____ in the spiritual

        ἐν Χριστῷ
    realm ___ _____.   Eph. 1:3

NOTES

A form of the word "is" was added after the first word.

The word ευλογησας is a participle. Up to now, you have translated participles by adding "ing". This is a past participle, so translate "one having blessed", or "who has blessed".

Exercise One

What English word looks like ευλογια, and means the "good words" spoken about someone at his funeral? (Copy the word, changing the ending:)

_____.

COMBINING ευ with χαρις

One customary meaning of χαρις is "grace":

...οὐ γὰρ ἐστε ὑπὸ νόμον ἀλλὰ ὑπὸ χαριν

_____ ____ ___ ____. Rom. 6:14

Another common meaning of χαρις is "thanks"

τῶ δε θεῶ χαρις

_____ who always leads us in triumph in Christ.
2 Cor. 2:14

Adding ευ to this second meaning gives us the usual word for thanksgiving

1. As a noun: ευχαριστια, ας, f

    μετα εὐχαριστιας
    ...foods, which God has created to be partaken ____ _____

    by believers and knowers of truth. 1 Tim. 4:3

2. As a verb

    ὁ Φαρισαιος   ὁ θεος,
    __ _____ standing by himself prayed these things: __ _____

    εὐχαριστῶ σοι ὁτι οὐκ εἰμι
    __ _____ ___ ____ _____ as others are... Luke 18:11

While they were eating, Jesus took bread, ____ καὶ εὐλογήσας* _____ broke and

gave ___ τοῖς ___ μαθηταῖς _____ saying, λάβετε take, φάγετε eat, ____ τοῦτό _____ ἐστιν

τὸ σῶμά μου _____. And taking the cup ____ καὶ εὐχαριστησας⁺ _____ gave ___ αὐτοῖς ____

λεγῶν _____ drink ἐξ αὐτοῦ ____ _____ πάντες _____ τοῦτο γάρ _____ ἐστιν _____ τὸ αἷμα μου _____ of

the covenant... Matt. 26:26-28

* These are both "past participles". Translate: "having...ed"
+ English word. Take the ending off ευχαριστια, spell it in English
  letters and you get another name for the Lord's Supper:_____.

FOUR WORD FAMILIES THAT MEAN "SPEAK"

Exercise Two

A. λογος (word)

____ 1. λογος (noun)

____ 2. λεγει (verb)

____ 3. απο (from) + λογια

____ 4. ευ (good) + λογος

____ 5. θεος (God) + λογος

____ 6. λογικος

____ 7. ομο (same) + λογεω

MATCHING:

a) Logical, reasonable. Based on thinking about words, not based on feelings or physical actions.
b) "word"
c) To say the same thing about yourself that God does: to "confess"
d) "says"
e) Words from a person who has been criticized: his "explanation". Theological explanations are called "apologies"; the study of how to stand up for your faith is called "apologetics"
f) A good word, blessing, eulogy
g) The study of God (theology)

SCRIPTURES BASED ON THE PREVIOUS WORDS

1. ᾿Εν ἀρχῇ ἦν ὁ λόγος, καὶ ὁ λόγος ἦν πρὸς τὸν θεόν,
___ beginning was __ _____ ___ __ _____ was with ___ ___

καὶ θεὸς ἦν ὁ λόγος
___ ___ ___ __ _____ . John 1:1

καὶ ὁ λόγος σάρξ
___ __ _____ flesh became, and lived among us... John 1:14

Who is the λογος mentioned in this passage? _____

(same thought is in Heb. 1:1 -- "God has spoken to us in his Son")

2. Εὐλογητὸς ὁ θεὸς καὶ πατὴρ τοῦ κυρίου ἡμῶν ᾿Ιησοῦ
___ ___ ___ ___ ___ ___ ___ ___ ___

Χριστοῦ, ὁ εὐλογήσας ἡμᾶς ἐν πάσῃ εὐλογίᾳ πνευματικῇ
___ __ _____ ____ __ ____ _____ _____ ,

ἐν Χριστῷ
in the heavenlies ___ _____ . Eph. 1:3

3. I beseech you, ᾱᵈᵉˡᵖᵒⁱ _____, by the mercies ᵗʰᵉᵒᵘ __ _____, to present your

bodies as a living sacrifice, well pleasing ᵗʰᵉᵒ ___ _____, which is

your λογικὴν _____ service. Rom. 12:1

4. If we say we have no ᵃᵐᵃʳᵗⁱᵃⁿ _____, we are lying to ourselves and the

truth is not in us. If we ᵒᵐᵒˡᵒᵍᵒᵘᵐᵉⁿ _____ our ᵃᵐᵃʳᵗⁱᵃˢ _____ (God) is

πιστὸς καὶ δίκαιος ᵃᵐᵃʳᵗⁱᵃˢ ᵏᵃⁱ
faithful ___ righteous to forgive us our _____ ___ make us

clean from all ᵃᵈⁱᵏⁱᵃˢ _____ . 1 John 1:8, 9

Exercise Three

| B. | The φη word family | | MATCHING |

B. The φη word family

___ 1. φημι (verb)

___ 2. φημη (noun)

___ 3. βλασφημεω

___ 4. προ (forth) + φη + της = προφητης (one who)

___ 5. προφητικος

___ 6. προφητεια

MATCHING

a) a speech or a report. Notice how the Greek word sounds like the English word "fame".
b) speak
c) one who speaks out about something God has told him; prophet.
d) prophetic
e) something a prophet would say; a prophecy
f) speak against (blaspheme)

FAMOUS SCRIPTURE QUOTES

5. (After one of Jesus' miracles): And the _____ of it went out

                                                  φήμη (above "_____")

unto all that land.   Matt. 9:26

6. We have the _____ _____ made more sure...because no
                 προφητικὸν λόγον

_____ of scripture is a matter of one's own interpretation;
προφητεία γραφῆς

because no _____ was ever made by an act of human will;
            προφητεία

but _____ moved by the _____ _____ spoke from
ἄνθρωποι   ἁγίου πνεύματος

θεοῦ
____.   2 Pet. 1:19-21

| C. | λαλεω - speak.   Noun-form: λαλια |

C. λαλεω - speak.   Noun-form: λαλια

    Ἐκ   γὰρ τοῦ   τῆς καρδίας τὸ στόμα λαλεῖ.

7. ___ ___ ___ fulness ___ ___ ___ ___ ___
                                              Matt. 12:34

    Εὐχαριστῶ τῷ θεῷ λαλῶ γλώσσαις   πάντων

8. ___ ___ ___ ___ ___ more than ___ ___
ὑμῶν
____.   1 Cor. 14:18

| D. | ῥῆμα, | ατος, | n. | word |

                                           τὸ δὲ ῥῆμα κυρίου

(All flesh is as) the flower of grass, ___ ___ ___ ___

μένει   τοῦτο δὲ ἐστιν τὸ ῥῆμα τὸ εὐαγγελισθὲν

___ forever; ___ ___ ___ ___   ___ ___   having been   -ed

εἰς ὑμᾶς

___ ___. 1 Pet. 1:25

καὶ ἡ μήτηρ αὐτοῦ   πάντα τὰ ῥήματα ἐν τῇ καρδίᾳ

___ ___ ___ ___ ___ kept ___ ___ ___ ___ ___ ___

αὐτῆς

___ ___. Luke 2:51

SALVATION - WORDS

Remember that σωτηρ means savior? The other related words are:

> verb: σωζω save / εσωθην* was saved / σωσω shall save
>
> *means aorist (a type of past) passive: "was saved"
>
> noun: σωτηρια, ας, f. salvation
>
> also found as σωτηριος m. and σωτηριον η.

"Save" implies there is something to be saved from. The following
scripture quotes are classifed according to what the problem is:

                    πιστει Νωε   σωτηριαν του
A FLOOD. by _____ ____ prepared...an ark for the _____ . __ __

οικου αυτου
_____ __ ____. Heb. 11:7

                              κυριε, σωσον,
A STORM. They awoke him saying _____ _____ or we perish.
                                                  Matt. 8:25

                    της πιστεως σωσει
SICKNESS. The prayer ____ _____ shall ____ the sick and will

      αυτον ο κυριος
raise _____ __ _____. James 5:15

                              Εαν μονον
(The woman said to herself) ____ _____ I touch his garment

      σωθησομαι   η πιστις
I shall be ____-ed ...Jesus said, courage, daughter, __ _____

σου   σεσωκεν   σε   και η γυνη   εσωθη   απο
____ has ____-ed ___. ____ woman was _____

της ωρας εκεινης
____ ____ _____. Matt. 9:21-22

              ο επιστρεψας   αμαρτωλον εκ πλανης οδου
DEATH. Know that the one ____-ing _____ ____ _____ ____

αυτου   σωσει   ψυχην αυτου εκ θανατου και καλυψει
__ __ will _____ ____ ____ __ _____ ____ _____

πληθος αμαρτιων
multitude ___ _____. James 5:20

                    Ιησουν, αυτος γαρ σωσει
SINS. You shall call his name _____ _____ _____ the people

απο των αμαρτιων αυτων
____ ____ _____ ____. Matt. 1:21

Many passages speak in a general way, where "save" seems to cover the entire area of freedom from sin and the gaining of an eternal relationship with God:

οὐ γὰρ ἀπέστειλεν* ὁ θεὸς τὸν υἱὸν εἰς τὸν κόσμον ἵνα
_____ _____ sent ___ _____ _____ ____ ____ _____ _____ ___

κρίνῃ τὸν κόσμον, ἀλλ' ἵνα σωθῇ ὁ κόσμος
he might ___ _____ _____ _____ ____ he might ____ _____

δι' αὐτοῦ.
_____. John 3:17

οἱ ὀφθαλμοί μου τὸ σωτήριόν σου.
___ _____ ____ have seen, __ _____ ____. Luke 2:30

* past tense of αποστελλω, which is related to αποστολος.

Exercise One

More uses for the word σωζω. Match each passage to the letter of the concept found on the next page.

τοῖς πᾶσιν   πάντα ἵνα πάντως τινὰς
____ 1. To all   I have become all things ___ by all ways some

σώσω.
I _____. 1 Cor. 9:22b

με ὁ κύριος ἀπὸ παντὸς ἔργου καὶ
____ 2. Will rescue ___ __ _____ ___ _____ _____ evil ____

σώσει
_____ me into his heavenly kingdom. 2 Tim. 4:18

σωθήσεται
____ 3. The one remaining unto the end shall be _____. Matt. 24:13

μετὰ φόβου καὶ   τὴν ἑαυτῶν σωτηρίαν
____ 4. _____ _____ _____ trembling ___ _____ _____ work out.
                                                     Phil. 2:12

ὁ λόγος γὰρ   μωρία
____ 5. __ _____ ___ of the cross to those perishing foolishness

ἐστίν, τοῖς δὲ σῳζομένοις ἡμῖν δύναμις θεοῦ
_____ _____ ___ being ____ _____ _____ ____

ἐστίν.
__ ____. 1 Cor. 1:18

____ 6. And cried (in a) ____ ____ saying, ____ ____ ____

   φωνῇ μεγάλη   ἡ σωτηρία τῷ θεῷ

 ἡμῶν ἐπὶ τῷ θρόνῳ καὶ

____ seated ____ ____ ____ ____ to the lamb. Rev. 7:10

 a) Something to be worked into your present experience

 b) As a worship-word

 c) Referring to conversion

 d) It will take endurance

 e) Referring to believers in general

 f) Looking ahead to eternal life

Exercise Two

Remember αλλος, other? A related word is αλλασσω to make other, to change, transform.

       καὶ ἀλλάξαι τὴν φωνήν μου

I wish I were present with you now ____ ____ ____ ____ ____

for I am perplexed. Gal. 4:20

Combine κατα + αλλασσω for the idea of exchange, used often for changing enemies into friends (reconciling).

| verb: καταλλασσω |
| noun: καταλλαγη |

        καταλλάξαντος ἡμᾶς

All these things are from God, the one _____ -ing ____

ἑαυτῷ διὰ Χριστοῦ   ἡμῖν   τῆς καταλλαγῆς

__ __ _____ and giving __ ___ the ministry ____ _____

    ἐν Χριστῷ καταλλάσσων κόσμον ἑαυτῷ μὴ λογιζόμενος

for God was ___ _____ -ing _____ ___ __ reckoning

αὐτοῖς τὰ παραπτώματα αὐτῶν, καὶ   τὸν λόγον τῆς

___ __ _____ _____ ___ ____ giving us ___ ____ ___

καταλλαγῆς

_____. 2 Cor. 5:18-19

> Combine απο + κατα + αλλασσω. The meaning is roughly the same as
> κατα + αλλασσω.

                              κατοικῆσαι* καὶ δι' αὐτοῦ ἀποκαταλλάξαι
In Him all the fulness "indwells", ____ ___ _____ to _____

τα πάντα εἰς αὐτόν   διὰ τοῦ αἱματος
_____ ___ _____ making peace ___ ___ _____ of his cross.
                                                  Col. 1:20

* This was one of the words from the οικος study.

221

SALVATION WORDS (Continued)

λυω = loosen

Jesus said, _____ ὑποκριται ! Each of you on the _____ σαββατω οὐ λυει his ox and

donkey from the manger? Luke 13:15

Ἀμην λεγω ὑμιν

___ ___ ___ ___ whatever you shall bind on earth shall be what is

bound in heaven, and whatever _____ λυσητε ἐπι της γης _____ shall be what is

loosed in heaven. Matt. 18:18

λυτρον = the price paid for release

Ὁ υἱος του ἀνθρωπου οὐκ

___ ___ ___ ___ ___ came to be served but to serve, and give

την ψυχην αὐτου λυτρον ἀντι πολλων

___ ___ ___ ___ ___ ___ . Matt. 20:28

λυτροω = release, ransom

Who gave himself for us ___ ἱνα λυτρωσηται ἡμας ἀπο πασης ἀνομιας

και καθαριση* cleanse ἑαυτω _ _ a people for his own possession, _____ ζηλωτην

καλων ἐργων

_____ . Titus 2:14

λυτρωσις = liberation

Not through the blood of bulls and calves, ___ δια δε του ἰδιου ___

αἱματος, _____ he entered once into the ___ ἁγια , having earned eternal αἰωνιαν

λυτρωσιν

_____ . Heb. 9:12

* cognate with English _____ a physical cleansing in medicine,
  an emotional cleansing in drama.

> απο + λυω is not used about eternal redemption, but about letting people go...physically:

ἀπέλυσεν αὐτοῖς τὸν Βαραββᾶν

Then _____ __ _____ ____ _____ . Matt. 27:26

...and spiritually:

κρίνετε   καταδικάζετε

Don't _____ and you won't be judged; don't _____, and

ἀπολύετε, καὶ ἀπολυθήσεσθε

you won't be condemned; _____ ____ you shall be _____ -en.
Luke 6:37

But the other form of this word, the noun απολυτρωσις, is used entirely in the New Testament to refer to eternal redemption:

All have sinned and fall short of the glory of God, but are justified

διὰ τῆς ἀπολυτρώσεως τῆς ἐν Χριστῷ Ἰησοῦ

freely by his grace ____ ____ _____ ____ ___ _____ _____ .
Rom. 3:23-24

Exercise One -- a word that is difficult to translate

Above the ark of the covenant were cherubim of glory, with their wings

τὸ ἱλαστήριον

covering ___ _____ . Heb. 9:5

This referred to the place of payment for sins in the Old Testament temple. Blood was sprinkled here, and the end results were that God's people had forgiveness.

In the New Testament, the location for payment of sins is a person:

ἱλαστήριον

Jesus, whom God set forth as a _____ through faith in his blood.
Rom. 3:25

Could be translated "means by which sins are forgiven".

Related word: ιλασμος (noun)

ἱλασμός

And He is the _____ for our sins... 1 John 2:2

Related verb: ἱλασκομα

(The publican said) __ ____ _____ ____, a sinner.   Luke 18:13

ὁ θεος ἱλασθητι μου

| The more common verb for "having mercy" is ελεεω |

Two blind men followed Jesus, crying and saying, _____ _____

ελεησον ἡμας,

υἱος Δαυιδ

_____ _____.   Matt. 9:27

And in the beatitudes:

ἐλεήμονες   ἐλεηθήσονται

Blessed are the _____, for they _____.   Matt. 5:7

The corresponding noun is ελεος

οὐκ ἐξ ἔργων

____ __ _____ which we have done ___ _____ ____ ____ ___

ἐν δικαιοσύνη ἀλλὰ κατὰ τὸ

αὐτου ελεος εσωσεν ἡμας

__ __ _____ he saved _____.   Titus 3:5

The following words are based on αγω (lead). Remember συν + αγω
gave us συναγωγη, the place where the Jews came together.

| αγορα = a secular place where people come together: the marketplace. |

τριτην ὡραν   αλλους   ἐν τῇ

And going out about the _____ _____ he saw _____ standing ___ __

αγορᾳ

_____ idle. Matt. 20:3

αγοραζω = doing a transaction that would take place in a market;
acquire by paying a price. (the past tense of this word starts with η)

(When the man finds the treasure he hides it) and out of his joy he goes and sells all ____ ____ ____ ____ ____ ____ ____.

ἔχει καὶ ἀγοράζει τὸν ἀγρὸν ἐκεῖνον

Matt. 13:44

Ye are not your own, ye were _____ with a price; therefore glorify

ἠγοράσθητε τιμῆς

God in your body. 1 Cor. 6:20

Worthy art thou...for you were slain, ____ ____ ____ ____ ____ ____

καὶ ἠγόρασας τῷ θεῷ ἐν τῷ

____ ____ from every tribe ____ ____ and people and ____.

αἵματι σου φυλῆς καὶ γλώσσης ἔθνους

Rev. 5:9

Exercise Two

Words based on ἱημι. This word which basically means "go", is not
found itself in the New Testament, but is found in combination with
απο. When απο is put in front of ἱημι, it is written in the form it
takes before vowels: αφ.

Verb:	αφιημι
Noun:	αφεσις

This word has many meanings. Can you guess from context?
Match each passage to the letter of the suggestions given here:

a) send away, dismiss   c) forgive

b) leave, go away from

____ 1. Then ____ _____ _____ _____ ____ and fled.

οἱ μαθηταὶ πάντες ἀφέντες αὐτὸν

Matt. 26:56

____ 2. I came from the Father and came ____ ____ _____ ; again

εἰς τὸν κόσμον

ἀφίημι τὸν κόσμον πρὸς τὸν πατέρα

_____ _____ and go ____ ____ _____. John 16:28

____ 3. Jesus, crying again with a ____ ____ ____ ____ ____

φωνῇ μεγάλῃ ἀφῆκεν τὸ πνεῦμα

Matt. 27:50

____ 4. If we confess our sins, he is faithful and righteous so that

αφη

he ____ our sins... 1 John 1:9

225

From the Lord's Prayer and following verses:

καὶ ἄφες ἡμῖν τὰ ὀφειλήματα

Give us this day our daily bread, ___ ____ __ __ ___ _____

ἡμῶν ὡς καὶ ἡμεῖς ἀφήκαμεν τοῖς ὀφειλέταις ἡμῶν

__ ___ ___ ____ _____ _____ _____. Matt. 6:11, 12

At the institution of the Lord's Supper:

τοῦτο γάρ ἐστιν τὸ αἷμά μου τῆς

_____ ____ ____ ___ ____ __ ___ of the covenant shed for many for

ἄφεσιν ἁμαρτιῶν.

_____ __ _____. Matt. 26:28

Exercise One

PEOPLE

The Family (οικειοι or πατρια)

ανθρωπος   μαμμη   παιδια or τεκνα

| nominative: | πατηρ |
| genitive: | πατρος |

| nominative: | ανηρ |
| genitive: | ανδρος |

μητηρ
μητρος

γυνη
γυναικος

| υιος | θυγατηρ | βρεφος |
| υιου | θυγατρος | βρεφους |

or

νηπιος,
α, ον
(adjec-
tive)

COGNATES

Write corresponding Greek word after each description:

a) Mammary. Pertaining to woman's breasts.   _____

b) Repatriate. Return to fatherland.   _____

c) Gynocologist. Doctor specializing on women.   _____

d) Nepotism. Granting favors to your relatives.   _____

e) Matriarch. Rule by mothers. Adds αρχη to
   the word above.   _____

f) Android. A man-like robot.   _____

SCRIPTURES

Ἐπεὶ οὖν τὰ παιδία κεκοινώηκεν αἵματος καὶ σαρκός, καὶ αὐτὸς
Since ___ ___ ___ share ___ ___ ___ also ___

partook of the same... Heb. 2:14

       τις γυνὴ   Μάρθα
A certain ____ named _____ served him.   Luke 10:38

                    ὁ ἄγγελος   ταῖς γυναιξίν μὴ φοβεῖσθε
(After the resurrection): __ _____ said __ ____ _____
                                                  Matt. 28:5

227

(From Peter's Pentecost sermon): Ἄνδρες Ἰσραηλῖται, ἀκούσατε τοὺς

_____ _____ _____ _____

λόγους τούτους. Ἰησοῦν τὸν Ναζωραῖον, ἄνδρα

_____ _____ _____ _____ _____ approved by God...
                                                    Acts 2:22

Αἱ γυναῖκες _____ τοῖς ἰδίοις ἀνδράσιν ὡς τῷ κυρίῳ, ὅτι
        submit

ἀνὴρ ἐστιν κεφαλὴ τῆς γυναικὸς ὡς καὶ ὁ Χριστὸς κεφαλὴ

_____ _____ _____ _____ _____ _____ _____ _____

τῆς ἐκκλησίας, αὐτὸς σωτὴρ τοῦ σώματος

_____ _____ _____ _____ _____ . Eph. 5:22-23

WORDS ABOUT SLAVES AND SERVANTS

δουλος
διακονος
λειτουργος
υπερετης
θεραπων
οικετης

παιδισκη

οἱ δοῦλοι, ὑπακούετε τοῖς κατὰ σάρκα[1] κυρίοις μετὰ φόβου καὶ

_____ _____ _____ _____ _____ _____ _____

                                    ὡς δοῦλοι Χριστοῦ ποιοῦντες
trembling, not as menpleasers but _____ _____ _____ _____ _____ -ing

τὸ θέλημα τοῦ θεοῦ ἐκ ψυχῆς[2]
_____ will _____ _____ _____ . Eph. 6:5

FOOTNOTES

1. according to the flesh, ie. here on this earth
2. from the soul, or from the heart; heartily, with all your might

228

Ἀμὴν Ἀμὴν λέγω ὑμῖν ὅτι πᾶς ὁ ποιῶν τὴν

Jesus answered, _____ _____ _____ _____ _____ _____ _____ _____ _____ _____

ἁμαρτίαν δοῦλος ἐστιν τῆς ἁμαρτίας

_____ _____ _____ _____ _____ . John 8:34

Ἰάκωβος θεοῦ καὶ κυρίου Ἰησοῦ Χριστοῦ δοῦλος ταῖς δώδεκα

James _____ _____ _____ _____ _____ _____ _____ _____

φυλαῖς ταῖς ἐν τῇ διασπορᾷ, χαίρειν

_____ _____ _____ _____ _____ greetings.   James 1:1

In the following example, the δουλος has a position of authority over
the rest of the household staff:

τίς ἄρα ἐστὶν ὁ πιστὸς   δοῦλος ὃν   ὁ κύριος

_____ _____ _____ _____ _____ and wise _____ _____ sets up _____ _____

ἐπὶ τῆς οἰκετείας αὐτοῦ

_____ _____ _____ _____ _____ to give them their food at the right time?
                                                        Matt. 24:45

Other forms related to δουλος

    Noun: δουλεια   bondage

    Verb: δουλευω   serve

    Verb: δουλοω   be in bondage

Οὐδεὶς οἰκέτης δύναται δυσὶ κυρίοις δουλεύειν   ἢ γὰρ

Not-one _____ is able _____ _____ _____ either

τὸν ἕνα μισήσει καὶ τὸν ἕτερον ἀγαπήσει... οὐ δύνασθε θεῷ

_____ _____ _____ _____ _____ _____ _____ _____ ye are able _____

δουλεύειν καὶ μαμωνᾷ

_____ _____ _____ . Luke 16:13

The last word above is a spelling in Greek letters of an Aramaic word.
(Aramaic, related to Hebrew, was the language spoken in Palestine in
the time of Jesus.) The meaning of the word: wealth, riches.

Words related to παις (child) -- genitive is παιδος

Nouns: παιδιον   child

παιδεια   nurture of children, education

παιδευτης and παιδαγωγος   both mean "instructor"

παιδισκης   female slave

Verb: παιδευω   instruct, chastise

παιδείας κυρίου
My son, do not despise the _____ __ _____ or faint when you're

ὃν γὰρ ἀγαπᾷ κύριος παιδεύει   πάντα
reproved; ___ ___ ____ _____ _____ and scourges _____

ὃν   ὃν   εἰς παιδείαν ὑπομένετε ὡς υἱοῖς ὑμῖν
υἱον ὃν   is
____ __ he receives. ____ _____ ye endure; ___ _____ _____

ὁ θεός   τίς γὰρ υἱός ὃν οὐ παιδεύει πατήρ
treating ____; ___ ___ ____ ___ ___ _____ _____?
                                                Heb. 12:5-7

διακονος and related words

(at the wedding of Cana): λεγει ἡ μητηρ αυτου τοις διακονοις, "Whatever he says to you, do!"

Other related words:

Verb: διακονεω   serve

Noun: διακονια   serving, service

Both are used in the following sentence:

ἡ Μαρθα   περὶ πολλὴν διακονίαν
_____ was distracted _____ _____ _____; she approached and

Κύριε, οὐ μέλει   σοι ὅτι ἡ ἀδελφή μου μόνην
said, _____ doesn't it matter __ ___ ____ ____ ___ _____

με   διακονεῖν;
___ has left __ _____   Luke 10:40

These words are often used to refer to Christian work:

                      ἀποστόλους   προφήτας   εὐαγγελιστάς

... and he gave some _____ some _____ some _____

                                      τῶν ἁγίων εἰς ἔργον

some pastors and teachers, for building up __ __ _____ ___ _____

διακονίας, εἰς οἰκοδομὴν τοῦ σώματος τοῦ Χριστοῦ

___ _____ ___ _____ __ _____ ___ _____ . Eph. 4:11-12

The English words "minister", "ministry" are often used to translate
these words. Apparently certain people in the early churches were
singled out for service, and received a title:

Παῦλος καὶ Τιμόθεος, δοῦλοι Χριστοῦ Ἰησοῦ πᾶσιν τοῖς ἁγίοις

_____ ___ _____ _____ _____ __ _____ ___ _____

ἐν Χριστῷ Ἰησοῦ

__ _____ _____ who are in Philippi ____ _____ ___

                               σὺν ἐπισκόποις* καὶ

διακόνοις

_____ . Phil. 1:1

The last word above is spelled in English as _____

* translate as "overseer". This word is explained later in this
  section.

Combine λειτος (public) + εργον, and you get λειτουργος. This word
is sometimes used to apply to the government, the "public servant":

For this reason you must pay taxes, $\underset{\text{_____}}{\text{λειτουργοὶ}}\ \underset{\text{\_\_\_}}{\text{γὰρ}}\ \underset{\text{\_\_\_\_}}{\text{θεοῦ}}\ \underset{\text{\_\_\_\_}}{\text{εἰσιν}}$

for this very thing. Rom. 13:6

Related words:

      Verb: λειτουργεω   serve, minister

      Noun: λειτουργια   service, ministration

      Adjective: λειτουργικος   serving, ministering

Here it is applied to angels:

Οὐχὶ πάντες εἰσὶν λειτουργικὰ πνεύματα, ἀποστελλόμενα εἰς
Are they not all _____ _____ sent out ____

διακονίαν...
_____ Heb. 1:14

About believers "serving" God through worship:

                                    λειτουργούντων
(Paul and others gathered at Antioch): as they were _____ -ing
τῷ κυρίῳ καὶ   τὸ πνεῦμα τὸ ἅγιον
__ ____ ___ fasting, _____ said... Acts 13:2

Referring to artifacts used in the worship of God:

And in the same way he sprinkled with blood both the tabernacle and all

                  τῆς λειτουργίας
the vessels ___ ___ _____. Heb. 9:21

English spelling of the last word (remove the αις and add "y")

_____ used to name the order of service in Christian
worship, and thus brings out the "corporate, public" character of
worship.

Combine ὑπερ (under) + ερετης (a rower), and you get a word that was first used to describe a member of a ship's crew.

Noun: ὑπηρετης   servant, assistant
Verb: ὑπηρετεω   serve

ὑπηρέτησαν
You know that these hands _____-ed to my needs and the needs of

those with me.   Acts 20:34

ὑπηρετῶν
Peter followed afar, and sat with the _____ and warmed himself

πρὸς τὸ φῶς
____ __ ____.   Mark 14:54

στρατηγὸς σὺν τοῖς ὑπηρέταις
Then the captain ____ _____ _____ went and brought them, without

violence...   Acts 5:26

English cognate of the word used above for captain:_____.
We use it to refer to military plans.

Apparently this same word was used to indicate an official in the synagogue:

βιβλίον   τῷ
(Jesus read from Isaiah), and closing the _____ he gave it __ __

ὑπηρέτη   καὶ πάντων οἱ ὀφθαλμοὶ ἐν τῇ συναγωγῇ
_____ and sat down; ____ _____ ___ _____ __ __ _____

αὐτῷ
were fixed ___ ___.   Luke 4:20

θεραπων and related forms

καὶ Μωϋσῆς μὲν* πιστὸς ἐν ὅλῳ τῷ οἴκῳ αὐτοῦ ὡς θεράπων
___ _____ ___ _____ __ ___ __ ____ _____ __ _____

εἰς μαρτύριον   Χριστὸς δὲ ὡς υἱος ἐπι
___ _____ of things spoken later; _____ __ __ ____ ___

τὸν οἴκον αὐτοῦ
___ _____ ___ ____.   Heb. 3:5-6

* When μεν and δε are in the same sentence, they can be translated
  "on the one hand...on the other hand..."

233

Related words:

    Noun: θεραπεια - service, including physical help, healing.

    Verb: θεραπευω - serve, also divine service (worship), and
                              physical help (heal).

τις αρα εστιν ο πιστος   οικονόμος ον   ο κύριος

____ ____ _____   _____ and wise _____ ___ sets up __ _____

επι της θεραπειας

____ ____ _____   to give them food in time. Luke 12:42

                         τους δώδεκα μαθητας αυτου

And calling to himself ____ _____ _____ __ ___ he gave authority

ωστε εκβαλλειν   πνευμάτων ακαθάρτων και θεραπευειν πασαν

____ _____ _____ _____ ___ _____ _____

illness and malady. Matt. 10:1

He spoke to them about the Kingdom of God, and healed those having

          θεραπειας
need ___ _____ . Luke 9:11

The English spelling of this last word, _____, we use
to refer to healing activites.

SOME TITLES OF OFFICIALS

ιερευς = priest
ιερον = temple

Exercise Five

Match the English derivatives:

____ 1. hieroglyphics (with
       γλυφω, "carve")

____ 2. Hierarchy (with
       αρχη, "chief)

____ 3. hieratic

a) The organizational pattern
   of religious officials

b) Pertaining to priests

c) Those Egyptian symbols
   known only to the priests

COMBINING επι (on, over) and σκοπεω (look, see)

As a verb:

1. The general ___ἐπισκοπει___ his army.

As a noun:

2. Titus appointed an ___ἐπισκοπον___ to watch over the Christians in Crete--he had to be blameless. (Titus 1:7)

3. An ___ἐπισκοπος___ is one who ___ἐπισκοπει___ large numbers of Christians.

What happened to the word ἐπισκοπος when Christianity reached England? (simplified explanation:)

___ἐπισκοπος___   4. Write the Greek word for one who supervises Christians.

_____ 5. The English took off the ending and first letter, leaving:

_____ 6. The English softened the sk sound to an sh sound:

_____ 7. They softened the opening p sound to a b sound:

_____ 8. Write the result in English letters:

_____ 9. After the church of England withdrew from the Catholic Church in the 1500's, it still wanted to keep these overseers or supervisors over groups of Christians and it still wanted to call them bishops. To describe the kind of church system they now had, they coined a word by taking the original Greek term for overseer and changing the ending. A method of church government that makes use of bishops is called an (fill in answer by 9.) system.

PEOPLE -- SUMMARY...

...of religious titles, including some new ones.

Exercise Six

Match the descriptions in the right-hand column to the two small blanks to the left of each Greek word. Then match the English translation from below the Greek words to the small blank at the right of each Greek word.

___ ___ 1. πρεσβυτερος ___
___ ___ 2. αποστολος ___
___ ___ 3. διακονος ___
___ ___ 4. προφητης ___
___ ___ 5. μαθητης ___
___ ___ 6. επισκοπος ___
___ ___ 7. ευαγγελιστας ___
___ ___ 8. ποιμην ___
___ ___ 9. κατηχουμενος ___

a) one who serves under others
b) supervisor, overseer
c) one who tends a flock; related to ποιμνη, which means "a flock"
d) older person
e) one who speaks forth a message from God
f) one who is sent out on a mission
g) one who is under discipline; a follower, learner
h) one who is taught; from κατα + ηχεω which means "to sound in the ears". (cf Eng. echo)
i) one who tells a good message; from ευ "good" + αγγελος "messenger"
j) presbyter
k) related to: αποστελλω --send forth
    αποστολη --expedition
l) related to "catechesis", an English word which means "the religious instruction program of the church". A "catechism" is a religious instruction book based on the question/answer method.

Match to these customary English translations:

A. Prophet
B. Evangelist
C. Deacon or Minister
D. Catechumen
E. Elder
F. Bishop
G. Apostle
H. Disciple
I. Pastor

m) related to: διακονεω --attend upon
    διακονια --aid, ministering
n) shepherd
o) made by combining φημι "speak" with προ "forth"
p) related to: ευαγγελιον --good news
    ευαγγελιζω --to proclaim good news
q) related to: μανθανω --learn
    μαθητευω --follow as a disciple
r) related to: επισκοπεω --look over
    επισκοπη --oversight, supervision

236

SCRIPTURES

κατηχημένος   τὴν ὁδὸν   τοῦ κυρίου
This man (had been) _____ ___ ____ ___ _____. Acts. 18:25

                                    καὶ ἐπὶ τῆς γῆς   οὖν
All power is given unto me in heaven ___ ___   ___. Going ____

μαθητεύσατε πάντα τὰ ἔθνη, βαπτίζοντες αὐτοὺς εἰς τὸ ὄνομα
_____ _____ __ ____ _____ _____ ___ __ _____

τοῦ πατρὸς καὶ τοῦ υἱοῦ καὶ τοῦ ἁγίου πνεύματος...
___ _____ ___ ___ ____ ___ ___ _____ _____. Matt. 28:18

YOU MAY ASK

Why didn't you say anything about the qualities of the different
servants--which one is considered a "bond-servant", etc.?

The answer is that this workbook is not a Bible dictionary or a
theological dictionary, but only an introduction to New Testament
words. There were no Bible quotes I could find that brought out the
differences between types of slaves. This matter depends on information
gathered from outside the Bible. At this point, you are able to use
some of the more advanced Theological dictionaries and get something
out of them.

Why didn't you devote a page to the three types of love?

    αγαπη, φιλια, & ερος?

1) Ερος is not even found in the New Testament.

2) Again, I could find no passages that clearly showed or contrasted
   the shades of difference between the two. In many instances, they
   mean about the same thing. This is a matter for theological
   dictionaries.

3) Incidentally, there is a fourth word for love, στοργη, which refers
   to natural family-type affection. It is not found in the New
   Testament, but its opposite is: (the last word in the following
   quote)

         φιλαυτοι   φιλαργυροι
For men shall be lovers-of-self, lovers of money, proud, arrogant,

βλάσφημοι,   ἀπειθεῖς ἀχάριστοι
_____, to parents _____, unthankful, unholy,

    ἀστοργοι...
3) _____... 2 Tim. 3:2-3

237

COGNATE ORIGINS

Why are some English words like Greek words?

   I. Sometimes it is because both the Greek and English words came
       from their common ancestor.

  II. Sometimes it is because Latin borrowed from Greek, and then the
       languages that are descendants of Latin, like French, came into
       the English language when French-speaking invaders conquered
       England in 1066.

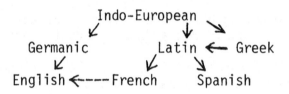

 III. Sometimes it reflects the fact that Latin borrowings from Greek
       were used to coin words needed for intellectual purposes.

  IV. Most recently, scientific words have been coined by taking roots
       directly from Greek and formulating new English words:

   V. There are also technical terms which came from Greek, but which
       underwent a lot of change and development as the English language
       itself changed over the years. Examples given in this workbook
       have been "bishop" and "church".

```
         Old English  ←————————  Greek
              ↓
           English
```

PART V

VERBS

You will:

1. survey the shades of meanings of verbs.

2. use charts to learn how to put the endings on
    verbs that express these shades of meaning.

3. learn how to use an analytical lexicon.

VERBS

In Part II, you learned the six "personal endings" which are added to verbs:

	singular		plural	
1st person -	I	-ω	we	-ομεν
2nd person -	you	-εις	ye	-ετε
3rd person -	he	-ει	they	-ουσι (ν)

Example: λεγω = I speak,   λεγουσι = they speak

These endings are for "present" tense. On the following pages, you will be introduced to different endings used for the other tenses (past, future, etc.)

In Part II, you were introduced to the infinitive (the basic sense of the verb without any personal ending), which we show in English by the use of the word "to": λεγειν = to speak. On the coming pages you will find additional infinitive endings and uses.

In Part II, you were told about participles, and you have been using the participle ending -ων: λεγων = speaking. You will learn more endings for participles and more uses for them here in Part V.

Other information about verbs you will learn includes:

1. Mood--shades of meaning indicated by different verb-endings.
2. Voice--such as "active", when the subject is doing the acting (I throw), and "passive", when the subject is receiving the action (I am being thrown).

VERB TENSES

The following chart lists six Greek verb tenses and their English meaning.

TENSE	DESCRIPTION	IDENTIFYING MARKS INCLUDE	EXAMPLE
Present	continuous action	The word in simple form, or with -ing on the end & preceded by a form of "be" (such as am, is, are).	I throw, or, more characteristically, I am throwing
Future	Action in future time, either continuous or a single act.	will or shall	I will throw

Continued next page

TENSE	DESCRIPTION	IDENTIFYING MARKS INCLUDE	EXAMPLE
Imperfect [3]	continuous action in past time	was plus -ing	I was throw-ing
Aorist [1]	an act	past form, or use of did [3]	I threw, or
Perfect [3]	a completed act with emphasis on existing present results		I did throw
Pluperfect	a completed act which had continuing results in the past.	had	I had thrown

1. In theory, aorist is used for a single act, whenever it happened. In actual use, aorist is the most common form used to describe single events in the past.

2. It is hard to differentiate Aorist from Perfect in English -- both of them sound like our "past tense."

3. The word "perfect" means completed. Imperfect tense then gets its name from the fact that it describes a continuous action, one that was not completed.

The following diagram illustrates the characteristics of the tenses:

```
                Past        Now         Future

Present                    --+--
Future                       |          -----
Imperfect       -----        |
Aorist          .(an event!) |
Perfect         .------------+
Pluperfect      .-----        |
                             |
```

Remember that each of the six tenses listed has six possible endings which stand for the six persons, making a total of 36 ways a verb can end. The following pages will add additional ways.

There is also a tense called "future perfect", which is translated "will have". Example: "I will have thrown."

Exercise One

MATCHING

Match the underlined English phrase to the Greek tense it would translate; in the other blank, match to the "person" used in the example:

___ ___ 1. He will give at the office.   a) Present

___ ___ 2. Ye were taking candy each time ye   b) Future
            walked past the counter.
                                                   c) Future Perfect

___ ___ 3. I wrote the letter you are now   d) Imperfect
            reading.
                                                   e) Aorist
___ ___ 4. We are being good.
                                                   f) Perfect
___ ___ 5. They will have arrived home by
            then.   g) Pluperfect

___ ___ 6. You gave a good speech.   Persons

___ ___ 7. He had eaten the cake before I   1s (1st singular)
            arrived.
                                                   2s
___ ___ 8. Ye shall see a light in the
            heavens.   3s

___ ___ 9. I was taking a shower.   1p (1st plural)

___ ___ 10. We built that house you're   2p
            looking at.
                                                   3p

Each underlined phrase above can be written as a single Greek word.

Exercise Two

Match the tense name to the "kind" of action it describes:

Tense Name   Kinds of Action

        ____ 1. Present   a) Completed

____ or ____ 2. Future   b) Single Act

        ____ 3. Imperfect   c) Continuing Action

____ and ____ 4. Aorist

        ____ 5. Perfect

        ____ 6. Pluperfect

Note: The perfect tense indicates continuing results, but not continu-
       ing action.

MOODS OF VERBS

The verb endings you learned in Part II were for the "INDICATIVE" mood--
they "indicate" what is going on: "I tell a story."

There are four additional moods, each with a different set of endings:

A. IMPERATIVE mood--used to give a command: "Tell a story!"

Scripture examples:

Eph. 4:30. λυπεω means grieve. "...and do not λυπεῖτε the Holy
   Spirit."
Eph. 4:28. κλεπτω means steal. "The one who stole, no longer
   κλεπτέτω ("let him steal").

B. SUBJUNCTIVE mood--used after the word "if": "If I should tell you
what I did, would you punish me?"

Here are eight examples of uses of the subjunctive. Remember that
the underlined portions can be said with a single word in Greek:

1. To exhort: "Let us believe"; "I command that you love one
   another."

2. To express purpose: "We came in order that we might see him."

3. Possibility: "If we go into the house, we will see him."

4. After "until" (when it hasn't happened yet): "Remain until I
   come."

5. Concerning fear: "I fear that he would come."

6. Warnings: "Do this lest you come into judgment."

7. Sentences using "whoever": "Whoever would want to save his life
   shall lose it."

8. Certain questions: "Shall I come?"

Scriptural examples: εχω means "have"

ἐχῃ

Eph. 4:28b. "Let him no longer steal, in order that he may have
   to give to the one in need."
Eph. 4:14. (The word used in this sentence is a form of "be.)

ὦμεν

"...in order that we no longer might be infants."

C. OPTATIVE mood--for wishing: "If only I could tell a joke."
Also used for wondering, and when the second part of a sentence
depends on a first part which is in the past: "I had gone, so that
I might see him leave.

243

Scriptural example:

Eph. 1:17. (using a form of the word that means "give"): "In order
that God <u>would give</u> you a spirit of wisdom..."
δώη

D. INFINITIVE mood--in Part II, you used it as a verb which comes after
the word "to": "I want <u>to tell</u> a story."

In Greek, it is often used after the word "the", and acts like a
noun. This is tricky to translate:

θέλειν
Rom. 7:18. "The <u>to wish</u> is present to me."

See how various Bible translations try to deal with this sentence.
RSV paraphrases it: "I can will what is right."

Exercise Three

SUMMARY

Here is an English sentence using all five moods.
Place the letter from the list below in each set of parentheses.

If anyone <u>should call</u>, (   ) <u>tell</u> (   ) them <u>I had decided</u> (   )

<u>to leave</u>, (   ) so I <u>could arrive</u> (   ) on time.

<u>Matching</u>:

a) indicative   c) subjunctive   e) infinitive

b) imperative   d) optative

NOTE: Concepts of "past" and "present" are only clearly expressed in
the indicative mood; the other moods bring out the character
("kind of action"--single act, continuing, or completed) but
not necessarily any time element.

Exercise Four

IDENTIFYING MOOD AND TENSE

Match the underlined part of each sentence to the correct term from each of the two lists below:

___ ___ 1. It's been worthwhile <u>to have been giving</u> to charities all year.

___ ___ 2. If he <u>should fall</u> to the ground, he would get up again.

___ ___ 3. She <u>might have made</u> the cake we see before us now.

___ ___ 4. The editor <u>had sent</u> the letter before I arrived.

___ ___ 5. We must preserve our resources, or else <u>we will have given</u> them all away by the time we need them.

___ ___ 6. They <u>are to send</u> their friends away immediately!

___ ___ 7. I wonder if he <u>would make</u> a fool of himself if he showed up next.

___ ___ 8. You must like <u>to be writing</u> letters all the time.

___ ___ 9. I wish God <u>would have been giving</u> me that kind of comfort all along.

___ ___ 10. They <u>should have moved</u> in long ago.

___ ___ 11. <u>Give</u> me a piece of pie, Mom.

Tenses	Moods
a) present	A. Indicative
b) future	B. Imperative
c) imperfect	C. Subjunctive
d) aorist	D. Optative
e) perfect	E. Infinitive
f) pluperfect	
g) future perfect	

VOICE OF VERBS

The examples described so far have been in "active" voice--which means the subject is doing the acting. Before we move on to "passive" voice, let's take a minute to summarize all the possible endings in "active" voice.

ACTIVE   The numbers indicate the number of endings in each category to
VOICE   match the six "persons".

Tenses:	Moods:				
	Indica-tive	Impera-tive	Subjunc-tive	Opta-tive	Infini-tive
PRESENT	6	4	6	6	1
FUTURE	6		6	6	1
IMPERFECT	6				
AORIST	6	4	6	6	1
PERFECT	6	4	6	6	1
PLUPERFECT	6				

A blank space on the chart means that particular possibility was not
actually used in Greek.

Note that imperative only needs four personal endings; "I" and "we"
are not used. There is only one infinitive for each tense.

If you add together all the possibilities, you will find there are
100 different ways to write a Greek verb.

PASSIVE VOICE

All 100 of these possibilities appear, with 100 different forms, in
"passive" voice (in which the subject is being acted upon). There is
also something called "middle" voice, which is used when the subject
acts upon himself. Fortunately, middle voice does not add another
100 endings, because "passive" and "middle" are formed identically in
some tenses. The passive voice has one tense that the active voice
does not have, the "future perfect".

The three voices then are:

ACTIVE	PASSIVE	MIDDLE
I threw the ball.	I was thrown for a loop.	I threw myself at his feet.

EXAMPLES OF PASSIVE VOICE FROM SCRIPTURE:

Present, indicative: In Christ you are being built together into a dwelling of God in the Spirit. Eph. 2:22

Aorist, indicative: ...which now has been revealed to the apostles and prophets...Eph. 3:5

Aorist, imperative: ...all bitterness let be gone from you. Eph. 4:31

Aorist, subjunctive: ...so that ye might be filled with all the fulness of God. Eph. 3:19

EXAMPLE OF MIDDLE VOICE

I do not cease to give thanks concerning you. Eph. 1:16

Exercise Five

IDENTIFYING VOICE

A.

_____ 1. I washed the dishes.   A. Active
_____ 2. I've been washed in the blood.   M. Middle
_____ 3. I washed myself.   P. Passive

B.

_____ 1. He is washing himself.
_____ 2. We will be clothed in His righteousness.
_____ 3. Ye have fed my lambs.
_____ 4. They will be washed by His word.
_____ 5. I am dressing myself.
_____ 6. You were being fed intravenously.
_____ 7. He washed your sins away.
_____ 8. We are being dressed because we can't do it ourselves.
_____ 9. They will feed themselves when they are able.

Exercise Six

IDENTIFYING VERB CHARACTERISTICS

Match the underlined phrase from each sentence to the correct term from each of the three lists below.

___ ___ ___   1. When ye <u>had given</u> the money, were ye still ashamed?

___ ___ ___   2. If you <u>would be built up</u> in faith, read His word.

___ ___ ___   3. I <u>will have made</u> four trips to the dentist by the time it's over.

___ ___ ___   4. Was it worth it <u>to have washed yourself</u> before eating?

___ ___ ___   5. They <u>would have been thrown</u> from their saddles if they hadn't hung on.

___ ___ ___   6. <u>Write</u> what I tell you to the seven churches.

___ ___ ___   7. If only I <u>could pass</u> that test tomorrow!

___ ___ ___   8. He <u>would have been rescued</u> if he had shouted for help.

___ ___ ___   9. You must have been patient <u>to have been building</u> that wall for so long.

___ ___ ___ 10. We <u>might have been declared</u> innocent had it not been for that witness.

Mood:	Tense:	Voice:
A. Indicative	a) present	X. Active
B. Imperative	b) future	Y. Middle
C. Subjunctive	c) imperfect	Z. Passive
D. Optative	d) aorist	
E. Infinitive	e) perfect	
	f) pluperfect	
	g) future perfect	

The following material summarizes all the possibilities for a Greek verb; the examples are all given in "first person", so each example given stands for six possibilities (except imperative, which has four; and infinitive, which has one).

SUMMARY OF VERB POSSIBILITIES

X = does not occur in Greek

ACTIVE

	INDICATIVE	IMPERATIVE	SUBJUNCTIVE	OPTATIVE	INFINITIVE
PRESENT	I throw. / I am throwing.	Throw! / Be throwing!	I should throw. / I should be throwing.	I would throw. / I would be throwing.	To throw / To be throwing
FUTURE	I will throw.	X	X	I might throw.	"to be going to throw"
IMPERFECT	I was throwing.	X	X	X	X
AORIST	I threw.	Throw!	I should have thrown.	I would have thrown.	To have thrown
PERFECT	I did throw. / I have thrown.	X	I should have thrown.	I would have thrown.	To have thrown
PLUPERFECT	I had thrown.	X	X	X	X

MIDDLE

	INDICATIVE	IMPERATIVE	SUBJUNCTIVE	OPTATIVE	INFINITIVE
PRESENT	I throw myself.	Throw yourself!	I should throw myself.	I would throw myself.	To throw myself
FUTURE	I will throw myself.	X	X	I might throw myself.	To be going to throw myself
IMPERFECT	I was throwing myself.	X	X	X	X

SUMMARY OF VERB POSSIBILITIES continued

MIDDLE (cont.)

	INDICATIVE	IMPERATIVE	SUBJUNCTIVE	OPTATIVE	INFINITIVE
AORIST	I threw myself.	Throw yourself!	I should have thrown myself.	I would have thrown myself.	To have thrown myself
PERFECT	I have thrown myself.	X	I should have thrown myself.	I would have thrown myself.	To have thrown myself
PLUPERFECT	I had thrown myself.	X	X	X	X

PASSIVE

	INDICATIVE	IMPERATIVE	SUBJUNCTIVE	OPTATIVE	INFINITIVE
PRESENT	I am being thrown.	Be thrown!	I should be thrown.	I would be thrown.	To be thrown
IMPERFECT	I was being thrown.	X	X	X	X
FUTURE	I will be thrown.	X	X	I might be thrown.	To be going to be thrown.
AORIST	I was thrown!	Be thrown!	I should have been thrown.	I would have been thrown.	To have been thrown
PERFECT	I have been thrown.	X	I should have been thrown.	I would have been thrown.	To have been thrown
PLUPERFECT	I had been thrown.	X	X	X	X
FUTURE PERFECT	I will have been thrown.	X	X	X	Shall have to be thrown

USING AN ANALYTICAL LEXICON

An analytical lexicon lists each word used in the New Testament separately--every time it appears with a different ending, it receives a different listing. You do not need to know all the details of forming Greek words in order to look them up in such a book. Let's go through the procedure together of tracking down the meaning of a word through the use of this type of lexicon.

Eph. 1:11 includes the word ἐκληρώθημεν.

If we look up the word, we find this entry:

ἐκληρώθημεν   1 pers. pl. aor. 1 ind. pass. . . . . . καλεω

We see at the far right that the word is a form of the word καλεω, which means call. The last abbreviation stands for "passive", so use the last third of the chart on the previous pages. Ind. stands for "indicative", so use the first column. Aor. stands for "aorist". When looking for the English meaning, you do not need to be concerned with the number found after the word "aorist". At the aorist location in the first column, the English example given is "I was thrown". Since the word we are concerned with means "call", simply substitute the word "call" for the word "throw", and you get "I was called". It states at the beginning of the lexicon entry that the word is "first person plural"--that is, the subject is "we". By substituting "we" for "I" in our translation, we arrive at the final translation: "we were called". Another example of using an analytical lexicon is given in the Appendix.

Summary of abbreviations used in an analytical lexicon

There are a few abbreviations in the book you don't have to use. After some words, you will see something like (§ 7 rem 1) or (tab B). This refers to "sections" (§) in the front of the book, which include "remarks" (rem.) and "tables" (tab.). This is only meaningful to the intermediate Greek student. Other places in the book refer to certain scholars and books to back up the information being given. You will find a list of these at the bottom right of the abbreviation page which comes right after the table of contents.

Following are abbreviations for the terms used in this book, which are the basic ones you will need to know:

abl.   =   ablative (shows separation)

acc.   =   accusative (direct object)

act.   =   active voice

aor.   =   aorist, a type of past tense

compar. =   comparative, used with adjectives to indicate "more"

dat.   =   dative (indirect object)

fem.   =   feminine

Abbreviations continued

fut.	=	future tense
gen.	=	genitive (possessive)
indic.	=	indicative (statement of fact)
inf.	=	infinitive (verb form that we translate using "to": to write)
imp. or imper. or imperat.	=	imperative (giving a command)
imperf.	=	imperfect tense (a type of past tense)
inst.	=	instrumental (expresses the means by which the action is accomplished)
loc.	=	locative (indicates the location or position of the noun it describes)
masc.	=	masculine
mid.	=	middle voice
neut.	=	neuter
nom.	=	nominative (subject of sentence)
part.	=	participle
pass.	=	passive voice
pers.	=	person (such as 2nd person = you, 3rd person = he)
perf.	=	perfect (a type of past tense)
pl. or plur.	=	plural
pluperf.	=	pluperfect (a type of past tense)
sing.	=	singular
subj.	=	subjunctive
superl.	=	superlative (used with adjectives to mean "most")
voc.	=	vocative (an ending put on a noun when you are speaking directly to that noun)

CONSTRUCTING GREEK VERBS

The chart on pages 255-257 shows how to make common verb forms in the indicative mood. Part II of the chart lists various sets of endings, labeled (a), (b), and so on. These endings are in sets of six, representing the six "persons", first person singular "I", second person singular "you", and so on.

Using this chart is only possible if you have information provided by a Greek lexicon (= Greek/English dictionary).

In the lexicon, you will notice that each verb is listed with six forms.[*] These are called the "six principal parts". They give you the information you need to construct the various forms of the verb. To see how these are used, here are the principal parts for the verb λυω (loose).

λυω λυσω ελυσα λελυκα λελυμαι ελυθην

The first principal part tells you what you need to know to construct present and imperfect tenses; the second, to construct future tenses; the third, aorist; the fourth and fifth, perfect; and the sixth, passive in aorist and future. These principal parts all have the first person ending attached. When you remove the ending, you are left with the "stem". You can then add whatever ending you need to the stem in order to construct the verb form that you want.

The right-hand half of the chart shows how to follow the instructions using λυω as an example. The third person singular is worked out for each tense and voice, as follows: The ending is removed from the principal part, and the third person ending is attached.

Exercise One

MATCHING from the verb construction chart. (These are all found in the sixth column of the chart.)

In the first blank, write the tense (present, future, etc.);
In the second blank, write the voice (active, passive, etc.);
In the third blank, write the letter of the English translation from the list at the right.

---

* Sometimes only the forms actually used in the New Testament are listed.

Tense	Voice			
_____	_____	___	1. ελυσατο	a) He was loosening himself.
_____	_____	___	2. λελυται	b) He loosened himself (simple act)
_____	_____	___	3. λυει	c) He had loosened
_____	_____	___	4. ελυετο	d) He has been loosened
_____	_____	___	5. ελελυκει	e) He will be loosened
_____	_____	___	6. λυεται	f) He is loosening
_____	_____	___	7. λυθησεται	g) He is being loosened

The instructions for IMPERFECT, in the fourth column of the chart, include the term AUG. For now, when you see this term, place an ε in front of the principal part, as you see has been done in the sixth column example for imperfect.

VERB CONSTRUCTION CHART FOR "INDICATIVE"

I. Instructions

If you want to make:

Example using λυω (=loosens)

TENSE	VOICE	PRINCI-PAL PART TO USE	ADD END-INGS FROM COLUMN	PRINCI-PAL PART LOOKS LIKE	THIRD PERSON SINGULAR WOULD BE	WHICH MEANS
Present	Active	1	a	λυω	λυει	he loosens, or he is loosening
Present	Middle	1	a	λυω	λυεται	he loosens himself
Present	Passive	1	a	λυω	λυεται	he is being loosened
Imperfect	Active	1	AUG* b	λυω	ελυε	he was loosening
Imperfect	Middle	1	AUG b	λυω	ελυετο	he was loosening himself
Imperfect	Passive	1	AUG b	λυω	ελυετο	he was being loosened
Future	Active	2	a	λυσω	λυσει	he will loosen
Future	Middle	2	a	λυσω	λυσεται	he will loosen himself
Aorist	Active	3	c	ελυσα	ελυσε	he loosened
Aorist	Middle	3	c	ελυσα	ελυσατο	he loosened himself
Perfect	Active	4	d	λελυκα	λελυκε	he has loosened
Pluperfect	Active	4	AUG f	λελυκα	ελελυκει	he had loosened
Perfect	Middle	5	d	λελυμαι	λελυται	he has loosed himself
Perfect	Passive	5	d	λελυμαι	λελυται	he has been loosened

* AUG. = "Augment", which means "put an ε in front, or if the word starts with a vowel, change the vowel. Just see the third principal part to see how it is done.

Continued next page

VERB CONSTRUCTION CHART FOR "INDICATIVE" continued

TENSE	VOICE	PRINCI-PAL PART TO USE	ADD END-INGS FROM COLUMN	PRINCI-PAL PART LOOKS LIKE	THIRD PERSON SINGULAR WOULD BE	WHICH MEANS
Aorist	Passive	6	e	ελυθην	ελυθη	he was loosened
Future	Passive	6	remove AUG, add "σ", and use endings from Col. (a)	ελυθην	λυθησεται	he will be loosened

II. Endings

	PERSON		(a) FOR PRESENT & FUTURE	(b) FOR IMPERFECT & SECOND AORIST	(c) FOR AORIST	(d) FOR PERFECT	(e) FOR AORIST PASSIVE	(f) FOR PLUPERFECT
A C T I V E	I	1	ω	ον	α	α	ην	ειν
	you	2	εις	ες	ας	ας	ης	εις
	he	3	ει	ε	ε (ν)	ε	η	ει
	we	1	ομεν	ομεν	αμεν	αμεν	ημεν	ειμεν
	you	2	ετε	ετε	ατε	ατε	ητε	ειτε
	they	3	ουσι (ν)*	ον	αν	ασι (ν) or αν	ησαν	εισαν
M I D D L E & P A S S I V E	I	1	ομαι	ομην	αμην	μαι		
	you	2	ῃ	ου or εο	ω	σαι		
	he	3	εται	ετο	ατο	ται		
	we	1	ομεθα	ομεθα	αμεθα	μεθα		
	you	2	εσθε	εσθε	ασθε	σθε		
	they	3	ονται	οντο	αντο	νται		

* The "ν" is sometimes added for a smooth connection to the next word.

257

Exercise Two

DRILL IN ADDING ENDINGS TO λυω

Step by step procedure:

1. Decide which tense and voice the example is in.
2. Select the correct principal part and remove the ending (unless the subject of your sentence is "I"; in that case, the correct ending is already on the principal part in most "active" examples.)
3. Decide which "person" the example calls for, and select the correct ending from the right column of endings.

As an example, let's construct the future middle form for the word λυω, and let's select "you" as the subject. We want to construct a form that will mean "you will loosen yourself". Future middle is the eighth row on the chart; we are told to use second principal part, and endings from column (a). After we remove the ending from the second principal part we are left with λυσ. Now we go to the endings columns; since we are making a "middle" form, we need an ending from the lower half of the column. The second person ending there is η; adding that to λυσ, the result is λυση, "you will loosen yourself".

Construct the form of λυω required to translate each phrase:

	Form of λυω	Tense	Voice	
1.	_____	_____	_____	- You were loosening
2.	_____	_____	_____	- She will loosen herself
3.	_____	_____	_____	- We have loosened
4.	_____	_____	_____	- Ye were loosened
5.	_____	_____	_____	- They are loosening themselves
6.	_____	_____	_____	- You will loosen
7.	_____	_____	_____	- It had loosened
8.	_____	_____	_____	- I am being loosened
9.	_____	_____	_____	- We loosened
10.	_____	_____	_____	- They have been loosened

MORE ABOUT "AUG"

The abbreviation stands for "augment", an addition or change at the beginning of the verb.

1. If the principal part starts with a consonant, place an ε at the beginning.

258

2. If the principal part starts with a vowel, it is changed to what is called a "long vowel". Here are some of the changes:

α or ε to η; ι to ει; ο to ω.

EXAMPLE: εγειρω means "I rise". To make imperfect, change ε to η, and add an ending from column (b); ηγειρον means "I was rising".

In other cases, you can find out the correct way to make the augment by looking at the third and sixth principal parts as listed in the lexicon, because those principal parts already have the augment attached.

EXAMPLE: οικοδομεω means "build". The third principal part is ῳκοδομησα, which shows us that adding the ε changed οι to ω. Put that ῳ at the beginning to construct your imperfect, add an ending from column (b), and the result is ῳκοδομεον, "I was building".

3. Another complication arises if your verb is a compound word. For example, απαγω, "lead away", is made of the word απο, "away", and αγω, "lead". The letter to be changed is the α on αγω, not the α on απο. The augment for α is η; the imperfect of απαγω then is απηγον. Again, in more complicated cases, the third or sixth principal part will show you how to augment the verb in question.

EXAMPLES WITH OTHER VERBS

Let's construct "he wrote", the aorist of γραφω (write). We will need the third principal part, which according to the lexicon turns out to be εγραψα. Our chart tells us that we need the endings from column (c). The first person ending is α. Removing that from the principal part, the stem turns out to be εγραψ. Now, from column (c), find and add the third person ending, ε, and the result is εγραψε, "he wrote".

SECOND AORIST

Some verbs form certain tenses in a different way. The same thing occurs in English. We have "regular" verbs, that form the past tense by adding -ed. Example: love, loved. We have other verbs that change within themselves to form the past. Example: throw, threw. When a Greek aorist is formed in a different way than the regular way, the formation is called "second aorist." The meaning is still the same, only the method of formation is different. If the formation is "second aorist", you will use endings from column (b) instead of column (c), (p. 270). How will you know when to do this? If your third principal part ends with ον, you will know that you are to use the endings from the column that is headed up that way, which is column (b). Another give-away is that regular (also called "first") aorists always have an σ before the ending (the aorist of λυω for example was ελυσα); second aorists never have this σ.

EXAMPLE: You decide to construct the form that means "we threw". You know that "throw" is βαλλω, so you look up βαλλω in the lexicon. The third principal part is εβαλον. You notice that it doesn't have an σ, and it ends with the ον, which shows you it is taking its endings from column (b). You remove the ending, obtaining the stem εβαλ; you add the ending for we, ομεν, and construct εβαλομεν, "we threw". For second aorist passive, use the same column as for first aorist passive. Forms called second future and second perfect also exist; and even some "third" forms.

Exercise Three

DRILL WITH VARIOUS VERBS

Here are the principal parts:

Write: γραφω   γραψω   εγραψα   γεγραφα   γεγραμμαι   εγραφην
Call: καλεω   καλεσω   εκαλεσα   κεκληκα   κεκλημαι   εκληθην
Drink: πινω   πιομαι   επιον   πεπωκα   πεπομαι   εποθην

1. He will write _____
2. They have been called (summoned)_____
3. He drank _____
4. We had drunk _____
5. He was called _____
6. We have written _____

"DEPONENT"

A verb is called "deponent" when it has a middle or passive form but an active meaning. The second principal part of "drink", above, is deponent. It looks like it has a passive ending, but it will be translated "I will drink". More about deponents later.

CONNECTING VOWELS

Sometimes you will notice a change in the vowels where the endings
connect with the principal part. Here is an example:

The lexicon entry for "love" is αγαπαω, so the stem is αγαπα. To
say "he loves", you would add ει. But that ει interacts with the α,
and the result is that the α cancels out the ε and the ι becomes
miniaturized; the result is αγαπα, "he loves".

This chart shows what happens when vowels interact with one another:

ε + diphthong = ε disappears.   ε + ο = ου   ε + ε = ει

α + ο = ω   α + ω = ω   α + ε = α   α + ο = α   α + ει = α
                                                           ι

ο + ε or ο or ου = ου   ο + α or ω = ω   ο + ι = οι

This workbook over-simplifies when explaining that endings can be
connected to principal parts. In actual fact, there is a connecting
vowel between the stem and the ending. A comprehensive, 40-page
explanation of this matter can be found in HANDBOOK OF NEW TESTAMENT
GREEK, © 1973 by William Sanford LaSor, Eerdmans Publishing Co.,
in Volume 2, starting on page B-85.

Since this matter will not be taken up in this workbook, simply
realize that some of the following examples will show slight variations from the endings given in the tables due to the connecting
vowels.

FORMING PRINCIPAL PARTS

If the verb follows regular patterns, your lexicon might not list the principal parts. Here is how they are constructed (basic concept):

Principal Part	Tense it Consists of	How it is Formed	Example with λυω
1.	Present	Stem + ending	λυω
2.	Future	Stem + σ + ending[1]	λυσω
3.	Aorist	Augment + stem + σ + ending	ελυσα
4.	Perfect	Reduplication[2] + aug. = stem + κ + ending	λελυκα
5.	Perfect passive	Red. + aug. + stem + ending	λελυμαι λελυμαι
6.	Aorist passive	Aug. + stem + θ[3] + ending	ελυθην

Footnotes:

1 When certain letters occur with σ, something happens. Sometimes this is common sense: If you take βλεπ, add σ and then the ending ω, you get βλεπσω. Obviously you can "save ink" by writing that πσ sound as ψ, and write βλεψω.

Here are some of the possibilities:

π, β, or φ + σ = ψ   κ, γ, or χ + σ = ξ

τ, δ, or θ simply disappear when σ is added.

Since your interest is in reading scriptures, your usual approach will be not to create a Greek word, but to work backward from a word you find in scripture and try to figure out its present tense form so you can look it up in a dictionary. For example, let's say you find a word, γραψω, but cannot find it in a dictionary. You surmise that the ψ might be there because an σ was added to a π, β, or φ to form a future tense. You try looking up γραπ, γραβ, and γραφ--and sure enough, you find there is a word γραφω.

When you come across the future of a verb whose stem ends in λ, ρ, μ, or ν, it will look something like present tense! The reason is that when these consonants interact with the σ used for future, they eliminate it. There is a change in accent, however. The first two principal parts of κρινω (judge) are κρίνω and κρινῶ.

2 Reduplication is formed either by:

(a) repeating the first letter of the stem in front of the augment. Example: since λυω starts with λ, we simply put another λ at the beginning.

(b) If the stem starts with certain sounds that we form in English by using "h" with a letter (ph, th, ch), the reduplication is the sound without the "h":

The reduplication of φ is π; θ becomes τ; χ becomes κ.

For example, the fourth principal part of φιλεω is πεφιληκατε.

3 Certain stem letters change before θ. If the stem ends in ζ, it is pretty hard to say ζθ, so the Greeks simply replaced that combination with an σ. Here are some of the possibilities:

κ or γ + θ = χ   π or β + θ = φ   ζ, τ, δ, or θ + θ = σ

Exercise One

The explanation above enables you to make the principal parts of some of the easier verbs.

Make the six parts of πιστευω (believe).
Now try πεμπω (send), referring to footnotes 1 and 3.
(Skip fourth and fifth parts, which are unusual.)

Exercise Two

VERBS IN SENTENCES

Generally you will not know the principal part of a verb before you look it up. The Word List on the next page contains only the present tense forms, which are the lexicon entries, so it is important to practice guessing at the present tense form when you see a word.

Instructions: Each sentence is preceded by two blanks. Find the verb in the sentence, and match it both to the Word List and to the list of Tenses.

καὶ αἱ χεῖρες ἡμῶν

____ ____ 1. That which we beheld, ____ ____ ____ ____ ____

ἐψηλάφησαν
_____ concerning ____ _____ ____ _____ ...
                                              1 John 1:1

τῆς πιστεως σώσει

____ ____ 2. The prayer of faith _____ the sick. James 5:15

                                                    καὶ

____ ____ 3. As the bridegroom was delayed, they all slumbered ____

ἐκάθευδον
_____. Matt. 25:5

263

____ ____ 4. We have fellowship ____ μετ' ἀλλήλων καὶ τὸ αἷμα ____

'Ιησοῦ τοῦ υἱοῦ αὐτοῦ καθαρίζει ἡμᾶς ἀπὸ
____ ____ ____ ____ ____ ____ ____ ____

πάσης ἁμαρτίας
____ ____ .   1 John 1:7

____ ____ 5. Courage, daughter, ἡ πίστις σου σέσωκέν σε
____ ____ ____ ____ ____ ____ .
Matt. 9:22

Word List   Tenses

A) σωζω   -- save   a) present

B) ψηλαφαω -- touch   b) future

C) καθαριζω -- cleanse   c) imperfect

D) καθευδω -- sleep   d) aorist

                         e) perfect

                         f) pluperfect

Exercise Three

SOME VARIETIES OF AORIST FORMS

Match the verb from the Bible verse with its present tense form from
the Word List and with the best description from the Word Forms List:

____ ____ 1. For no one ever ἐμίσησεν _____ his own flesh... Eph. 5:29

____ ____ 2. For God so ἠγάπησεν τὸν κόσμον _____ ___ _____. John 3:16

____ ____ 3. οὐχ ὅτι ἔλαβον ____ ____ already _____ or already have been made

complete. Phil. 3:12

____ ____ 4. πάντες γὰρ ἥμαρτον ____ ____ _____ and fall short of the glory of

God. Rom. 3:23

____ ____ 5. Then ἀπέλυσεν αὐτοῖς τὸν βαρραβᾶν _____ ___ ____ _____. Matt. 27:26

264

_____ _____ 6. As the father has sent me into the world, καγὼ _____ _____

ἀπέστειλα αὐτοὺς εἰς τὸν κόσμον

_____ _____ ____ ____ _____. John 17:18

Word List

A) αποστελλω -- send

B) απολυω   -- release

C) αγαπαω   -- love

D) αμαρτανω   -- sin

E) μισεω   -- hate

F) λαμβανω   -- take, obtain

Word Forms List

a) It has a prefix, so the ε (the augment) is found after the prefix rather than at the beginning of the word.

b) A "second aorist"--same meaning as any other aorist, but with no σ and using endings from column (b) on page 257. Also illustrates a letter removed from the stem of the present.

c) A word that started with a vowel, so adding the augment changed the vowel.

d) Second aorist, in a word with a prefix.

e) Second aorist, in a word that started with a vowel.

f) Ordinary aorist; regular augment at the beginning, with σ and endings from (c) on page 257.

Exercise Four

THREE VERY COMMON BUT UNUSUAL VERBS

You will see these often in the New Testament.

Learn by guessing:

Answer choices: a) he saw   c) said   e) we know

                  b) knows   d) we saw

_____ 1. He answered and ειπεν to them.

_____ 2. They answered and ειπαν to him.

_____ 3. Walking along the sea, εἶδεν two brothers. Matt. 4:18

_____ 4. Where is he born King of the Jews? εἴδομεν his star in the East... Matt. 2:2

The next word is aorist in form, but present in meaning (deponent):

____ 5. Your Father οἶδεν what you need before you ask. Matt. 6:8

____ 6. ...came to him by night and said, ραββί, οἴδαμεν you are a
teacher sent from God. John 3:2

COMMENTS

1. ειπον (I said) is a second aorist form; it is the third principal
part of λεγω. Not that one can form ειπον from λεγω, but rather,
the Greeks simply used a different word in order to express the
aorist of "speak". We do the same type of thing in English. Our
present tense words about "being" are: is, are; past tense words
are: was, were. These were originally from two different word
families. There is a present tense form of the "was" word
family, but it has fallen into disuse.

2. ειδον (I saw) is second aorist, the third principal part of οραω,
see.

3. οιδα has a different background. It is in perfect tense, but it
is translated as though it were present.

The subjunctive first person is ειδω (I would or should know).

The imperative second person is ισθι (Know ye).

The pluperfect forms are translated as though they were imperfect:
ηδειν translated "I was knowing".

Exercise Five

MIDDLES AND PASSIVES -- EXAMPLES

Match the verbs with their present tense forms from the Word List and
their tense and voice from the Word Uses List.

____ ____ 1. We are more than conquerors through him who loved us.

πέπεισμαι γάρ ὅτι οὔτε θάνατος οὔτε ζωή

_____ ____ ____ ____ _____ ____ ____...will

separate us from the love of God... Rom. 8:38

οὐ παύομαι

____ ____ 2. (Since I heard of your faith and love) ___ _____

ὑπέρ ὑμῶν

giving thanks ____ ____   Eph. 1:16

266

ἐν ἑαυτῇ

____ ____ 3. She said to herself, if only I touch his garment

σωθήσομαι

_____ . Matt. 9:21

ἐσώθη ἀπὸ τῆς ὥρας ἐκείνης

____ ____ 4. ...and the woman ____ ____ ____ ____ .

Matt. 9:22

πρὸς τὸν πατέρα

____ ____ 5. I bow my knee ____ ____ ____ from whom every

ὀνομάζεται

fatherhood _____ . Eph. 3:14-15

Word List

A) ονομαζω -- name

cognate to English
onomatopeia (words
that imitate natural
sounds.

B) πειθω -- persuade

C) παυω -- cease

D) σωζω -- save

Word Uses List

a) present middle

b) present passive

c) future passive

d) aorist passive

e) perfect passive

DEPONENT VERBS

By this term, lexicon entries will point out that certain verbs receive
middle or passive endings but are translated as though they were active.
A give-away is that the lexicon entry itself will show the verb with a
passive ending:

μαρτυρομαι

These things therefore I say and _____ in the Lord... Eph. 4:17

θεαομαι = behold (related word θεατρον, cognate to English theater.

This one could also be explained as a "middle" form, since you
see "for yourself." The point is it is called "deponent"
because its lexicon entry is not in "active" form.

EXAMPLE (in imperfect tense):

That which was from the beginning, which we have heard, which our eyes

ἐθεασάμεθα

have seen, which we have _____ and our hands have touched....

1 John 1:6

ψευδομαι = lie

ἐὰν   ἔχομεν   μετ᾽ αὐτοῦ
____ we say _____ fellowship ____ _____ and walk in the darkness,

ψευδόμεθα
__ _____ and do not do the truth.   1 John 1:6

Here is the same verb in another tense. The form is middle, the translation is active:

                                    οὐκ ἐψεύσω ἀνθρώποις ἀλλὰ
Why did you plan this in your heart? ____ _____ __ _____ _____

τῷ θεῷ
__ ___   Acts. 5:4

Some verbs are deponent in one tense, but not in another.

Exercise One

VERB EXAMPLES: MIXED TENSES AND VOICES.

Match the verbs from these sentences with their present tense form
from the Word List and its tense and voice from the Form List:

____ ____ 1. You did not so learn Christ, εἴ γε αὐτὸν ἠκούσατε ___ _____ _____

and in him were taught. Eph. 4:21

____ ____ 2. When he'd received the vinegar ὁ Ἰησοῦς εἶπεν _____ ____

Τετέλεσται

_____. John 19:30

____ ____ 3. Knowing that οὐ δικαιοῦται ἄνθρωπος ἐξ ἔργων

νόμου

__ _____ but through faith... Gal. 2:16

____ ____ 4. Then the righteous ἀποκριθήσονται αὐτῷ saying, Lord,

when did we see you hungry? Matt. 25:37

____ ____ 5. Ἐπίστευσεν δὲ Ἀβραὰμ τῷ θεῷ, καὶ ἐλογίσθη αὐτῷ

εἰς δικαιοσύνη

_____. Rom. 4:3

____ ____ 6. Having heard the king, ἐπορεύθησαν and the star went

before them. Matt. 2:9

____ ____ 7. If they don't hear Moses and the prophets, not ἐάν ___

τις should rise ἐκ νεκρῶν πεισθήσονται ___ ___ _____. Luke 16:31

____ ____ 8. (He'll be born) ἐν βηθλεὲμ τῆς Ἰουδαίας οὕτως

γὰρ γέγραπται

__ _____ by the prophet. Matt. 2:5

___ ___ 9. ...did not deem it robbery to be equal with God, _____ ἀλλὰ

ἑαυτὸν ἐκένωσεν

_____ _____, taking the form of a servant.

Phil. 2:7

___ ___ 10. That which was from the beginning, __ _____ __ ὃ ἀκηκόαμεν, ὃ

ἑωράκαμεν τοῖς ὀφθαλμοῖς ἡμῶν

___ ___ _____ __ _____ __ __. 1 John 1:1

___ ___ 11. No man can serve two masters; the one _____ and the μισήσει

___ ___ other _____. Luke 16:13 ἀγαπήσει

___ ___ 12. Beware of _____ which _____ ____ ____ ψευδοπροφητῶν ἔρχονται πρὸς ὑμᾶς

in sheep's clothing. Matt. 7:15

___ ___ 13. Ye are not your own _____ ____ therefore ἠγοράσθητε τιμῆς

glorify God... 1 Cor. 6:20

___ ___ 14. He who endures to the end _____. Matt. 24:13 σωθήσεται

Word List

A) αποκρινομαι = answer
B) σωζω = save
C) μισεω = hate
D) αγαπαω = love
E) πειθω = persuade
F) πιστευω = believe
G) λογιζω = reckon
H) αγοραζω = buy
I) ακουω = hear
J) κενοω = deprive of power, empty; source of theological term "kenosis", Christ's emptying of power as he became man.

K) οραω = see
L) γραφω = write
M) τελεω = finish
N) δικαιοω = make right
O) πορευομαι = go
P) ερχομαι = come

Forms

a) present, deponent
b) present, passive
c) future
d) future, deponent
e) future, passive
f) aorist
g) aorist, deponent
h) aorist, passive
i) perfect

Exercise Two

INFINITIVES

You have learned the ending ειν. λεγειν = to speak. Another infinitive ending is αι. The following chart shows examples of infinitive endings added to principal parts:

A List of Infinitives of the verb λυω:

		Active	Middle	Passive
Present	=	λυειν	λυεσθαι	λυεσθαι
Future	=	λυσειν	λυσεσθαι	λυθησεσθαι
Aorist	=	λυσαι	λυσασθαι	λυθηναι
Perfect	=	λελυκεναι	λελυσθαι	λελυσθαι

MATCHING

____ 1. λελυσθαι   a) to have loosed

____ 2. λελυκεναι   b) to be about to loose

____ 3. λυσαι   c) to be loosing one's self

____ 4. λυθησεσθαι   d) to have been loosed

____ 5. λυσειν   e) to be being loosed

____ 6. λυεσθαι   f) to be about to be loosed

                                     g) to loose

An example of the passive infinitive (based on δικαιοω: make right):

                    δικαιοῦσθαι

For we reckon man _____ by faith without deeds of the law.

                                                Rom. 3:28

Translation: "To have been made right."

The infinitive can be used as a noun; in such cases the word for "the" can be placed in front of it, as in το ποιειν. "The to-make" (from the phrase "το ποιειν") is obviously not smooth English; your paraphrase might end up something like, "the act of making" or "the making process".

EXAMPLE

For God is the one working in you, both (in regards to)

τὸ θέλειν καὶ τὸ ἐνεργεῖν

_____ _____ ___ ___ _____ for His good pleasure. Phil. 2:13

Since the infinitive has past and future forms, as well as present, it can express when something takes place, compared to when the main action of the sentence takes place. Prepositions may be added to make these relationships even more clear. The following list is excerpted from NEW TESTAMENT GREEK MADE FUNCTIONAL, © 1972 by Fred Nofer; Pages 132-133. Used by permission.

Preposition and "the" Placed Before Infinitive	Possible English Translation
μετα το	after
εν το	as or while
πριν or προ + "the"	before

Other relationships that can be shown:

εις το	in order to (shows purpose)
ωστε	so that (shows result)
δια το	because (shows cause)

Exercise Three

INFINITIVE EXAMPLES

You are not expected to understand why the stem changes developed, but only to recognize the words as infinitives. Try to match them to the chart. (Forms List and Word List on p.273.) You will see it is not always obvious to English speakers why the writers chose the tense they did. Remember that present is usually chosen for "continuation", aorist for speaking of an event without regard to time, and perfect for an event with a definite start and repercussions in the future.

Start by trying to work the word "to" into your translation; after you have said it somewhat literally, you can paraphrase into more acceptable English if needed:

σῶσαι
____ ____ 1. Christ came into the world ____ ____ sinners.
1 Tim. 1:15

κραταιωθῆναι
____ ____ 2. That he may give you the ability _____ through

κατοικῆσαι τὸν Χριστὸν
____ ____ 2b. his spirit in your inner man, _____ _____

διὰ τῆς πίστεως ἐν ταῖς καρδίαις ὑμῶν

____ _____ __ ____ ____
Eph. 3:17

___ ___ 3. Unless you remain on the ship, you will not be able

σωθῆναι

___ __ _____. Acts 27:31

ἀνανεοῦσθαι

___ ___ 4. Put off the old man corrupted by deceit, _____

in the spirit of your mind. Eph. 4:23

περιπατῆσαι

___ ___ 5. I beseech you worthily _____ of the calling with

which you are called.   Eph. 4:1

Examples with the word "the" before the infinitive:

θεὸς γάρ ἐστιν ὁ ἐνεργῶν   ἐν ὑμῖν καὶ

___ ___ 6. ____ ____ _____ the working-one ___ ___ _____

τὸ θέλειν καὶ τὸ ἐνεργεῖν ὑπὲρ

___ ___ _____ _____ _____ ____ his good pleasure.
                                              Phil. 2:13

___ ___ 7. The eyes of your heart being enlightened

εἰς τὸ εἰδέναι ὑμᾶς

_____ _____ what is the hope of his calling.
                                              Eph. 1:18

Word List

a) περιπατεω = walk
b) οιδα   = know; the form
        used is based on ειδω
c) ανανεοω   = transform
        (see the word νεο in it?)
d) κραταιοω   = strengthen
e) σωζω   = save
f) κατοικεω   = dwell within
g) ενεργεω   = work, do
h) θελω   = will, want

Forms List

A) Present
B) Present Passive
C) Aorist
D) Aorist Passive
E) Perfect

FORMING THE IMPERATIVE

I. INSTRUCTIONS

This is the way the endings work out with the word λυω. There will be vowel changes with other verbs.

TO FORM:	VOICE	USE: PRIN. PART	PLUS ENDING	PRIN. PART IS	SECOND PERSON	EXAMPLE (a command to you)
PRESENT continuity	Active	1	g	λυω	λυε	loosen!
	Middle	1	g	λυω	λυου	loose yourself!
	Passive	1	g	λυω	λυου	be loosened!
AORIST simple event	Active	3	h	ελυσα	λυσον	The English
	Middle	3	h	ελυσα	λυσαι	language does
	Passive	6	j	ελυθην	λυθη	not have simple
						equivalents for
PERFECT effect continues	Active	4	i	λελυκα	λελυκε	these; translate
	Middle	5	i	λελυμαι	λελυσο	the same as you
	Passive	5	i	λελυμαι	λελυσο	would for present.

II. ENDINGS TO USE

Only four endings are needed in each category, since there are no first person forms. Note that the augment is removed from the aorist.

	PERSON		(g)	(h)	(i)	(j)
ACTIVE	Singular	2	ε	ον	ε	
		3	ετω	ατω	ετω	
	Plural	2	ετε	ατε	ετε	
		3	ωσαν	ωσαν	ωσαν	
MIDDLE & PASSIVE	Singular	2	ου	αι	σο	ητι
		3	εσθω	ασθω	σθω	ητω
	Plural	2	εσθε	ασθε	σθε	ητε
		3	εσθωσαν	ασθωσαν	σθωσαν	ητωσαν

A scripture example: λυπεω = grieve

and μὴ λυπεῖτε the Holy Spirit... Eph. 4:30   (second person plural)
    Note vowel change. According to the vowel change chart on page 261,
    ε + ε = ει

Exercise One

IMPERATIVE EXAMPLES

Match the Greek verb from each sentence with its present tense from
the Word List and its tense and voice from the Form List:

                          μαθητεύσατε πάντα τὰ ἔθνη
____ ____ 1. Going, therefore, _____ _____   _____ bap-

           tizing them in the name of...   Matt. 28:19

                     μνημονεύετε ὅτι
____ ____ 2. Wherefore _____ ____ you were then without

           Christ. Eph. 2:11

____ ____ 3. Don't fear when people harm you for doing right, rather
                ἁγιάσατε
               _____ Christ in your hearts. 1 Pet. 3:15

                                    ἁγιασθήτω
____ ____ 4. Our Father who art in heaven, _____ thy name.
                                                      Matt. 6:9

                     ἀρθήτω
____ ____ 5. All bitterness..._____ from you... Eph. 4:31
           ὁ ἄγγελος   Μη φοβεῖσθε
____ ____ 6. _____ said to the women, _____!
                                                      Matt. 28:5

Word List

A) αιρω   = remove
B) ἁγιαζω   = related to ἁγιος--make holy, sanctify, regard with reverence
C) μνημονευω = remember, cognate to English Mnemonics (a system of
                 memorizing) and the anamneses, the remembering part
                 of a communion prayer

Continued next page

Word List continued			Forms List

Word List continued | Forms List

D) μαθητευω = related to μαθητης
"instruct, disciple"

E) φοβεω = fear

a) present active

b) aorist active (aorist used for emphasis)

c) aorist passive

d) present middle

AN EXAMPLE OF A PASSIVE IMPERATIVE

This example also demonstrates the idea of the present tense as giving the idea of continuous action.

πληροῦσθε

Do not be drunk with wine...but _____ with the Spirit. Eph. 5:18

The dictionary entry is πληροω, "fill". Since the form is passive, that means it is not something you do, but something that someone else does to you. However, since it is imperative (command), that means you must have the ability to either allow or prohibit the process from happening—you are commanded to let it happen. And since it is present, it suggests the idea of a continuous process, as a way of life. The passage could be translated, "And be ye continually being filled..."

While on the subject of imperatives, I would like to mention something else about nouns. There is an ending we haven't talked about yet, used when you are talking directly to someone. It is called the vocative case. It often ends with the letter ε: If talking to Paul, you would call him Παυλε. In other instances, the vowel of the nominative is changed: Jesus addressed the Father in John 17:25 as πατὲρ δίκαιε (righteous father).

κύριε σῶσον

The disciples woke him saying, _____ _____ or we perish. Matt. 8:25

FORMING THE SUBJUNCTIVE

Remember that the endings may differ as they interact with the vowels in a particular verb-stem. These endings will fit with the word λυω. Remove the augment from the aorist indicative.

PERSON		(k)	(1)
Singular	1	ω	ωμαι
	2	ης	η
	3	η	ηται
Plural	1	ωμεν	ωμεθα
	2	ητε	ησθε
	3	ωσι	ωνται

		USE: PRIN. PART	PLUS ENDING	PRIN. PART IS	EXAMPLE WITH λυω THIRD PERSON SINGULAR	
TO FORM	VOICE					WHICH MEANS
PRESENT	Active	1	k	λυω	λυη	he might loosen
	Middle	1	1	λυω	λυηται	he might loosen himself
	Passive	1	1	λυω	λυηται	he might be loosened
AORIST	Active	3	k	ελυσα	λυσῃ	he might have loosened
	Middle	3	1	ελυσα	λυσηται	he might have loosened himself
	Passive	6	k	ελυθην	λυθη	he might have been loosened
PERFECT	Active	4	k	λελυκα	λελυκη	he might have loosened
	Middle	5	*	λελυμαι	λελυμενος η	he might have loosened himself
	Passive	5	*	λελυμαι	λελυμενος η	he might have been loosened

---

* This form is expressed with two words: the participle (in this case λελυμενος) plus the ending from column (k) as a separate word.

A Scripture Example: πληροω = fill

"...in order that _____ all things." Eph. 4:10
(above blank: πληρώσῃ)

    It is aorist, which indicates a one-time filling. (The idea of past-ness is not necessarily implied in any but the indicative mood forms.)

OPTATIVE

Because it is seldom used, a chart will not be given. Many of the forms stand out because of οι or αι as the connecting vowels between stem and ending, as in this example:

Μὴ γένοιτο   "may it never be." Rom. 6:2

Here is an optative based on the word "give". Translate as "would give":

ἵνα ὁ θεὸς ... δῷη ὑμῖν πνεῦμα σοφίας... Eph. 1:17

Exercise Two

PRACTICE WITH SUBJUNCTIVE ENDINGS

Match the correct Greek verb with each of these English sentences:

____ 1. You might have loosened yourself.
     (completed action)

____ 2. He might have been loosened.
     (simple action)

____ 3. We might loosen.

____ 4. They might have loosened themselves.
     (simple action)

____ 5. I might have been loosened.
     (completed action)

____ 6. You might be loosened.
     (or, might be being loosened).

____ 7. We might have loosened ourselves.
     (simple action)

____ 8. They might have loosened.
     (completed action)

a) λυωμεθα

b) λυσωνται

c) λελυμενος ῃς

d) λελυκωσι

e) λελυμενος ῳ

f) λυθῃ

g) λυῃ

h) λυωμεν

Exercise Three

SUBJUNCTIVE EXAMPLES

Translate using words like might, may, should:

_____ _____ 1. My children, ταῦτα γράφω ὑμῖν ἵνα μὴ ἁμάρτητε
_____ _____ _____ _____ _____ _____ _____.
1 John 2:1

_____ _____ 2. Who gave himself for us ἵνα λυτρώσηται ἡμᾶς
_____ _____ _____ from

_____ _____ lawlessness and καθαρίσῃ ἑαυτῷ
_____ _____ _____ a people for his own

possession. Titus 2:14

_____ _____ 3. What we have heard and seen we announce to you ἵνα
_____

καὶ ἔχητε μεθ᾽ ἡμῶν
_____ you fellowship _____ _____ _____ 1 John 1:3

Ἐὰν εἴπωμεν ὅτι ἁμαρτίαν οὐκ ἔχομεν
_____ _____ 4. _____ _____ _____ _____ _____ _____ we deceive

ourselves and the truth is not in us. 1 John 1:8

_____ _____ 5. We have believed in Jesus ἵνα δικαιωθῶμεν ἐκ
_____ _____

πίστεως Χριστοῦ καὶ οὐκ ἐξ ἔργων νόμου
Gal. 2:16
_____ _____ _____ _____ _____ _____ _____

_____ _____ 6. ...that whosoever believes in him μὴ ἀπόληται ἀλλ᾽
_____ _____ _____

ἔχῃ ζωὴν αἰώνιον
_____ _____ _____ _____ _____. John 3:16

The little word αν is sometimes used in connection with statements that
are "iffy." You don't necessarily have to translate the word itself,
but make sure the character of the entire sentence is affected by it.

εἴπῃ
_____ _____ 7. And whoever _____ against the son of man, it will be

ὃς δ᾽ ἂν εἴπῃ
forgiven him; _____ _____ _____ against the Spirit, it

will not be forgiven. Matt. 12:32

Continued next page

_____ _____ 8. Whoever _____ _____ _____ his life shall lose it.

θέλῃ σῶσαι

Matt. 16:25

_____ _____ 9. To all people I have become _____ _____ _____

πάντα, ἵνα πάντως

_____ _____. 1 Cor. 9:22

τινὰς σώσω

_____ _____ 10. _____ _____ _____ _____ and my words remain in you,

Ἐὰν μείνητε ἐν ἐμοὶ

_____ _____ ask whatever _____ and it shall be done for you.

θέλητε

John 15:7

Word List

A) ειπον = say
B) εχω = have
C) δικαιοω = make right
D) απολλυμι = perish
E) ἁμαρτανω = sin
F) μενω = remain
G) σωζω = save
H) θελω = want
I) λυτροω = release
J) καθαριζω = cleanse

a) Present; therefore stress on the continuing action of the verb.

b) Aorist, illustrating that in the subjunctive mood aorist does not indicate past, but a simple reference to an event.

c) Second aorist. If it were a present, more of the present stem would remain.

d) Aorist middle. Looks like a passive ending, but no sense of passive in the meaning of the sentence.

e) The θ is a give-away that it is aorist passive.

ANOTHER TYPE OF VERB

There is a completely different set of endings for a group of verbs called μι - verbs. Some of these verbs are unusual in that they have reduplication in the present tense, as well as in the perfect tense.

EXAMPLE: The word for "give" has the stem δο.

Placing the reduplication at the front makes it into διδο.

The endings are:

PERSON	SINGULAR	PLURAL
1	μι	μεν
2	ς	τι
3	σι	ασι

Adding the endings, with allowance for interaction of connecting vowels:

1	διδωμι	διδομεν
2	διδως	διδοτε
3	διδωσι	διδοασι

Other common μι-verbs are

τιθημι = put

αφιημι = let go (this is the usual word for "forgive")

ιστημι = cause to stand

Exercise One

Can you match these despite variations in connecting vowels?
(Watch out for a final ν added to one example.)

____ 1. διδωσι   a) they forgive

____ 2. ισταμεν   b) you cause to stand

____ 3. αφιεισι   c) he gives

____ 4. τιθεμεν   d) we place

____ 5. τιθησιν   e) you forgive

____ 6. ιστης   f) we cause to stand

____ 7. διδασι   g) she places

____ 8. αφιης   h) they give

Principal parts of διδωμι are (Note some do not have reduplication):

διδωμι   δωσω   εδωκα   δεδωκα*   διδομαι   εδοθην

This chart is a selection of some μι-verb endings, using διδωμι as an example:

Tense	Voice	Mood	Principal Part To Use	Reduplication?	Augment?	Ending From Column	Example
PRESENT	ACT	IND	1	yes	no	above	διδωμι
PRESENT	ACT	IMPER	1	yes	no	o	διδου
PRESENT	ACT	SUBJ	1	yes	no	p	διδω
PRESENT	PASS	IND	1	yes	no	d	διδομαι
PRESENT	PASS	IMPER	1	yes	no	r	διδοσο
PRESENT	PASS	SUBJ	1	yes	no	l	διδωμαι
IMPERFECT	ACT	IND	1	yes	yes	n	εδιδουν
IMPERFECT	PASS	IND	1	yes	yes	b	εδιδομην
AORIST	ACT	IND	3	no	yes	d	εδωκα
AORIST	MID	IND	3	no	yes	b	εδομην
AORIST	PASS	IND	6	no	yes	e	εδοθην
SECOND AORIST	ACT	IND	stem	no	yes	n	εδων
SECOND AORIST	ACT	IMPER	stem	no	yes	s	δος
SECOND AORIST	ACT	SUBJ	stem	no	yes	p	δω

Some infinitives:

    present -- διδοναι "to be giving" (continuous)
    aorist -- δουναι "to give"   (simple statement)

* Note that κ is used instead of σ.

NEW COLUMNS OF ENDINGS

VOICE	PERSON		(n)	(o)	(p)	(s)
ACTIVE	Singular	1	ων		ω	
		2	ως	ου or θι	ως	ς
		3	ω	οτω	ω	τω
	Plural	1	ομεν		ωμεν	
		2	οτε	οτε	ωτε	τε
		3	οσαν	οτωσαν	ωσι	τωσαν

VOICE	PERSON		(d)	(r)	(l)
MIDDLE & PASSIVE	Singular	1	μαι		ωμαι
		2	σαι	σω	η͜ι
		3	ται	σθω	ηται
	Plural	1	μεθα		ωμεθα
		2	σθε	σθε	ησθε
		3	νται	σθωσαν	ωνται

EXAMPLES WITH μι-VERBS

If you being evil know how ___ _____ διδόναι good gifts...   Matt. 7:11

(from the Lord's Prayer) ____ δός us this day our daily bread.
                                              Matt. 6:11

God so loved the world that _____ ἔδωκεν his only son...   John 3:16

Ἐμοὶ ___ ____, the least ___ ___ ___ _____ πάντων ἁγίων ἐδόθη ἡ χάρις αὕτη _____ _____... Eph. 3:8

Son of man came to serve and ___ ___ _____ _____ δοῦναι τὴν ψυχὴν αὐτοῦ as a ransom for

many.   Matt. 20:28

The following examples use the word ἀφιημι, "let go". Expect some vowel changes.

I came from the father and come ____ ____ _____ again __ _____ ____
εἰς τὸν κόσμον ἀφίημι τὸν

κόσμον
_____ and go to the father.   John 16:28

AORISTS:

Jesus, crying with a ____ _____ _____ ___ _____.   Matt. 27:50
φωνῇ μεγάλῃ, ἀφῆκεν τὸ πνεῦμα

He is _____ ____ _____ ____ _____ our sins.   1 John 1:9
πιστὸς καὶ δίκαιος ἵνα ἀφῇ
      (column (p) with a different vowel)

(from the Lord's Prayer) ____ _____ us our debts, as we _____ our
καὶ ἀφες ἀφήκαμεν

debtors.   Matt. 6:12
      (column (s) with a connecting vowel. p. 283)

ALL THE FORMS OF "TO BE", "I AM", ETC.

PRESENT	INDICA-TIVE	IMPERA-TIVE	SUBJUNC-TIVE	OPTA-TIVE	INFINI-TIVE
	I am, etc.	Be!	That I might be	That I would be	"to be"
I am	εἰμί		ὦ	εἴην	εἶναι
you are	εἶς or εἰ	ἴσθι	ἧς	εἴης	
he is	ἐστί	ἔστω	ἦ	εἴη	
we are	ἐσμέν		ὦμεν	εἴημεν	
ye are	ἐστέ	ἔστε	ἦτε	εἴητε	
they are	εἰσί	ἔστωσαν	ὦσι	εἴησαν or εἶεν	

Continued on next page.

FUTURE	INDICATIVE	OPTATIVE	INFINITIVE
	I will be	That I may be about to be	about to be
I will be	ἔσομαι	ἐσοίμην	
you will be	ἔσῃ	ἔσοιο	ἔσεσθαι
he will be	ἔσται	ἔσοιτο	
we will be	ἐσόμεθα	ἐσοίμεθα	
ye will be	ἔσεσθε	ἔσοισθε	
they will be	ἔσονται	ἔσοιντο	

IMPERFECT	INDICATIVE ONLY		
I was	ἤμην or		ἦν
you were	ἦσθα		
he was	ἦν		
we were	ἤμεθα or		ἦμεν
ye were	ἦτε		
they were	ἦσαν		

Differentiate these forms from the feminine forms of "the" by the fact that the word "the" does not have an accent mark; only the "breathing" mark.

NO PERFECT, AORIST, OR PLUPERFECT

Exercise Two

MATCHING WITH MEANINGS OF "TO BE"

____ 1. εστε   a) you will be

____ 2. εστωσαν   b) you were

____ 3. ειην   c) we might be

____ 4. εσῃ   d) they are to be!

____ 5. εσοιο   e) about to be

____ 6. ἦς   f) ye are

____ 7. ισθι   g) ye would be

____ 8. ὦμεν   h) you are to be!

____ 9. ειητε   i) I would be

____ 10. εσεσθαι   j) you may be about to be

Exercise Three

EXAMPLES OF "TO BE" IN VARIOUS TENSES

Match the tenses below to these two possibilities:

a) present subjunctive   b) imperfect

            Ἐν ἀρχῇ ἦν ὁ λόγος

____ 1.   ___ _____ ___ __ _____   John 1:1

                             ὦμεν

____ 2.   In order that no longer ____ infants, tossed to and fro...
                                            Eph. 4:14

            καὶ ταῦτά τινες ἦτε

____ 3.   ___ _____ ___ ___ _____ but you were washed... 1 Cor. 6:11

                     ἵνα ὦσιν

____ 4.   I sanctify myself, ____ ____ sanctified in truth. John 17:19

                                      καὶ ἤμεθα

____ 5.   Doing the will of the flesh and understanding, ____ _____

                τέκνα

         by nature _____ of wrath.   Eph. 2:3

           καὶ ταῦτα γράφομεν ἡμεῖς ἵνα   ᾖ

____ 6.   ___ _____ _____ _____ ___ our joy ____ full.
                                                    1 John 1:4

A VERY COMMON DEPONENT VERB

that means about the same as "is":   (Matching possibilities found
                                       on next page)

γίνομαι = become, am

                 ἐγένετο

____ 7.   And _____ in those days... Luke 2:1

                     γίνεται

____ 8.   After two days _____ the passover...   Matt. 26:2

          Γίνεσθε

____ 9.   _____ therefore imitators of God... Eph. 5:1

          τοῖς πᾶσιν γέγονα πάντα, ἵνα πάντως τινὰς σώσω

____ 10.   ___ _____ _____ _____ __ _____ _____ _____
                                         1 Cor. 9:22

_____ 11.   Ἐὰν μείνητε ἐν ἐμοὶ καὶ τὰ ῥήματά μου ἐν ὑμῖν
      _____   _____ _____ _____   _____ _____ _____ _____

μείνῃ,   θέλητε καὶ γενήσεται ὑμῖν
_____   ask whatever   _____ _____ _____ _____ _____ _____ .

                                      John 15:7

Match examples 7 through 11 to:

c)   present

d)   imperative

e)   aorist (it's second aorist: there is an augment, but no σ.)

f)   perfect. It is a second perfect because while there is redupli-
     cation, there is no letter κ.

g)   future

PARTICIPLES

So far you have learned the ending ων, as in λεγων, "saying". There are many more endings used to make participles.

1. Participles are made from the principal parts of verbs.

2. Like verbs, they appear in various tenses (present, perfect, etc.) and voices (active, passive, etc.). They do not appear in Imperfect and Pluperfect.

3. The participle receives endings from the noun chart to indicate whether it is nominative, genitive, etc., and whether it is singular or plural. The ων ending you have used happens to be nominative, and you have seen it used when it happens to be the subject of the sentence, or to describe the subject.

    λυων
The man loosening the ropes is my friend.

If the word which the participle is describing is plural, the participle uses one of the plural endings from the chart of noun endings in Part II (p. 98). In our example, the ending will be from the third column (third declension) and will be from the fifth row (Nominative plural, p. 126):

    λυοντες
The men loosening the ropes were my friends.

If the word which the participle is describing is not the subject of the sentence but has some other function, the participle ending will again change, using the appropriate ending from column three of the noun chart.

Exercise One

MATCHING   (refer to noun-ending chart in Part II--p.126, column III)

____ 1. I sold the slave loosening the ropes to a new master.

____ 2. I have the lunch of the man loosening the ropes.

____ 3. I spoke to the man loosening the ropes.

____ 4. I spoke to the men loosening the ropes.

a) λυουσι
(dative singular)

b) λυοντα
(accusative singular)

c) λυουσι
(dative plural)

d) λυοντος
(genitive singular)

CHART OF PARTICIPLE ENDINGS

The masculine and neuter endings are from third declension, the feminine from first:

SINGULAR:	Masculine	Feminine	Neuter
Nominative	ων	ουσα	ον
Genitive	οντος	ουσης	οντος
Dative	οντι	ουση	οντι
Accusative	οντα	ουσαν	ον

PLURAL:			
Nominative	οντες	ουσαι	οντα
Genitive	οντων	ουσων	οντων
Dative	ουσι	ουσαις	ουσι
Accusative	οντας	ουσας	οντα

(The endings above are also the exact forms of the present participle of ειμι, "I am", so they can all be translated "being".)

Exercise Two

CONSTRUCTING THE PARTICIPLES BASED ON THE WORD λυω, "LOOSEN"

Fill in the blanks.

Present stem is λυ. Adding singular masculine endings, the result is:

_____ 1. Nominative

_____ 2. Genitive

_____ 3. Dative

                     etc. (The approach given continues through the Accusative and the plurals.)

For singular feminine, the result is:

_____ 4. Nominative

_____ 5. Genitive

_____ 6. Dative

                     etc.

Examples 1 through 6 would be translated "loosing" (or "loosening").

To make future; the stem (from the second principal part) is λυσ.

Singular masculine:

_____ 7. Nominative

_____ 8. Genitive

_____ 9. Dative

etc.

There is no single word in English that can be used to translate a Greek future participle. One way to express the thought is to use the phrase "about to": λυσων = about to loosen.

In Greek, participles are not formed in the imperfect tense.

Exercise Three

PRESENT TENSE EXAMPLES

The following sentences make use of four different verbs (use the endings just as they are): "be", "loose", "believe", and "speak".

To work these out, first write the stem of the underlined word. Then decide if it is masculine, feminine, or neuter, singular or plural, and go to the corresponding column of the endings-chart. Then decide if it is subject, genitive, dative, etc., and select the ending from the correct row. All these are in present tense.

_____ 1. This is the house of the man loosening that screw.

_____ 2. I wrote a letter to the girls being at college.

_____ 3. I spoke to the men, believing they were the winners.

_____ 4. The car, being by the hydrant, received a ticket.

_____ 5. I appreciate the words of the man speaking to us now.

_____ 6. I sent roses to her, the girl believing I had overlooked her birthday.

_____ 7. I removed the doorknob of the door, the one being open.

_____ 8. The men loosing the rope fell overboard.

a) λεγοντος

b) λυοντες

c) λυοντος

d) ον

e) ουσαις

f) οντος

g) πιστευοντων

h) πιστευουση

Exercise Four

TO FORM AORIST

    1) use the third principal part as listed on page 253, but remove the augment.
       ελυσα less ε = λυσα; stem then is λυσ

    2) use the endings from page 289, but use the letter α instead of the connecting vowels used on the chart. For example, write οντα as αντα; write ουσαν as ασαν.

    3) Change the masculine nominative singular ending from ν to ς .

Masculine: _____ 1. Nominative

           _____ 2. Genitive

           _____ 3. Dative

                                  etc.

Feminine: _____ 4. Nominative

           _____ 5. Genitive

           _____ 6. Dative

                                  etc.

TO FORM PERFECT

    1) do not use the letter ν. (Write οντος as οτος.)

    2) use ς instead of ν in masculine nominative singular. Otherwise, use the endings as they are.

    3) use fourth principal part (λελυκ-).

Masculine: _____ 7. Nominative

           _____ 8. Genitive

           _____ 9. Dative

                                  etc.

For feminine, use υι as the connector, and take the endings not from the participle chart but from the noun chart in Part II, first declension.

Feminine: _____ 10. Nominative

           _____ 11. Genitive

           _____ 12. Dative

                                  etc.

Both the aorist and perfect participles are translated "having loosed". The difference in shade of meaning does not appear in English; you are to keep in mind that perfect refers to completed actions with continuing results, while aorist is a simple statement.

Exercise Five

MATCHING

____ 1. The girls <u>having loosed</u> each
others hair went to bed. (completed)

____ 2. I spoke to the man <u>about to</u>
<u>loose</u> the rope.

____ 3. I spoke to the man <u>having loosed</u>
his grip for a moment. (simple)

____ 4. I have the address of the girl who
<u>loosed</u> the dog. (completed)

a) λυσοντι

b) λελυκυιας

c) λυσαντι

d) λελυκυιαι

Exercise One

FORMING PASSIVE PARTICIPLES

To make aorist passive, the connecting vowel is ε or ει, and the nominative ending is εις. To form examples which mean "was loosened", use the sixth principal part of λυω, ελυθην. stem: λυθ.
Use the chart on page 289.

Aorist Passive
Masculine:

_____ 1. Nominative

_____ 2. Genitive

_____ 3. Dative

etc.

For the other passive, and the middle forms: take the ending off the indicative form, add a connecting vowel and the syllable μεν, and endings from this pattern:

SINGULAR:	Masculine	Feminine	Neuter
Nominative	ος	η	ον
Genitive	ου	ης	ου

...and so on, using second declension for masculine and neuter and first declension for feminine, as shown on the chart from page 126.

Present Passive
Masculine:

_____ 4. Nominative

_____ 5. Genitive

_____ 6. Dative

etc.

Feminine:

_____ 7. Nominative

_____ 8. Genitive

_____ 9. Dative

etc.

Present passive would be translated "being loosed".
Aorist and perfect passive would be translated "having been loosed".
The middle voices would be translated "loosing one's self", etc.

Exercise Two

PARTICIPLES IN VARIOUS TENSES, VOICES, "CASES" & GENDERS

Match the Greek participles from the Word List below with their
English equivalent.

_____ 1. I wrote to the ones <u>about to be
believing</u>.

_____ 2. I helped the girl <u>being spoken
to</u>.

_____ 3. The bone, <u>having been</u> in the
dog's mouth, was crushed.

_____ 4. The dentist inspected the status
of the teeth <u>having been loosened</u>.

_____ 5. I spoke to the girls (the ones
<u>having been</u> in Europe).

_____ 6. I fired him (the man <u>having been
written</u> on the report).

_____ 7. I spoke to my wife, <u>having been
loosed</u> from her chores.

_____ 8. This is the gathering of them,
the ones <u>having believed</u> in God.

Word List

a) ον

b) γραφεντα

c) πιστευσαντων

d) πιστευσουσι

e) ουσαις

f) λεγομενην

g) λυθειση

h) λυθεντας

Obviously, the sentences above are not written in usual English style.
We would rephrase them in translating:

1. I wrote to the ones who would believe.

2. I helped the girl who was being addressed.

3. The bone which had been in the dog's mouth was crushed.

etc.

This is the kind of rephrasing you will do when you translate a Greek
participle into acceptable English.

HERE ARE SOME OF THE PARTICIPLE USES YOU WILL SEE IN THE UPCOMING
SCRIPTURE EXAMPLES

1. When the participle is used as an adjective, it has to match the
    ending on the noun it is describing. If I want to say "of the
    living God", I take the verb for live (ζω). With nominative end-
    ing it would be ζων, which I could use with the subject of a
    sentence. With the genitive ending, (see p. 284) it would be ζοντος,
    so ζοντος θεου would be "of living God". Adding the word for "the" =
    ζοντος θεου, "of the living God".

    The participle, like an adjective, can be placed after the noun,
    with each word having its own word "the":

    του θεου του ζοντος = of the living God.

    τω ζοντι θεω or τω θεω τω ζοντι = to the living God

2. When there is no noun provided, then the participle acts as a
    noun, and I add the word "one" or "thing" as I translate.

    ὁ ζων   =   the living one

    του ζοντος   =   of the living one

    τοις ζουσι   =   to the living ones

    των αγαπαντων   =   of the loving ones

3. In both cases described above, there can be added words that go
    with the participle.

    A prepositional phrase can be added: (underlined below)

    του εν ναον ζοντος θεου or }
                                       = of the living-in-the-temple God.
    του θεου του ζοντος εν ναον }

    A direct object can be added: (underlined below)

    του αγαπαντος παντα θεου or }
                                       = of the loving-everyone God.
    του θεου του αγαπαντος παντα }

4. Sometimes a participle with the other words in its portion of the
    sentence is put in the genitive case as a way of setting off that
    part from the rest of the sentence.

    λεγοντος θεου, ακουω = God speaking, I listen (literal)

                            = While God is speaking, I listen.
                               (smooth English)

    As you look at the participle examples coming up, don't be dis-
    couraged if you are not able to explain why every single letter is

the way it is; you simply have not been given that much instruction on these matters. You can be proud of yourself if

1. you can figure out which words are the participles; and
2. you can match them to the words at the bottom of the page.

Give yourself an extra pat on the back if you can guess the tense. Proceed like this:

1. If it has the endings on the chart on page 289, it has to be active, so that rules out middle and passive (except that it could be aorist passive).

2. If its letters are like the spelling in the Word List, it is probably present. The only other possibilities I have given examples for are aorist and perfect.

3. If the beginning of the word is tampered with, it is probably perfect (since there are no augments or reduplications anywhere outside indicative mood, except for perfects.)

4. I did not give you the principal parts, which will slow you down; you might remember that aorists have an σ added to the stem (if it is a second aorist, you are sunk). Aorist passives include a θ . Expect vowel changes after these letters.

5. You can't tell middles from passives anyway; they look the same (except for aorists, which do look different). So if you see a word with μεν in it, and the sense of the sentence does not indicate anyone doing anything to the subject, it is probably middle.

Exercise Three

PARTICIPLE EXAMPLES FROM SCRIPTURE (Match to Word List & Tense List on following page)

                    Παῦλος τοῖς ἁγίοις τοῖς οὖσιν ἐν Ἐφέσῳ

___ ___ 1. _____ __ __ _____   _____ __ ____.
                                      Eph. 1:1
(the participle is dative because it is being used to describe the word "saints", which is dative. Word for word: Paul to the saints, the ones being in Ephesus.

Could you find the ending? Remember that ν can be added to endings for smoothness.

                               πιστεύοντες
___ ___ 2. Whatever you ask in prayer _____ you shall

receive.   Matt. 21:22

(the participle is nominative plural because the subject is you--plural.)

296

_____ _____ 3. According to the ruler of the authority of the air,

τοῦ πνεύματος τοῦ νῦν ἐνεργοῦντες

_____ _____ ____ _____ _____ in the sons of

disobedience. Eph. 2:2

The participle is genitive to match "spirit" which is genitive. Word for word: of the spirit, the one now working...   It is common to translate a participle into English by making up a phrase that starts with "who": the spirit who is now working. This is not a word-for-word translation, but it does bring out the meaning.

_____ _____ 4. For all have sinned and fall short of the glory of God,

δικαιούμενοι

_____ freely by his grace. Rom. 3:24

(Passive participle of "make right" = being made right)

τὴν δύναμιν

_____ _____ 5. ...to do all we ask or think according to _____ _____

τὴν ἐνεργουμένην ἐν ὑμιν...

_____ ___ _____. Eph. 3:20

ἀκούσαντες τὸν λόγον

_____ _____ 6. You, _____ ____ _____ of truth, were sealed by

the Spirit. Eph. 1:13

_____ _____ 7. (We are those) serving the spirit of God, boasting in

καὶ οὐκ ἐν σαρκὶ πεποιθότες

Christ, ____ ____ ___ _____ _____. Phil. 3:3

Γράφομεν   πεπληρωμένη
_____ _____ 8. _____ these things so our joy might be _____
                                              1 John 1:4

Word List

A) ακουω = hear
B) ενεργεω = work
C) ειμι = am (being)
D) δικαιοω = make right

E) πειθω = convince
   (put confidence)
F) πληροω = fill
G) πιστευω = believe

Tense List

a) present
b) present middle
c) present passive
d) aorist
e) aorist passive
f) perfect
g) perfect passive

297

MORE PRACTICAL EXAMPLES

In the next example, the first word "the" goes with the participle, and they are both in the genitive; the second word "the" goes with "all things", and is the plural direct object of the participle:

____ ____ 9. According to the purpose τοῦ τὰ πάντα ἐνεργοῦντος _____
                                                                    Eph. 1:11

____ ____ 10. You are the οἰκεῖοι θεοῦ _____ __ ____, ἐποικοδομηθέντες _____ on the

foundation of the apostles...   Eph. 2:19, 20

____ ____ 11. Paul to the church in Corinth, ἡγιασμένοις ἐν Χριστῷ _____ ___ _____

Ἰησοῦ,
_____ called saints...   1 Cor. 1:2

____ ____ 12. ...that he sent his only-begotten son, ἵνα πᾶς ὁ ____ ____

πιστεύων εἰς αὐτὸν
_____ ___ _____ might not perish but have eternal

life. John 3:16

____ ____ 13. I do not cease giving thanks ὑπὲρ ὑμῶν _____ _____, remembrance

ποιούμενος
_____ in my prayers...   Eph. 1:16

(in genitive because it is a sentence portion of its own, set off from the main sentence)

____ ____ 14. Are they not all ministering πνεύματα, ἀποστελλόμενα _____, _____

for serving? Heb. 1:14

Εὐλογητὸς ὁ θεὸς καὶ πατὴρ τοῦ κυρίου ἡμῶν
____ ____ 15. _____   _____ _____ _____ _____ ____ _____ _____

Ἰησοῦ Χριστοῦ ⌈ὁ εὐλογήσας⌉ ἡμᾶς ἐν πάσῃ εὐλογίᾳ
_____ _____ _____ ____ ___ ____ _____

πνευματικῇ
_____...   Eph. 1:13

ABOUT THE BRACKETED PART:

(the participle has its own word "the" since it is acting like an adjective would act to describe the subject of the sentence. Word for word: the having-blessed-(us with every spiritual blessing)-one

298

_____ _____ 16. (The word) is foolishness to those perishing, τοῖς δὲ _____ _____

σῳζομένοις _____ it is the δύναμις θεοῦ _____ __ ____. 1 Cor. 1:18

'Εγὼ ἁγιάζω ἐμουτόν

_____ _____ 17. ___ _____ _____ for my followers ἵνα ___ also they

might be ἡγιασμένοι _____ in truth. John 17:19

Word List   Tense List

A) ἁγιαζω   = make holy, sanctify   a) present

B) εποικοδομεω = build upon   b) present middle

C) σωζω   = save   c) present passive

D) ενεργεω = work   d) aorist

E) πιστευω = believe   e) aorist passive

F) ευλογεω = bless   f) perfect

G) αποστελλω = send   g) perfect passive

H) ποιεω   = do

COMPARING PARTICIPLE AND MAIN VERB OF THE SENTENCE

The participle can express action occuring during, before or after the event expressed by the main verb of the sentence.

A present participle expresses action during the main verb.

Example: λυων το τεκνον, εβλεψα τον ανθρωπον.

          is translated with sentence (b) below.

The three possible translations:

          (a) After loosing the child, I saw the man
          (b) While loosing the child, I saw the man.
          (c) Before loosing the child, I saw the man.

An aorist participle indicates action before the main verb.

Example: λυσας το τεκνον, εβλεψα τον ανθρωπον.
          is translated with sentence (a) above.

A perfect participle would always express completed action before the main verb.

Example: λελυκως το τεκνον, εβλεψα τον ανθρωπον.

   corresponds to sentence (a), above

The future participle would always express action after the main verb.

Example: λυσων το τεκνον, εβλεψα τον ανθρωπον.

   corresponds to sentence (c), above

Information from NEW TESTAMENT GREEK MADE FUNCTIONAL, © 1972 by H. Fred Nofer, page 88.

PARTICIPLES WITH "BE"

When a participle is used, plus some form of "to be", ειναι, (or similarly-used words such as γινομαι, "to become"), the result can be translated using English helping-verbs:

Αυτος   ἠν   διδασκων   =   he was teaching.
         ↓   ↓
      "to be" in   participle
      imperfect   in present
      tense   tense

Here is a more complete chart of the possibilities, taken from the book by Nofer, page 92.

Form of Participle	Form of "to be"	Resulting Translation Will Sound Like
Present	Present	Present
Present	Imperfect	Imperfect
Present	Future	Future
Perfect	Present	Perfect
Perfect	Imperfect	Pluperfect
Perfect	Future	Future-perfect

An example: Εγω   εσομαι   λελυκως
                      ↓   ↓
                "to be" in   λυω (loose) as
                future   a participle in
                tense   perfect tense

This sentence corresponds to the last option on the chart above, and the translation would therefore sound like a future-perfect:

   "I shall have loosed."

Exercise Four

EXAMPLE WITH FOUR DIFFERENT USES OF THE WORD ἔχω "HAVE"

After translating match each form of εχω with the best description
from the list following the scripture passage.

Jesus, looking at him, loved him, and said to him, "You lack one thing;

              ἔχεις   ἕξεις
go, sell what ____ ____ ( ) and give to the poor, and ____ ____

____ ( ) riches in heaven, and come follow me." But he, saddened

                                    ἦν   ἔχων
by these words, went away grieving, for ____ ____ _____ ( )

many possessions. And looking around, Jesus said to his disciples,

                            ἔχοντες
"How hard it is for the ones _____ ( ) riches to enter into the

kingdom of heaven."   Mark 10:21-23

a) participle   c) future $(\chi + \sigma = \xi)$

b) participle + form of "be"   d) present

Exercise Five

THE VERB FORMS OF FIRST JOHN CHAPTER ONE

Meanings for words you do not know--look up in your English Bible.

          ἦν   ἀκηκόαμεν
That which ___ from the beginning, which _____, which our eyes
ἑωράκαμεν   ἐθεασάμεθα   ἐψηλάφησαν
_____ which _____ and our hands _____ concerning the
                            ἐφανερώθη   ἑωράκαμεν   μαρτυροῦμεν
word of life...and the life _____, and _____ and _____
    ἀπαγγέλομεν   ἦν
and _____ to you the eternal life which ___ with the father and

ἐφανερώθη   ἑωράκαμεν   ἀκηκόαμεν ἀπαγγέλλομεν

_____ to you...that which _____ and _____ _____

                   ἔχητε

also to you, in order that you also _____ fellowship with us. And our

           (no "is"--must be added)

fellowship ___   with the father and with his son

         γράφομεν   ᾖ

Jesus Christ. And _____ these things in order that our joy ____

πεπληρωμένη   ἀκηκόαμεν

_____. And this is the message which _____ from him and

ἀναγγέλλομεν   ἐστιν   ἐστιν

_____ to you, that God _____ light, and darkness _____ not

           εἴπωμεν   ἔχομεν

in him at all. If _____ that _____ fellowship with him and

περιπατῶμεν   ψευδόμεθα   ποιοῦμεν

_____ in darkness, _____, and _____ not the truth.

      περιπατῶμεν   ἐστιν   ἔχομεν

But if _____ in the light, as he _____ in the light, _____

                                        καθαρίζει

fellowship with one another and the blood of Jesus his son _____

          εἴπωμεν   ἔχομεν   πλανῶμεν

us from all sin. If _____ that _____ no sin, _____ ourselves

      ἐστιν   ὁμολογῶμεν   ἐστιν

and the truth _____ not in us; if _____ our sins, _____

                     ἀφῇ   καθαρίσῃ

faithful and righteous in order that ___ our sins and _____ us

                  εἴπωμεν   ἡμαρτήκαμεν,

from all unrighteousness. If _____ that not _____,

ποιοῦμεν   ἐστιν

_____ him a liar, and his word _____ not in us.

List the words that are

a) subjunctive, present tense (translate with "might", etc.)

b) deponent (looks like passive, but translated as if it were active.)

c) aorist.

d) perfect (shown by κ)

e) participle

A COLLEGE COURSE

It is the writer's hope that you will now be interested enough, and self-confident enough, to continue in Greek by taking an academic course or by working through a standard Greek textbook. What will you learn in such a course that you do not already know?

1. Rules about accents.

2. Rules about the changes that occur when various letters come together.

3. Grammatical terms.

4. More detailed rules of usage for words.

5. Vocabulary. Your vocabulary so far is almost entirely limited to cognates; but you do not know hundreds of words that are not cognates.

6. Memorization of endings.

CONTINUING ON YOUR OWN -- See Appendix

TOPICAL INDEX

(In Order of Appearance)

A WORD TO THE GREEK SPECIALIST

Here are some of the principles used in this workbook:

1. The vocabulary is based on cognates, so that the student does not have to consciously memorize meanings. I have tried to avoid false etymologies in setting forth these cognates. The few words I have used which are not cognates were chosen because they helped me use pictures (οικος) or to lay the groundwork for word studies in Part IV (χαρις). While virtually all the commonly used cognates (for example, those listed in the frequency lists of Bruce Metzger) are used, I also had to use many words which occur but seldom in the New Testament in order to keep to the ideal of using cognates. The vocabulary is also strictly limited to words actually used in the New Testament. The only exceptions are in some compound words used as illustrations to bring out the meaning of a New Testament word. (στελλω, ιστημι)

2. The approach to grammar: second declension masculine endings are used to introduce case meanings, adjectives, and the article, pronouns, and prepositional phrases; and all this is done using the minimum vocabulary (second declension cognates). Then a chart is used to introduce the fact that there are other endings, but there is little drill or exercise on these endings. Accent rules are conspicuously absent from this workbook. Contraction rules and vowel and stem changes are given only passing reference.

    The assumption is that the person using this book will either go on to an academic course, or will learn to make use of an analytical lexicon. Regarding verbs, only present tense is used until Part V. However, the notion that there is such a thing as a participle is introduced early, and the masculine singular participle is used often in the scriptural examples.

    I'm sure my decision to minimize grammatical terminology will at times seem to cause more difficulties than it is avoiding, particularly as one struggles through my circumlocutions. Typical of these decisions is postponing the use of the correct names for the cases. After much consideration, I decided not even to use a common word like "appositive". The guiding principle was: if something is self-evident, don't bother to give it a name. The same decision was made in regard to usage and word-order rules. Scriptures are simply quoted and the student is able to see for himself that the writers put the words in a different order from the customary English order. The overriding consideration was: avoid getting bogged down; the goal is that the student will want to study further in other, more academic works.

I am aware that languages today are taught without word-for-word translation to English, and that the approach used in the scriptural examples will seem far from modern teaching practice. The excitement of the non-scholar when he begins to grasp the meaning of portions of sentences has confirmed for me the approach I have taken here, for the purposes of this volume.

However, I have made much use of the idea of having the student grasp the overall meaning of sentences simply by recognizing the vocabulary, without stopping to analyse the endings.

LESSON ONE

Exercise One:	Exercise Two:		Exercise Three:	
The words sound like	The words sound like		The words sound like	
bed	pet	rope	lips	log
dotted	pot	road	lap	ring
bet	top	robe	pill	gear
dad	pit	crib	call	map
bat	tip	drip	land	lamp
tab	dip	dart	plan	rim
cat	pop	cart	sell	men
kit	pope	cork	sink	milk
cot	boat	parrot	star	mask
kid	toad	pin	pencil	grass
bit	code	can	spot	most
cab	coat	pan	sled	leg
boss	rat	bone	gas	goal
cost	rabbit	coat	glas	man
dot	bred	cone	pig	mar

Exercise Four:

I.		II.		III.		IV.	
	c		h		d		i
	e		j		a		j
	f		l		c		g
	a		g		e		h
	b		k		b		f
	d		i				k

LESSON TWO

Exercise One:	Exercise Two:			Exercise Three:			
1-a	I. 1-b	II.	5-h, k	I. 1-c	II.		5-g
2-a	2-c		6-e, l	2-b			6-f
3-a	3-a		7-i, o	3-d			7-h
4-b	4-d		8-g, m	4-a			8-i
5-b			9-f, n				9-j
			10-j, p				10-e
							11-k

LESSON TWO continued

Exercise Four:

1-b (ι as in pin or machine, never as in like)
2-a (α is short, as in father)
3-a
4-b (ε is short, as in let)
5-a (each α has to be pronounced separately)
6-b (αυ as in cow, never as awe)
7-b (αι as in aisle)
8-a

Six Greek Words -- house   = οικος   rock = πετρα
                   scorpion = σκορπιος   lamp = λαμπας
                   book   = βιβλος   lion = λεων

 9-b
10-b
11-a
12-a
13-a
14-b

Exercise Five:

1-a   6-b
2-b   7-a
3-b   8-b
4-a   9-a
5-a   10-b

LESSON THREE

Exercise One: Exercise Two: Exercise Three:

1-c   1-c   phone   phonograph   phantom
2-e   2-d   photograph   Philadelphia   Phil
3-b   3-b
4-f   4-e
5-a   5-f
6-d   6-a

LESSON THREE continued

Exercise Four:

English words -- thumb   thorn   thread
Bible Names   -- Martha   Nathan   Bethlehem (no "h" in Greek)

Exercise Five:

1-c	5-f	9-c
2-a	6-h	10-d
3-g	7-d	11-b
4-e	8-b	12-a
		13-e

Exercise Six:

1-c
2-b
3-a
4-e
5-f
6-d

Exercise Seven:

1-b	6-a
2-b	7-b
3-a	8-a
4-a	9-a
5-a	10-no (man and orphan in house)
	11-no (rock and stone on house)

Exercise Eight:

1-a	12-f
2-b	13-a
3-a	14-g
4-a	15-d
5-a	16-h
6-b	17-b
7-b	18-e
8-a	19-c
9-b	20-k
10-a	21-i
11-b	22-j

LESSON FOUR

Exercise One:

1-e	μικρος + σκοπος	10-g	εν + εργον	A- 4
2-g	μικρος + μετρον	11-d	μονος + λιθος	B-13
3-f	σοφος + μωρος	12-j	μονος + λογος	C-10
4-a	τιμιος + θεος	13-h	φιλος + σοφια	D-14
5-i	μικρος + κοσμος	14-a	φιλος + ανθρωπος	
6-c	θεος + σοφος	15-c	φωτος + γραφω	
7-b	μακρος + σκοπος	16-e	ανθρωπος + λογος	
8-h	κοσμος + λογος	17-i	βιος + λογος	
9-d	μακρος + κοσμος	18-b	μεγα + λιθος	
		19-f	λιθος + γραφω	

LESSON FIVE

Exercise One:

1-b	10-d
2-c	11-g
3-a	12-b
	13-e
4-b	14-a
5-c	15-f
6-a	16-c
	17-j
7-c	18-m
8-a	19-h
9-b	20-o
	21-k
	22-n
	23-l
	24-i

Exercise Two:

1-a
2-b
3-b
4-a
5-a
6-b
7-b
8-b

LESSON SIX

Exercise One:

1-f	φωνη	9-n	πλαστος	17-x	θανατος
2-c	γαλακτος	10-l	ανθρακος	18-q	λευκος
3-h	φως	11-i	νεκρος	19-u	γερων
4-a	σκληρος	12-p	κλεπτω	20-w	ιδιος
5-d	τοπος	13-m	δενδρον	21-s	εσωτερος
6-g	νεος	14-o	ακουω	22-v	μελας
7-b	φοβος	15-k	γραμμα	23-r	μεγας
8-e	σκολιος	16-j	ορθος	24-t	κρανιον
				25-y	τραυμα

LESSON SEVEN

Exercise One:

1-k	9-b
2-m	10-p
3-n	11-d
4-i	12-e
5-j	13-c
6-o	14-f
7-a	15-g
8-h	16-l

Exercise Two:

1-b	4-f	10-i	16-b
2-c	5-a	11-k	17-d
3-a	6-d	12-j	18-a
	7-c	13-m	19-e
	8-b	14-h	20-f
	9-e	15-g	21-c

LESSON SEVEN continued

Exercise Three:

1-b	15-e
2-b	16-d
3-a	17-c
4-b	18-b
5-b	19-a
6-a	20-k
7-b	21-f
8-b	22-i
9-a	23-g
10-b	24-h
11-a	25-j
12-b	26-o
13-b	27-m
14-a	28-n
	29-l

LESSON EIGHT

Exercise One:

		Exercise Two:	
1-c	a. επι	1-d	9-f
2-a	b. παρα	2-e	10-b
3-i	c. εν	3-n	11-k
4-h	d. απο	4-m	12-i
5-g	e. δια	5-j	13-c
6-e	f. εκ	6-l	14-h
7-b	g. προς	7-a	15-o
8-f	h. αντι	8-g	
9-d	i. εις		

LESSON NINE

Exercise One:

1-d	7-j	13-o	17-v	23-t
2-e	8-k	14-l	18-s	24-u
3-a	9-g	15-p	19-r	25-x
4-c	10-i	16-m	20-y	
5-b	11-h		21-q	
6-f	12-n		22-w	

LESSON NINE continued

Exercise Two:

man	– ανθρωπος	law	– νομος	see	– σκοπεω
write	– γραφω	treasure	– θησαυρος	shining	– φανερος
skin	– δερμα	seed	– σπορα	throne	– θρονος
grave	– ταφος	earth	– γη or κοσμος		

Exercise Three:

1-g	7-h	11-l	18-v
2-j	8-c	12-n	19-u
3-e	9-f	13-t	20-y
4-d	10-a	14-s	21-x
5-i		15-r	22-w
6-b		16-m	23-k
		17-o	24-z

LESSON TEN

Exercise One:

paradox
exodus

Exercise Two:

1-c	5-i
2-b	6-h
3-a	7-e
4-d	8-g
	9-f

Exercise Three:

1- anoints
2- anointed
3- anoint
4- anoint
   Christ

Exercise Four:

Charismatic

Exercise Five:

psychic, psychology
pseudonym, pseudo

Exercise Six:

1-b	4-f
2-a	5-g
3-c	6-d
	7-e
	8-h

Exercise One:

see - σκοπεω   stomach - στομαχος   skull - κρανιον
body - σωμα   hear - ακουω   stomach area - γαστηρ, γαστρος
white - λευκος   head - κεφαλη   rip or tear - σχιζω
bone - οστεον   brain - φρην   eye - οφθαλμος
mouth - στομα   chest - στηθος   heart - καρδια
skin - δερμα, δερματος hand - χειρ   chair - καθεδρα
foot - πους, ποδας

1-e	ποδας		6-g	οστεον
2-c	φρην		7-j	καθεδρα
3-i	οφθαλμος		8-f	γαστρος
4-k	δερματος		9-a	χειρ
5-b	δερμα		10-h	σχιζω + φρην
			11-d	στηθος + σκοπεω

Exercise Two:

1-c
2-a
3-d
4-b

Exercise Three:

1-c ὁλος
2-a ὁμος
3-b εσχατος
4-f ἡγεμον
5-e Μιχαηλ
6-g σχολη
7-h ἑτερος
8-d ὁμος

Exercise Four:

type
hymn
myths
Greek υ became English "y"
but for David, υ became "v"

Exercise Five:

1-f	9-i
2-n	10-k
3-c	11-j
4-a	12-e
5-d	13-l
6-b	14-m
7-h	15-o
8-g	

Exercise Six:

1-f	6-e
2-a	7-c
3-h	8-d
4-g	9-j
5-b	10-i

LESSON TWELVE

Exercise One:

1- βοτανη		13- θερμη	+ μετρος
2- ιρις		14- ανεμος	+ μετρος
3- χρυσος		15- ῾ιππος	+ ποταμος
4- αστηρ		16- αστηρ	+ λογος
5- ῾ηλιος		17- αστηρ	+ νομος
6- σπερμα, σπορος		18- πετρα	+ λογος
7- κρυσταλλος		19- λιθος	+ γραφω
8- ποταμος		20- ιχθυς	+ λογος
9- πετρα		21- χλορος	+ φυλλα
10- πνευμα		22- αγρος	+ νομος
11- ῾ιππος, ποταμος		23- δενδρον	+ λογος
12- αγρος		24- ξυλος	+ φωνη

Exercise Two:

Word for word -- Jesus
Christ
of God
Son
Savior

In usual English word order --
Jesus Christ, Son of God, Savior

Exercise Three:

1-c	δεκα
2-f	πρωτος
3-i	῾εξ
4-a	πρωτος
5-h	μυριαι
6-d	χιλιοι
7-g	δεκα
8-b	πεντε
9-e	δευτερος

Exercise Four:

1-d	8-k
2-f	9-l
3-b	10-p
4-g	11-o
5-e	12-j
6-c	13-h
7-a	14-i
	15-n
	16-m
	17-t
	18-s
	19-r
	20-q

LESSON THIRTEEN

Exercise One:

angel

Exercise Two:

1-b   3-b
2-a   4-c
           5-a

Exercise Three:

evangelist
evangelize

Exercise Four:

1-b
2-c
3-d
4-a

Exercise Five:

1-d
2-c
3-a
4-e
5-b
6-f
7-g

Exercise Six:

1- angel
2- anchor
3- larynx

Exercise Seven:

1. c   5. g   9. j
2. d   6. h   10. l
3. a   7. e   11. i
4. b   8. f   12. k

LESSON FOURTEEN

Exercise One:

I.   1- 5   II.   1- 4   7- 6   III.   1- 7   6- 2
      2- 1   2-12   8- 9   2- 4   7- 6
      3- 3   3- 7   9-11   3- 1   8- 3
      4- 2   4- 2   10-10   4- 9   9- 5
      5- 4   5- 1   11- 8   5- 8
                         6-13   12- 5
                                     13- 3

LESSON FIFTEEN

Exercise One:

1-a b a
2-a b c a d e a
  rocks
  man head
3-a, d b a, f c a, e
  past
4-e d f c g
  a h
  b

Exercise Two:

1- say
2- word
3- says
4- say
5- saying words

Exercise Three:

1- call
2- calls

Exercise Four:

I.   1-b
     2-a
     3-c

II. 4-b
     5-b
     6-a
     7-a

III.   8-d
     9-i
   10-a
   11-k
   12-f
   13-h
   14-b
   15-l
   16-j
   17-c
   18-g
   19-e

Exercise Five:

1-a   7-d
2-b   8-f
3-a   9-c
4-a   10-g
5-b   11-i
6-b   12-e
      13-h
      14-j
      15-k

LESSON SEVENTEEN

Exercise One:

1-c
2-f
3-a h g
4-e
5-d
6-b
7-g

LESSON EIGHTEEN

Exercise One:

I.		II.		III.		IV.		V.	
	1-c		4-c		7-c		10-c		13-c
	2-a		5-b		8-a		11-a		14-b
	3-b		6-a		9-b		12-b		15-a

Exercise Two:

1-b
2-e
3-f
4-d
5-h
6-a
7-c
8-g

Exercise Three:

1-b	9-b	21-o
2-a	10-f	22-p
3-a	11-a	23-n
4-b	12-d	24-m
5-b	13-h	25-t
6-b	14-e	26-s
7-b	15-c	27-q
8-b	16-g	28-r
	17-l	
	18-k	
	19-i	
	20-j	

Exercise Four:

1-Pp				
2-Ds				
3-Os	Ss			
4-Os	Ps			
5-Ds				
6-Os	Os	Ps		
7-Sp	Ps			
8-Op	Op			
9-Op				
10-Op				
11-Os	Pp	Os	Ps	
12-Op				
13-Ps				
14-Ps				

LESSON NINETEEN

Exercise One:

1- Men throw stones.
2- Brother writes words.
3- God speaks to Philip.
4- Brothers speak to lepers.
5- I write to Mark.
6- He writes to Paul.
7- I throw stone.
8- You write words.
9- Brothers write law of God.
10- Mark speaks word of men.
11- Slave writes to men of God.
12- Lepers speak to slaves of Paul.
13- We speak words of God to men.
14- They speak word of law to Philip.
15- I want to speak words.
16- He teaches to write words.
17- Cornelius writes book in house.
18- God loves men in world.
19- Slaves speak to scorpion on house.
20- Nicodemus writes to brother on stone.

21- Men of God write words of book
to brothers of Paul in house
of prophets.
22- Brothers of lepers speak words
of God to men of God in house
of God.

LESSON TWENTY

Exercise One:

1- τιμιους

2- μονω   σοφω

3- πρωτοι   εσχατοι

5- αλλος   δευτερος

6- νεκρων

7- ομοιον

Exercise Two:

1-f C
2-e F
3-d A
4-c D
5-b E
6-a B
7-g C

Exercise Three:

1-d		9- ὁ	m
2-h		10- του	l
3-g		11- τω	j
4-e		12- τον	o
5-f		13- οἱ	p
6-c		14- των	k
7-a		15- τοις	i
8-b		16- τους	n

LESSON TWENTY-ONE

Exercise One:

first - πρωτος   large - μεγας   temple - (n) ναος
second - δευτερος   small - μικρος   grave - (n) ταφος
third - τριτος   other - αλλος   dead   -   νεκρος

full   - πληρους   numbers - (n) αριθμοι
medium - μεσος
empty - κενος

Exercise Two:

1-d	5-h	9-k	13-n	17-y
2-f	6-e	10-j	14-p	18-z
3-a	7-b	11-l	15-i	19-w
4-g	8-c	12-o	16-m	20-x
				21-v
				22-t
				23-u
				24-q
				25-s
				26-r

Exercise Three:

1- The first man, in the house, speaks a word.
2- The second man writes words in the temple.
3- The third man sees the dead man.
4- The first man throws the small stone in the house.
5- The second man hears the word of the first man.
6- The other man sees the empty tomb.
7- The men throw hard stones.
8- The brother writes a crooked word.
9- Mark says a hard word of the law to the holy brothers.
10- We speak good words of the holy God to the apostles.
11- They speak a new word of God to the wise men.

Exercise Four:

ολον   αγιοις   αγιων   μονος   νεον

LESSON TWENTY-TWO

Exercise One:

I.   1-e   II.   7-c
     2-c   8-f
     3-f   9-a
     4-d   10-e
     5-a   11-d
     6-b   12 b

Exercise Two:

1-b
2-a
3-e
4-d
5-c
6-g
7 f

Exercise Three:

A- with
B- after

Exercise Four:

1-b
2-e
3-a
4-d
5-f
6-c

LESSON TWENTY-SIX

Exercise One:

1-b
2-d
3-a
4-c

Exercise Two:

1-d	8-d
2-b	9-a
3-d	10-d
4-d	11-d
5-b	12-a
6-d	13-c
7-a	14-e

LESSON TWENTY-SEVEN

Exercise One:

1-b	5-g
2-d	6-i
3-a	7-h
4-c	8-e
	9-f

LESSON TWENTY-EIGHT

<u>Exercise</u> <u>One</u>:

1-e
2-a
3-f
4-c
5-b
6-d

LESSON THIRTY

<u>Exercise</u> <u>One</u>:   <u>Exercise</u> <u>Two</u>:

1-e   1-b   5-b
2-c   2-b   6-b
3-h   3-a   7-a
4-a   4-a   8-a
5-d
6-g
7-f
8-b

LESSON THIRTY-TWO

<u>Exercise</u> <u>One</u>:

I. 1-b   II. 4-f
    2-c   5-g
    3-a d   6-e

LESSON THIRTY-THREE

Exercise One:

1- call
2- calls
3- called
4- called
5- calling
6- called one

Exercise Two:

1-c
2-a
3-b

Exercise Three:

A- call out
B- calls out
ecclesiastical

Exercise Four:

Kyrie

Exercise Five:

1- kuriak
2- kurk
 - kirk
3- church

LESSON THIRTY-FOUR

Exercise One:

adjective

Exercise Two:

cross out---love
            -peace
            -faith
            -word
            -apostle
            -Lord

LESSON THIRTY-FIVE

Exercise One:

economy
ecumenical

LESSON THIRTY-SIX

Exercise One:

I.		II.		III.		IV.		V.	
	1-B		5-H		9-K		13-N		17-S
	2-C		6-F		10-J		14-P		18-T
	3-A		7-E		11-L		15-0		19-R
	4-D		8-G		12-I		16-M		20-Q

VI.		VII.	
	21-W		25-Y
	22-V		26-AA
	23-U		27-Z
	24-X		28-DD
			29-BB
			30-CC

Exercise Two:

1-c
2-a
3-d
4-b
5-e

Exercise Three:

apothecary
pyromaniac

LESSON THIRTY-SEVEN

Exercise One:

cross out---holy
       -love
       -faith
       -saint
       -lordship
       -believe

Exercise Two:

criterion

Exercise Three:

critic

LESSON THIRTY-EIGHT

Exercise One:

1-e	4-c
2-a	5-d
3-b	6-f

Exercise Two:

1-b	4-a
2-b	5-c
3-c	6-b

LESSON THIRTY-NINE

Exercise One:

homily

Exercise Two:

metamorphosis
scheme

Exercise Three:

1-b	f	επι	+	στρεφω
2-b	e	μετα	+	νους
3-a	d	ὁμο	+	λογος

Exercise Four:

1-c g i
2-d j n
3-b f
4-e k
5-a m
6-h l

LESSON FORTY

Exercise One:

eulogy
eucharist

Exercise Two:

1-b
2-d
3-e
4-f
5-g
6-a
7-c

Exercise Three:

1-b
2-a
3-f
4-c
5-d
6-e

LESSON FORTY-ONE

Exercise One:

1-c
2-f
3-d
4-a
5-e
6-b

LESSON FORTY-TWO

Exercise One: Exercise Two:

catharsis   1-b
                       2-b
                       3-a
                       4-c

LESSON FORTY-THREE

Exercise One: Exercise Two:

a- μαμμη   deacon
b- πατρος
c- γυναικος
d- νηπιος
e- μητρος
f- ανδρος

LESSON FORTY-FOUR

Exercise One: Exercise Two: Exercise Three: Exercise Four:

liturgy   strategy   therapy   1-c
                                                     2-a
                                                     3-b

Exercise Five: Exercise Six:

1- oversees or looks over, etc.   1-d j E
2- overseer or supervisor   2-f k G
3- overseer...oversees, or any other words   3-a m C
   with similar meaning.   4-e o A
                                               5-g q H
5- piskop   6-b r F
6- pishop   7-i p B
7- bishop   8-c n I
8- bishop   9-h l D
9- episcopal

LESSON FORTY-FIVE

Exercise One:		Exercise Two:	Exercise Three:
1-b	3s	1-c	c
2-d	2p	2-b or c	b
3-f	1s	3-c	a (pluperfect)
4-a	1p	4-a and b	e
5-c	3p	5-a	d
6-e	2s	6-a	
7-g	3s		
8-b	2p		
9-d	1s		
10-f	1p		

Exercise Four:

1-e	E
2-d	C
3-e	D
4-f	A
5-g	A
6-a	E
7-b	D
8-a	E
9-c	D
10-e	C
11-a	B

Exercise Five:

A.
1-A
2-P
3-M

B.
1-M
2-P
3-A
4-P
5-M
6-P
7-A
8-P
9-M

Exercise Six:

1-A	f	X
2-D	a	Z
3-A	g	X
4-E	e	Y
5-C	d	Z
6-B	a	X
7-D	b	X
8-C	d	Z
9-E	c	X
10-C	e	Z

LESSON FORTY-SIX

Exercise One:

1-	aorist	middle	b
2-	perfect	passive	d
3-	present	active	f
4-	imperfect	middle	a
5-	pluperfect	active	c
6-	present	passive	g
7-	future	passive	e

Exercise Two:

1- ελυες	imperfect	active	
2- λυσεται	future	middle	(she is 3rd person)
3- λελυκαμεν	perfect	active	
4- ελυθητε	aorist	passive	
5- λυονται	present	middle	
6- λυσεις	future	active	
7- ελελυκει	pluperfect	active	
8- λυομαι	present	passive	
9- ελυσαμεν	aorist	active	
10- λελυνται	perfect	passive	

Exercise Three:

1- γραψει	(future active)
2- κεκληνται	(perfect passive)
3- επιε	(aorist active)
4- επεπωκειμεν	(pluperfect active)
5- εκληθη	(aorist passive)
6- γεγραφαμεν	(Perfect active)

LESSON FORTY-SEVEN

Exercise One:

πιστευω	πεμπω
πιστευσω	πεμψω (from πεμπσω)
επιστευσα	επεμψα
πεπιστευκα	-----
πεπιστευμαι	επεμψθην (π changes to φ before θ)
επιστευθην	

Exercise Two:	Exercise Three:	Exercise Four:	Exercise Five:
1-B d	1-f E	1-c	1-B e
2-A b	2-c C	2-c	2-C a
3-D c	3-b F	3-a	3-D c
4-C a	4-e D	4-d	4-D d
5-A e	5-a B	5-b	5-A a or b both
	6-d A	6-e	possible: "Is
			named" or
			"names itself"

LESSON FORTY-EIGHT

Exercise One:

1-I f	9-J f
2-M i	10-I i
3-N b	K i
4-A d	11-C c
5-F f	D c
G h	12-P a
6-0 g	13-H h
7-E e	14-B e
8-L i	

Exercise Two:

1-d
2-a
3-g
4-f
5-b
6-c and e

Exercise Three:

1-e C
2-d D
-f C
3-e D
4-c B
5-a C
6-g A and h A
7-b E

LESSON FORTY-NINE

Exercise One:

1-D b
2-C a
3-B b
4-B c
5-A c
6-E d

Exercise Two:

1-c
2-f
3-h
4-b
5-e
6-g
7-a
8-d

Exercise Three:

1-E c	8-H a
2-I d	9-G b
-J B	10-F c
3-B a	-H a
4-A c	
5-C e	
6-D c	
B a	
7-A b	

LESSON FIFTY

Exercise One:

1-c
2-f
3-a
4-d
5-g
6-b
7-h
8-e

Exercise Two:

1-f
2-d
3-i
4-a
5-j
6-b
7-h
8-c
9-g
10-e

Exercise Three:

1-b	7-e
2-a	8-c
3-b	9-d
4-a	10-f
5-b	11-g
6-a	

LESSON FIFTY-ONE

Exercise One:

1-b
2-d
3-a
4-c

Exercise Two:

1- λυων
2- λυοντος
3- λυοντι

4- λυουσα
5- λυουσης
6- λυουσῃ

7-λυσων
8-λυσοντος
9-λυσοντι

Exercise Three:

1-c
2-e
3-g
4-d
5-a
6-h
7-f
8-b

Exercise Four:

1- λυσας
2- λυσαντος
3- λυσαντι

4- λυσασα
5- λυσασης
6- λυσασῃ

7- λελυκως
8- λυλυκοτος
9- λελυκοτι

10- λελυκυια
11- λελυκυιας
12- λελυκυια

Exercise Five:

1-d (perfect feminine plural)
2-a (future)
3-c (aorist)
4-b (perfect feminine genitive)

LESSON FIFTY-TWO

Exercise One:

1- λυθεις
2- λυθεντος
3- λυθεντι

4- λυομενος
5- λυομενου
6- λυομενῳ

7- λυομενη
8- λυομενης
9- λυομενῃ

Exercise Two:

1-d
2-f
3-a
4-h
5-e
6-b
7-g
8-c

Exercise Three:

1-C a
2-G a
3-B a
4-D c
5-B b
6-A d
7-E f
8-F g
9-D a
10-B e
11-A g
12-E a
13-H b
14-G c
15-F d
16-C c
17-A g

Exercise Four:

a- ἔχοντες
b- ἦν ἔχων
c- ἕξεις
d- ἔχεις

Exercise Five:

a- ἔχητε
- ᾖ
- εἴπωμεν
- περιπατῶμεν
- ὁμολογῶμεν
- ἀφῇ
- καθαρίσῃ

b- ψευδόμεθα

c- ἐθεασάμεθα
- ἐφανερώθη
(passive)
- ἐψηλαφήσαν

d- ἀκηκόαμεν
- ἑωράκαμεν
- ἡμαρτήκαμεν
(these are
irregular in
that they do
not start
with a redu-
plication.)

e- πεπληρωμένη
(perfect
participle)

Using Reference Books

In learning how to use Greek lexicons and other reference books, we will continue our learning-by-doing approach. We will follow six basic steps in doing a word study from the Greek New Testament.

1. Choose a word in a specific text. We will use "fellowship" from Phil. 3:10.

2. Write a definition of your study-word (fellowship) according to its context.

3. Find the Greek word from which your English word is translated. We will look at two different ways to do this.

   (a) Look up your study-word in a concordance. We will use Strong's Exhaustive Concordance. Find your study-word's dictionary number in the right-hand column. See Figure 1. Look up the Greek word for fellowship under dictionary entry 2842. See Figure 2. Two other fine concordances are Young's Analytical Concordance to the Bible and The New Englishman's Greek Concordance to the New Testament.

Figure 1

fellowservants
M't 18:28 went out, and found one of his *f.*   4889
     31 So when his *f* saw what was done,   "
  24:49 And shall begin to smite his *f,*   "
Re   6:11 their *f* also and their brethren,   "
fellowship
Le   6: 2 or in *f,* or in a thing taken *8667, 3027
Ps 94:20 of iniquity have *f* with thee,   2266
Ac   2:42 and *f,* and in breaking of bread,   2842
1Co   1: 9 were called unto the *f* of his Son   "
   10:20 that ye should have *f* with devils.*2844
2Co   6:14 what *f* hath righteousness with   3352
   8: 4 upon us the *f* of the ministering   2842
Ga   2: 9 and Barnabas the right hand of *f ;*   "
Eph   3: 9 see what is the *f* of the mystery, *   "
   5:11 And have no *f* with the unfruitful 4790
Ph'p 1: 5 your *f* in the gospel from the first 2842
   2: 1 of love, if any *f* of the Spirit,   "
   3:10 and the *f* of his sufferings,   "
1Jo   1: 3 ye also may have *f* with us: and   "
   3 truly our *f* is with the Father,   "
   6 If we say that we have *f* with him,"
   7 light, we have *f* one with another. "
fellowsoldier
Ph'p 2:25 and companion in labour, and *f,*   4961
Ph'm   2 and Archippus our *f,* and to the   "

Greek word for "fellowship"
dictionary number
root meaning
other meanings
other translations in NT

Figure 2

2839. κοινός **kŏinŏs,** *koy-nos';* prob. from *4862;* common, i.e. (lit.) shared by all or several, or (cer.) profane:—common, defiled, unclean, unholy.

2840. κοινόω **kŏinŏō,** *koy-nŏ'-o;* from *2839;* to make (or consider) profane (cer.):—call common, defile, pollute, unclean.

2841. κοινωνέω **kŏinōnĕō,** *koy-no-neh'-o;* from *2844;* to share with others (obj. or subj.):—communicate, distribute, be partaker.

2842. κοινωνία **kŏinōnia,** *koy-nohn-ee'-ah;* from *2844;* partnership, i.e. (lit.) participation, or (social) intercourse, or (pecuniary) benefaction:—(to) communicate (-ation), communion, (contri-) distribution, fellowship.

2843. κοινωνικός **kŏinōnikŏs,** *koy-no-nee-kos';* from *2844;* communicative, i.e. (pecuniarily) liberal:—willing to communicate.

2844. κοινωνός **kŏinōnŏs,** *koy-no-nos';* from *2839;* a sharer, i.e. associate:—companion, × fellowship, partaker, partner.

2 pronunciation guides

(b) Find your study-word in an interlinear New Testament; many are available. Our sample in Figure 3 is from The Interlinear Literal Translation of the Greek New Testament. You will find each English word directly under its Greek equivalent. Figure 1 shows Phil. 3:10-11. (See p.303)

τῇ πίστει, 10 τοῦ γνῶναι αὐτὸν καὶ τὴν δύναμιν τῆς ἀνα-
faith,   to know   him   and the   power   of ²resur-
στάσεως αὐτοῦ, καὶ ᵉτὴν‖ κοινωνίαν ᶠτῶν‖.παθημάτων.αὐτοῦ,
rection   ¹his,   and the   fellowship   of his sufferings,
ᵍσυμμορφούμενος‖ τῷ.θανάτῳ.αὐτοῦ, 11 εἰ.πως   καταντήσω
being conformed   to his death,   if by any means I may arrive
εἰς τὴν ἐξανάστασιν ʰτῶν‖ νεκρῶν. 12 οὐχ ὅτι ἤδη   ἔλαβον,
at the   resurrection   of the dead.   Not that ²already ¹I received,

331

(2) continued

Now that we have found the Greek word for fellowship from Phil. 3:10, we will look up its meaning in an analytical lexicon, <u>The Analytical Greek Lexicon Revised</u>. An analytical lexicon lists every form of every Greek word used in the New Testament while general lexicons will list only one main form. Determining which entry explains your word in these lexicons can be difficult if your word differs greatly from the form in the lexical entry. To find the meaning of our word <u>koinonian</u> (fellowship), follow the numbers in Figure 4. Number 8 is our destination. The <u>koinonia</u> entry lists Phil. 3:10 under the first of its four definitions.

Figure 4

κοινῆς, gen. sing. fem. . . . . κοινός
κοινοῖ, 3 pers. sing. pres. ind. act. . . κοινόω
κοινόν, acc. sing. masc. . . . . κοινός
κοινόν, nom. and acc. sing. neut. . . id.

⑦ κοινός], ή, όν, (§ 7. tab. F. a) *common, belonging equally to several*, Ac. 2. 44; 4. 32; in N.T. *common, profane*, He. 10. 29; *ceremonially unclean*, Mar. 7. 2; Ac. 10. 14, et al.

κοινόω, ῶ, fut. ώσω, perf. κεκοίνωκα, aor. 1, ἐκοίνωσα, (§ 20. tab. T) *to make common*; in N.T. *to profane, desecrate*, Ac. 21. 28; *to render ceremonially unclean, defile, pollute*, Mat. 15. 11, 18, 20; *to pronounce unclean ceremonially*, Ac. 10. 15; 11. 9.

κοινωνός, οῦ, ὁ, ἡ, (§ 3. tab. C. a. b) *a fellow, partner*, Mat. 23. 30; Lu. 5. 10; 1 Co. 10. 18, 20; 2 Co. 8. 23; Phile. 17; He. 10. 33; *a sharer, partaker*, 2 Co. 1. 7; 1 Pe. 5. 1; 2 Pe. 1. 4.

κοινωνέω, ῶ, fut. ήσω, perf. κεκοινώνηκα, aor. 1, ἐκοινώνησα, (§ 16. tab. P) *to have in common, share*, He. 2. 14; *to be associated in, to become a sharer in*,

Ro. 15. 27; 1 Pe. 4. 13; *to become implicated in, be a party to*, 1 Ti. 5. 22; 2 Jno. 11; *to associate one's self with by sympathy and assistance, to communicate with in the way of aid and relief*, Ro. 12. 13; Gal. 6. 6.

⑧ κοινωνία, ας, ἡ, (§ 2. tab. B. b, and rem. 2) *fellowship, partnership*, Ac. 2. 42; 2 Co. 6. 14; Gal. 2. 9; Phi. 3. 10; 1 Jno. 1. 3, et al.; *participation, communion*, 1 Co. 10. 16, et al.; *aid, relief*, He. 13. 16, et al.; *contribution in aid*, Ro. 15. 26.

κοινωνείτω, 3 pers. sing. pres. imper. . κοινωνέω
κοινωνέω, ῶ], fut. ήσω, (§ 16. tab. P) . . κοινός ⑥
④ κοινωνία], ας, ἡ, (§ 2. tab. B. b, and rem. 2) ⑤id.
κοινωνίᾳ, dat. sing. . . . . ③ κοινωνία
① κοινωνίαν, acc. sing. . . . . ②id.
κοινωνίας, gen. sing. . . . . id.
κοινωνικός], ή, όν, (§ 7. tab. F. a) . . κοινός
κοινωνικούς,ᵃ acc. pl. masc. . . . κοινωνικός
κοινωνοί, nom. pl. masc. . . . . κοινωνός
κοινωνόν, acc. sing. masc. . . . id.
κοινωνός], οῦ, ὁ, ἡ, (§ 3. tab. C. a. b) . . κοινός
κοινωνοῦντες, nom. pl. masc. part. pres. . κοινωνέω
κοινωνούς, acc. pl. masc. . . . . κοινωνός
κοινῶσαι, aor. 1, infin. act. . . . κοινόω

4. Compare your definition of your study-word from Step 2 with the dictionary/lexicon definition from Step 3. Write down any new insights.

5. Research other uses of your Greek study-word (<u>koinonia</u>) from the New Testament. Do this by studying the other uses of this word by the same author (Paul wrote Philippians), and the uses of this word by other New Testament authors. Here are two ways to locate the other uses of your study-word.

   (a) If you are using <u>Strong's Exhaustive Concordance</u>, study the other verses listed under the entry "fellowship" that have the same dictionary number, 2842.

   (b) If you are using a lexicon, study the other verses listed in the definitions of <u>koinonia</u>.

After studying these other verses, write a paragraph comparing the various uses of your word by the author of your study-text (Phil. 3:10). Write at least another paragraph on uses of this word by other New Testament authors.

Here are some other reference books which can give you valuable insight at this point in your word study.

An Expository Dictionary of New Testament Words by W.E. Vine is written especially for the Greek novice and is widely recommended. All entries are alphabetized in English. See Figure 5.

As your knowledge of Greek grows, you will find Arndt and Gingrich's Greek-English Lexicon of the New Testament and Other Early Christian Literature very helpful. It is well known for its thorough definitions of New Testament words and also includes insight from other writings of that time period, both Christian and secular. See Figure 6. This figure shows less than one-tenth of the total entry for koinonia.

Figure 5

FELLOWSHIP
A. Nouns.

1. KOINŌNIA (κοινωνία), (a) communion, fellowship, sharing in common (from koinos, common), is translated "communion" in 1 Cor. 10 : 16 ; Philm. 6, R.V., "fellowship," for A.V., "communication ;" it is most frequently translated "fellowship ;" (b) that which is the outcome of fellowship, a contribution, e.g., Rom. 15 : 26 ; 2 Cor. 8 : 4. See COMMUNION, CONTRIBUTION, etc.

Note : In Eph. 3 : 9, some mss. have koinōnia, instead of oikonomia, dispensation, R.V.

2. METOCHĒ (μετοχή), partnership (akin to No. 3, under FELLOW), is translated "fellowship" in 2 Cor. 6 : 14.¶ In the Sept., Ps. 122 : 3, "Jerusalem is built as a city whose fellowship is complete."¶ The word seems to have a more restricted sense than koinōnia. Cp. the verb form in Heb. 2 : 14.

3. KOINŌNOS (κοινωνός) denotes a partaker or partner (akin to No. 1) ; in 1 Cor. 10 : 20 it is used with ginomai, to become, " that ye should have communion with," R.V. (A.V., " fellowship with "). See COMPANION, PARTAKER, PARTNER.

Figure 6

κοινωνία, ας, ἡ (Pind.+; inscr., pap., LXX, Philo [Mos. 1, 158 of communion w. God]; Joseph.; loanw. in rabb.).
1. *association, communion, fellowship, close relationship* (hence a favorite expr. for the marital relationship as the most intimate betw. human beings Isocr. 3, 40; BGU 1051, 9 [I AD]; 1052, 7; POxy. 1473, 33; 3 Macc 4: 6; Jos., Ant. 1, 304. But s. also Diod. S. 10, 8, 2 ἡ τοῦ βίου κ.=the

When you want as much information as possible on a Greek word, go to the Theological Dictionary of the New Testament by Gerhard Kittel and Gerhard Friederich. Many scholars consider this massive ten-volume to be the best theological dictionary ever compiled. Kittel is so thorough that he gives 11 pages to discussing koinonia and closely related words.

6. Now you are ready to look at a commentary in your word-study. Going to a commentary was maybe your first impulse, but that can hinder your study as it gives you another person's ideas about truth rather than allowing the Holy Spirit to guide you first. Look up the section in the commentary that discusses your study text, and compare the commentator's conclusions with your own. Also read his comments on any other related passages. Every commentator will carry his personal bias into his writing even though he tries to be open-minded. Therefore, it is wise to compare commentators with each other. We have included the segment from Adam Clarke's Commentary on the Bible which deals with Phil. 3:10-11. See Figure 7.

Figure 7

10. *That I may know him.* To be the true and promised Messiah, and experience all that salvation which He has bought by His blood. *And the fellowship of his sufferings.* Christ died, not only as a Victim for sin, but as a Martyr to the truth. No creature can have *fellowship* with Him in His vicarious sufferings; as a martyr to the truth, Paul wished to imitate Him.

11. *The resurrection of the dead.* That is, the resurrection of those who, having died in the Lord, rise to glory and honor; and hence Paul uses a peculiar word which occurs nowhere else in the New Testament. The words, as they stand in the best MSS., are as follows: "to that resurrection which is of the dead."

Following is a list of eight more books which will help you delve into the meanings of Greek words as you study the New Testament:

New Testament Words by William Barclay; SCM Press, Ltd., Bloomsbury St., London; first published 1964. Selected words are discussed, such as "love" and "covenant", in five- to six-page articles.

Greek Words and Hebrew Meanings by David Hill; Cambridge, England; 1967. He discusses several words that are of importance in understanding salvation, including the words, propitiation, redemption, and righteousness. For each word he explores the meaning of the Hebrew word upon which the concepts is based. Then he examines changes in these concepts during the centuries just preceding Christ, and interprets the word as it is used by each New Testament author.

Lexical Aids for Students of New Testament Greek by Bruce M. Metzger; Princeton, NJ; many editions since 1946.
This work includes a list of the most frequent words in the Greek New Testament (a handy memorizing guide) and word lists classified according to their roots (all the words based on a given word). This book also explains the meaning of various prefixes and suffixes.

Synonymns of the New Testament by Richard C. Trench; Wm. B. Eerdman's Publishing Co., Grand Rapids, MI; first published in 1880, first Eerdman's reprint in 1958.
Each section discusses two or more New Testament words similar in meaning and shows the differences in meaning between them. The entries are not arranged alphabetically, but there is an alphabetical index in the back. Articles flow in a conversational style and utilize secular Greek writings as well as the New Testament for insights.

Christian Words by Nigel Turner; subtitled "Concise Word Studies to Help Anyone Understand the Unique Vocabulary of the Greek New Testament"; Thomas Nelson Publishers, Nashville, TN; 1981
Words are listed in alphabetical order in English. Most of the articles then compare what the corresponding Greek word means in secular writings and in Christian literature. The five-page article on "fellowship" deals with five words related to koinonia.

Word Pictures in the New Testament by A.T. Robertson; 6 Volumes; first published by 1933; Broadman Press, Nashville, TN.
The book discusses selected phrases in their order of appearance in the New Testament. Comments range from a single sentence to half a page. It also explains the significance of the vocabulary and verb tenses in these phrases.

Word Studies in the Greek New Testament by Kenneth Wuest; The three-volume edition published by Eerdmans in 1973 includes his studies on various books from the New Testament. He comments on some Greek words from each verse and includes his personal translation of each sentence.

The New International Dictionary of New Testament Theology, Colin Brown,
general editor (translated from a German original of 1967); three
volumes; English language edition copyright 1975 by Zondervan Corp.,
Grand Rapids, MI.
In this work, words are listed alphabetically in English. The articles
then treat the Greek words which that particular English word translates. As an example of the scope of the book, the article "Fellowship"
explains two Greek words, the word for "have" (four pages) and the
word koinonia (five pages).

The following three books offer many insights gained from understanding Greek grammar in the Greek New Testament.

Light from the Greek New Testament by Boyce W. Blackwelder; The
Warner Press, Anderson, IN; 1959.

The Practical Use of the Greek New Testament by Kenneth S. Wuest;
Copyright 1946 by the Moody Bible Institute of Chicago; revised by
Donald L. Wise and reissued in 1982.
Both Blackwelder's and Wuest's works are organized according to
grammatical categories with sections on verbs, on nouns, etc. Each
section explains Bible verses by its related grammatical principles.
Blackwelder also adds much additional information about word-meanings.

Grammatical Insights into the Greek New Testament by Nigel Turner;
T & T Clark, Edinburgh, England; 1965.
Each chapter is devoted to a different author of New Testament books
(Paul, John, etc.) and the insights gained from studying the style
of that particular author. Major emphasis is given to clearing up
difficult passages. For example, Did Jesus mean "yes" when he said
to the high priest at his trial, "You have said so."? What is meant
in First John where it says that a Christian does not sin?

A few final hints:

Before buying reference books, experiment with a few at your church
or public library. Trying a few will help you decide what you want
and do not want in a reference book.

Your local Christian bookstore can order just about any reference
book you desire.

Whenever you use an unfamiliar reference book, first study the author's
guidelines on how to make the best use of his book.